best hikes with dogs
WESTERN WASHINGTON

Dan A. Nelson

THE MOUNTAINEERS BOOKS

Published by
The Mountaineers Books
1001 SW Klickitat Way, Suite 201
Seattle, WA 98134

First printing 2002, second printing 2003, third printing 2003, fourth printing 2003

Published simultaneously in Great Britain by Cordee, 3a DeMontfort Street, Leicester, England, LE1 7HD

Printed in Canada

Project Editor: Laura Slavik
Editor: Erin Moore
Cover and Book Design: Ani Rucki
Layout: Ani Rucki
Mapmaker: Moore Creative Design
Photographer: All photographs by the author unless otherwise noted
Illustrator: Ani Rucki (featuring Tiny, the super star, and a cameo appearance by Addison)

Cover photograph: *Sam* Fogstock Images © Rob Casey
Frontispiece: *Grace, overlooking Ferguson Lake* Dean Cass

Library of Congress Cataloging-in-Publication Data
Nelson, Dan A.
    Best hikes with dogs in western Washington / Dan Nelson.— 1st ed.
        p.   cm.
    ISBN 0-89886-829-7 (pbk.)
    1. Hiking with dogs—Washington (State), Western—Guidebooks. 2. Trails—Washington (State), Western—Guidebooks. 3. Washington (State),
Western—Guidebooks. I. Title.
    SF427.455 .N45 2002
    796.51'09797—dc21

                                    2002005065

DEDICATION

To Parka,
who is more than a mere dog—
she is my true friend and companion.

And to Dr. Randy Acker of the Sun Valley Animal Center,
who made it possible for Parka to join me on the trail.
His skilled hands repaired genetic damage in the joints of all
four of Parka's legs before she was two years old,
saving her from a pain-filled life as a house-bound cripple.

Parka as a puppy on lower Pilots Trail on Tiger Mountain

CONTENTS

Part 1: Hiking with Your Dog

Part 2: The Trails

Olympics

North Cascades

Central Cascades

South Cascades

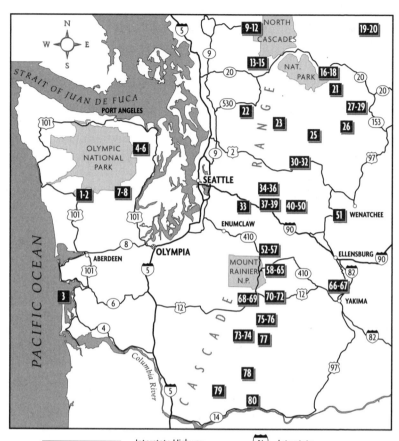

AUTHOR'S NOTE

Dogs were an important part of my life until I went to college. School wasn't a time or place for pets, and for four years, I had none. I missed them. After graduation, I moved to a small apartment in western Washington and, though I would have loved to have a dog then, it just wasn't feasible. I like larger sporting breeds and the water dogs in particular—Labrador retrievers and golden retrievers. But these dogs need large yards in which to play and romp—not small apartments without private outdoor spaces. Still, I wanted a companion animal, a pet of some kind. So, while working as a newspaper reporter, I stuck to that apartment and I learned to live with cats.

A few years ago, the time was right to get a dog. Donna and I had a modest home with a large fenced backyard. We had the time to devote to raising and training a puppy, and we had both gone long enough without a dog. Donna wanted a large canine companion with whom to run in the evenings when I was late getting home, and we both wanted a dog with whom to share the trails.

So, one Halloween Day, we went to pick up Parka, an eight-week-old yellow Labrador. Parka proved to be a wonderfully intelligent and loving pet, quickly learning basic dog-necessities (she was housebroken in just a week or two) and her primary skills (sit, stay, and heel were picked up almost immediately). Unfortunately, we soon learned she wasn't 100 percent healthy. By the time she was five months old, she developed a periodic limp. Initial medical diagnosis: growing pains. Two months later, the limping was more frequent and more pronounced. A new vet and a new diagnosis: malformed cartilage in the middle joints of her front legs (the elbows). A genetic problem resulted in the cartilage refusing to bond to the bone, leaving loose folds of torn cartilage pinched and crumpled in the joint. The treatment came as three options: do nothing, and leave Parka crippled and constantly in pain; put her down, and get a new puppy; or, the third option, fix her condition with expensive orthoscopic surgery.

Donna and I had bonded strongly with this smart, loving pup, but we seriously weighed the options. Fortunately, friends put us in touch with a wonderful veterinary surgeon in Sun Valley, Idaho, who specializes in these types of procedures for sporting breeds especially. Randy Acker has built a national reputation as a leading orthopedic surgeon for field dogs, and after consulting with him on the phone, Donna and I agreed to try the surgery. The cost in Sun Valley was less than a third the price we were quoted from western Washington vet hospitals, and the Sun Valley Animal Hospital came with strong recommendations from friends who own and breed field trial dogs worth tens of thousands of dollars. And even though we thought we had lost the chance to have a dog hiking companion, we wouldn't lose Parka as a living companion.

To cut to the chase, Parka got her surgery—both elbows endured a procedure that basically involved removing the poorly formed cartilage and any loose bone fragments that might have been chipped off into the joint by the grinding action of the joint. A series of tiny holes were then drilled into the exposed bone to spur the growth of new, reparative cartilage, which would be weaker than normal joint cartilage but at least would provide some cushion in the joint. Within a few weeks of the surgery, Parka was moving pain free—until her left rear leg went out.

It seems that when the elbows are genetically flawed like this, the hind legs are often problematic, and Parka suffered the canine equivalent of a torn ACL—her CrCL was ripped and the culprit was a badly aligned leg joint. The solution this time was more drastic—it was called a TPLO, or tibial plateau leveling operation. The end of Parka's tibia would be cut off and repositioned to remove the excessive stress on the ligament. The repositioned bone parts would then be bolted together with a steel plate and surgical screws. Again, Randy Acker performed the procedure. Before she was a year old, Parka had had three legs surgically repaired. Yet she was strong and active, and on her first birthday we enjoyed a modest 5-mile hike together that September weekend.

Within months, though, Parka had a new limp. This time it was her right rear leg. Same symptoms, same diagnosis. One last trip to Sun Valley in late spring that year (I was getting in some great hiking, skiing, and snowshoeing trips in that beautiful mountain valley while Parka was being treated), and Parka was done with surgery. She faced a lifetime of pills (the doctor recommended a daily dose of glucosamine and chondroitin—two compounds found to aid the regeneration and restoration of cartilage and joint flexibility in humans and animals), yet she had four legs operated on with four successes. But what kind of dog would she be? Would I ever have a dog with whom to share regular hiking and my love of the trails?

After acknowledging the genetic joint ailments she suffered, Donna and I had accepted the fact that Parka would never be an active dog. Her last surgery was in March when she was about 18 months old. Yet by August that year, Parka was backpacking with me. A year later, as she turned three years old, she was out hiking with both Donna and me, enjoying long 20-mile outings, then demanding an hour of swimming at the end of the trail. As I write this, I hear her chasing Donna through the yard in a rambunctious game of soccer.

In short, she is stronger and healthier today than most dogs born with perfect joints.

I have always been a dog person, and I have always enjoyed hiking and sharing the wild backcountry with canine companions. But when I spend a day afield with Parka, the experience is especially sweet and special. She has endured so much pain and discomfort, but even at her worst moments, she wanted nothing so much as to go walking with me. Today, she can go hiking and she does it without pain and without any limitations. She is a true trail hound.

NOTE: The Cascade and Olympic Mountains often receive some of the most severe weather in the country. The storms of October 2003, which brought high winds and substantial rainfall, damaged countless roads and trails throughout Washington State. The U.S. Forest Service, operating with little budgetary support from Congress, tries to inventory the damage after each storm and make plans for repairs. But because their recreational budgets are stretched so tight, there is little the agency can do to quickly repair damaged trails. Before setting out for any hike, therefore, you should contact the appropriate land management agency (listed in the heading material for each trail in this book) to learn the current condition of the trail you'd like to visit. And while you're at it, call your senator or representative to let them know you'd like to see higher levels of funding for recreational programs on federal lands.

PREFACE

Through the last decade, the population of the United States—particularly the western states—has exhibited remarkable growth in two areas: hiking and dog ownership. Today, there are more hikers than ever before, and there are also more dog owners than at any time in history. That means the intersection of those two population segments—hikers with dogs—is booming, too.

Despite this growing affinity for dogs as pets, canines on trails continue to be a contentious issue. Some hikers feel domestic dogs have no place in the wilderness, citing cases of dogs attacking or molesting other hikers, harassing wildlife, and fouling trails and campsites. Yet, as with any trail user group, a small segment of the group creates the problems. With some care, understanding, and education, dogs can be tremendous trail users.

The key is education not only for the dogs and the dog owners but also for the general hiking public who will surely, at some time or another, encounter dogs on trails. People with sentiments against dogs on trails will successfully push for dog bans if dog owners continue to let their canines run freely up the trails, chasing wildlife (which, depending on the species pursued, could be a state or federal offense, punishable by sizable fines and/or jail time for dog owners) and harassing other hikers. And any unwanted approach of a hiker by a dog can be considered harassment.

Yet hikers create a dangerous precedent when they start advocating for the ban of some users—even canine trail users—merely because some of those users are behaving badly. With dogs already banned from some trails, trail "purists" are setting their sights on other bothersome uses. There are calls to outlaw trail runners on some trails, to ban certain styles of climbing (e.g., eliminate the use of fixed anchors anywhere in designated wilderness, and limit the amount of chalk used on big wall routes), and to severely limit the number of day hikers in some wildernesses.

The question is whether dogs are harmful to the natural environment, and the answer clearly is "no more so than hikers." Just as there are responsible and irresponsible hikers, there are responsible and irresponsible dog owners. Dogs who are well controlled by their owners and picked up after by their owners can be among the least intrusive types of trail

Ed Henderson and Katie on Mount Defiance

users. Animals restrained by leash or by good training stay on the trail, and they do no damage to the hard-packed tread (at least, far less than their two-legged friends). They don't trample vegetation at campsites (to the degree humans tend to do). They are no more of a threat to water quality than other hikers (dogs should be led at least 200 feet from water sources when they need to defecate, and their waste should be buried—in other words, dogs should adhere to the same guidelines as humans). Done right, dogs can actually help hikers see more wildlife with less impact to those wild critters.

That has been my own experience hiking with dogs. A well-trained dog—one who doesn't bark, who stays at heel or walks calmly on a short (less than ten feet) leash, and who obeys my vocal and hand-signal commands—increases my wildlife viewing opportunities substantially. That is, after all, why many dog breeds were created: to increase the likelihood of seeing animals during a hunt.

That's not to say dog owners should just rush out and hit the trail. Indeed, some wild areas are off limits by regulation to dogs, such as national parks and monuments. Know the land management rules before you set out. The hikes in this book were chosen because dogs are allowed. However, trail regulations and trail conditions can change. Hikers should contact the land manager before every hike to find out the current regulation status and condition of the route. But what I would like to focus upon here are special considerations that dog owners must always bear in mind when traveling with their four-legged friends. Hiking in the Cascades is one of the most enjoyable pursuits you'll ever experience, but it can also be one of the most deadly. All that beautiful, natural wilderness poses great danger to ill-prepared and unsuspecting hikers and their canines. A stroll through a sunny wildflower meadow at 6000 feet in the North Cascades can become a nightmare struggle through a slippery, sodden field of mud in a matter of moments. Thunderstorms can develop and blow in with little or no advance warning.

Hikers who plan to spend a day on the trail may twist an ankle while crossing a talus slope and end up having to the spend the night, waiting while someone makes the long hike out, summons medical personnel, and then leads them back to you. Dogs many sprain a knee or elbow, tear a pad, encounter a porcupine, or fall off a ledge.

The key to having an enjoyable and safe hike is being prepared—both you and the dog—not just for the conditions you expect to encounter but for the unexpected conditions, as well.

PART 1

Hiking with Your Dog

*If a dog will not come to you
after having looked you in the face,
you should go home and
examine your conscience.*

— *Woodrow Wilson*

Hitting the trail with your dog seems an easy, carefree undertaking. But there are some important issues to consider, and preparations to make, before heading out. The following will help you and your dog stay safe and make sure that you have a good time and don't affect the good times of other hikers.

Good Dogs Require Good Owners

Dogs provide many hours of joy and satisfaction to their owners. But dog ownership also brings many responsibilities. All too often, people fail to live up to these responsibilities, and the result is that the dogs suffer—as do responsible dog owners, who bear the brunt of negative feelings engendered by badly behaved dogs and their owners.

It is baffling that some dog owners fail to meet these requirements. The responsibilities aren't onerous—you must, first and foremost, care for your dog, feed it, and keep it healthy. You must also provide regular exercise and recreation for the dog and focus on training for obedience and manners. Owners who live up to these responsibilities will be rewarded with a good dog. Those who fail end up with a dog that exhibits unwelcome and unacceptable behaviors. In short, a "bad dog."

Dogs that are properly trained and respected will generally be acceptable to the public. It is when folks fail to meet these requirements that we see "bad dogs." That is, I generally agree with the notion that bad dogs are a result of bad owners, but I also accept the fact that some dogs just aren't trainable or are the result of selective breeding to bring out antisocial, aggressive behaviors. This needs to be considered when you go out to select a new puppy, or when you adopt an older dog. The general breed-traits of your dog will give a good indication of how that dog may react not only toward people but also toward other dogs. Aggressive traits can often be mitigated with strong, consistent training. Likewise, even the gentlest breed can be made to be aggressive and mean with improper training. I've known gentle, loving bullterriers and rottweilers and a few very nasty and aggressive Labrador retrievers. So in the end, the behavior of your dog almost always is a direct reflection on you and your ability to live up to the responsibilities of dog ownership.

If your dog is well behaved, well mannered, and responsive to commands, then you can and should be out hiking with her. The best way to keep trails and public lands open and accessible to dogs is to make sure that the dogs we see on those trails are good dogs, led by good owners.

Health Concerns for Your Dog

We all have this perception in our minds that dogs are tough, athletic creatures capable of running all day with no trouble. For some dogs, that may be true. But canines aren't much different than humans when it comes to physical fitness. Dogs who do nothing but lie around the living room—or the backyard—all day can't be expected to hike up a steep mountain trail with no ill effects, any more than a human couch potato can. They'll get stiff and sore and suffer cramped muscles, bruised and blistered toes, and annoying bug bites just like you and me.

To avoid that, you and your dog must stay active. Regular daily exercise and aerobic activity is essential to staying in shape. It doesn't have to be anything extreme or outrageous. A morning walk of 30 minutes or so will do wonders for both of you. You should start a new exercise program slowly—begin with a walk of 10 or 15 minutes and slowly lengthen the distance and quicken your pace. Within several weeks, you can be covering 2 or 3 miles at a fast walking pace (more if you set aside at least an hour each morning). This will help build and maintain muscle tone, improve circulation and lung capacity, and toughen and strengthen the dog's footpads, so they are less likely to tear or blister on the trail.

If your dog is a novice trail hound, you'll want to introduce him to trails slowly. Make your first several outings short day hikes so the dog can become accustomed to the trails and the vertical gains and losses. Let him develop muscle and experience on the trails. You can progressively increase outing length, but remember this: it is always the second day of hiking when muscles cramp and stiffen. So if you are planning a backpacking trip, go easy on Fido or he may wake up in the morning so stiff and sore that he'll refuse to move from camp. Your choices then are limited: Poke, prod, or bribe the dog into motion; carry the aching beast; or stay in camp a little longer. You can also

Devo gets shaky and cold without his vest. (Kelly McCaffrey)

Gnarly tree on Fifes Ridge Trail

help relieve some of the aches and pains with medications—even simple aspirin—that are explained in detail in the first-aid section of this book.

By maintaining a regular, fairly rigorous exercise routine throughout the year, you and your dog will become fit enough to enjoy the trails, rather than just survive them.

Permits and Regulations

The importance of setting a good example can't be understated. Not only must we make sure that our dogs behave properly but if we want the trails to remain open and accessible to us, we need to follow the rules ourselves. And there are plenty of rules these days. It seems as if we can't set out the door and onto the trails without first making sure we are not breaking the rules. In an effort to keep our wilderness areas wild and our trails safe and well-maintained, the land managers—especially the National Park Service and the U.S. Forest Service—have implemented a sometimes complex set of rules and regulations governing the use of public lands.

It also must be stressed that even when the rules are based on faulty information or outright misinformation, those regulations must be obeyed—at least until they can be overturned. For instance, the National Park Service bans dogs from most, if not all, wilderness park units partly because dogs were once believed to be the primary agent in the spreading of *giardia* cysts in water supplies. We now know that all animals, including humans and native wildlife, can be carriers of *giardia*. In short, any person entering the backcountry may be assisting in the spreading of these illness-producing protozoan cysts. Yet, even though dogs have been cleared of the blame for the spread of *giardia*, they are still banned from national park trails. The Park Service also cites possible harassment to wildlife, a legitimate concern when dog owners allow their dogs to run uncontrolled on trails.

Other agencies are generally more lenient toward dogs, though there are still some areas where they are restricted. The rules throughout Washington vary widely through the different forests and regions of the state. The first hard-and-fast rule is that dogs are not permitted on any trails in Mount Rainier and Olympic National Parks, and they are allowed only on the Pacific Crest Trail in the North Cascades National Park. In general, dogs are allowed on trails open to horses and many trails open only to hikers, with a few notable exceptions. Dogs are outright banned on the trails in and around the Enchantment Lakes Basin. The dog ban stems from the fact that the basin is extremely fragile and even human access there is severely restricted and regulated. Further, on all trails accessed off Interstate 90, leashes are required.

Although most dogs are hiking under their own power, occasionally a hiker will bring along a small, toy-sized breed. The rules and regulations governing dogs on trails apply equally to these smaller dogs even when they are carried by their owners. A ban on dogs means *no* dogs, whether they are walking or riding in a backpack.

No special permits are needed for dog hikers. All trail users, however, are required to purchase a Region 6 Forest Pass from the U.S. Forest Service to use any trailhead within the USFS Region 6 forests—that is, all national forests in Washington and Oregon. The passes sell for $5 per day or $30 for an annual pass.

When the trail enters wilderness areas, hikers must pick up and fill out a wilderness permit at the trailhead registration box (sometimes located along the trail at the wilderness boundary). For the time being, these permits are free and unlimited, at least on the trailheads covered in this book.

Go Lightly on the Land

With ever-growing populations of people, and dogs, on the earth, we each must work harder to ensure that we leave our pristine wild lands as undisturbed as possible. That means following the tenets of Leave No Trace camping and hiking, and you must apply those tenets to your dog as well.

As the name implies, the goals of Leave No Trace hiking are simply to eliminate as many signs of human (and canine) passage in wild country as possible. A national nonprofit organization, Leave No Trace, works to educate hikers, backpackers, horse packers, mountain bikers—and all other outdoor recreationists—about Leave No Trace practices and works to minimize the impacts of humans and their animals on wild lands.

The basic guiding principles of Leave No Trace are the following:

- Plan ahead and prepare
- Travel and camp on durable surfaces
- Pack it in, pack it out
- Properly dispose of what you can't pack out
- Leave what you find
- Minimize use and impact of fire

By working out the details of your trips before you ever leave home, you solve many problems before they have a chance to develop. Planning ahead includes designing an outing agenda that matches your skills and expectations. If you undertake an adventure that exceeds your skill level, you are more likely to end up in a situation where you put yourself at risk and, to ensure your personal safety, are forced to damage the environment such as by igniting large fires for warmth or by signaling. By planning trips from the start that match your skills, you avoid these difficulties, and both you and the wilderness benefit.

Preplanning also means preparing the gear you will need for yourself and your dog. Prepackaged food should be transferred out of the bulky, excessive packaging in which it comes. Store it instead in reusable bottles, or small, resealable plastic bags. This saves weight in your pack and reduces the risk of litter being left behind in the woods. For your gear, you can reduce your impact by dressing appropriately. For example, sturdy, waterproof boots and gaiters keep your feet and legs dry, enabling you to stay on the main trail when it is wet or muddy rather than stomping out secondary trails around the mudholes.

What you do in camp could be among the most important things you do as far as leaving no trace. Everyone loves to sit around a campfire, letting the orange flames hypnotize them and stir a wealth of thoughts and dreams. Unfortunately, if everyone who entered the wilderness were to build a fire, the campsites would be filled with charcoal and the forests would soon be picked clean of dead wood, leaving hordes of small critters with nowhere to scrounge for food (the insects that live and feed in dead wood provide meals for an army of birds and animals). So, fires should be left to the car campgrounds with their structured fire pits and readily available supplies of firewood. Backcountry campers should stick to small pack stoves, even where regulations allow campfires.

Hikers must also remember that anything packed in must be packed out, even biodegradable items such as apple cores or orange rinds. The

Katie has summitted several of Washington's mountains, including Bandera Peak. (Ed Henderson)

phrase, "leave only footprints, take only pictures," is a worthy slogan to live by when visiting the wilderness.

Give some thought to your campsites. When hardened sites are available, use them. Restricting campers to one or two sites around a lake prevents the shoreline from being trampled and stripped of its vegetation. If there are no established sites, choose a rocky or sandy area where you won't damage fragile vegetation. If you must camp in a meadow, choose a location with good drainage and limit the amount of time that your tent is set up. Rather than pitch the tent immediately upon reaching your camp, leave it in its stuff sack until you are done with dinner; then set it up. First thing next morning, break camp before breakfast—this helps prevent the plants under the tent from being smothered and, most of the time, even though they are a bit bent and crumpled, they will soon spring back up again.

Using water bladders—large, flexible water containers that hold anywhere from two liters to two gallons—allow you to comfortably camp well back from water sources, where you'll do less damage to fragile shorelines. An added bonus to this is that your dog will spend less time romping through the muddy shores and playing in the lakes, so when it's time to crawl into the tent, you don't have a wet mutt rolling on your sleeping bag. Keep your camps at least 100 feet away from lakeshores and streambanks. This not only lets other hikers—and animals—get to the water without having to bypass you but it helps keep the water clean.

Being aware of the needs of others goes a long way to keeping the wilderness setting intact and enjoyable. Chances are, when you get to your destination at trail's end, you and your dog won't be the only hikers there. Leave No Trace recommends that you minimize the visual impact of your camp. By avoiding brightly colored tents and packs, and opting instead for neutral colors and earth tones in your gear, you minimize the likelihood that others will see you and your camp. This helps provide a sense of solitude and privacy for all wilderness users. To further enhance that sense, visit the backcountry in small groups and during seasons or days of the week when fewer people will be on the trails.

You can also minimize the visual impact through site selection. That rocky bench overlooking the mountains across the valley might seem the perfect place for a tent, but what if you set up there and someone comes along behind and just wants to sit and enjoy the view for a few moments? With your camp established on the viewpoint, other hikers will feel uncomfortable stepping up for a look at that vista. It's a much better idea to set up well back from the most scenic locations so that you can still walk to them from camp and enjoy them but also so others can share the trail with you.

Another important Leave No Trace principle focuses on the business of taking care of personal business. The first rule of backcountry bathroom etiquette says that if an outhouse exists, use it. This seem obvious, but all too often, folks find backcountry toilets dark, dank affairs and they choose to use the woods rather than the rickety wooden structure provided by the land manager. It may be easier on your nose to head off into the woods, but this disperses human waste around the popular camping areas. Privies, on the other hand, keep the waste concentrated in a single site, minimizing contamination of area waters. The outhouses get even higher environmental marks if they feature removable holding tanks that can be air lifted out. These johns and their accompanying stack of tanks aren't exactly aesthetically pleasing, but having an ugly outhouse tucked into the corner of the woods is better than finding toilet paper strewn throughout the woods.

When privies aren't provided, the key factor to consider is location. You'll want to choose a site at least 200 to 300 feet from water, campsites, and trails. A location well out of sight of trails and viewpoints will give you privacy and reduce the odds of other hikers stumbling onto the site after you leave. Other factors to consider are ecological: a good surrounding of vegetation, with some direct sunlight, will aid decomposition.

Once you pick your place, start digging. The idea is to make like a cat and dig and bury your waste. You need to dig down through the organic duff into the mineral soil below—a hole six to eight inches deep is usually adequate. When you've taken care of business, refill the hole and camouflage it with rocks and sticks—this helps prevent other humans, or animals, from digging in the same location before decomposition has done its job.

Dogs, too, can learn from their feline friends. Dog waste must either be packed out or buried in a "cathole." Make sure your canine stays well clear of all waterways when taking care of its business, too.

By monitoring our own activities and reducing our individual impact, we add to the enjoyment of all wilderness users and ensure the long-term health of the environment we all love.

Good Canine Trail Etiquette

Anyone who enjoys backcountry trails should recognize their responsibility to those trails and to other trail users. We each must work to preserve the tranquility of the wild lands not only by being sensitive to the environment but by paying attention to other trail users as well.

As a hiker, you are responsible for your own actions. As a dog owner, you have an added responsibility: your dog's actions. When you encounter other trail users, whether hikers, climbers, trail runners, bicyclists, or horse riders, the only hard-and-fast rule is to observe common sense and simple courtesy. It's hard to overstate just how vital these two things—common sense and courtesy—are to maintaining an enjoyable, safe, and friendly situation on our trails when different types of trail users meet.

With that "Golden Rule of Trail Etiquette" firmly in mind, here are other techniques to smooth encounters on the trail:

- Hikers who take their dogs on the trails should have their dog on a leash—or under very strict voice command—at all times. Strict voice command means the dog immediately heels when told, stays at heel, and refrains from barking.
- When dog owners meet any other trail users, dog and owner must yield the right-of-way, stepping well clear of the trail to allow the other users to pass without worrying about "getting sniffed."
- When dog meets horse, the dog owner must first yield the trail

but also must make sure the dog stays calm, does not bark, and makes no move toward the horse. Horses can be easily spooked by strange dogs, and it is the dog owner's responsibility to keep his or her animal quiet and under firm control. Move well off the trail (downhill from the trail when possible) and stay off the trail, with your dog held close to your side, until the horses pass well beyond you.

- When hikers meet other hikers, the group heading uphill has the right-of-way. There are two general reasons for this. First, on steep ascents, hikers may be watching the trail before them and not notice the approach of descending hikers until they are face-to-face. More importantly, it is easier for descending hikers to break their stride and step off the trail than it is for those who have fallen into a good, climbing plod. If, however, the uphill hiker is in need of a rest, they may choose to step off the trail and yield the right-of-way to the downhill hikers, but this is the decision of the climbers alone.

- When hikers meet other user groups, the hikers should move off the trail. This is because hikers are generally the most mobile and flexible users; it is easier for hikers to step off the trail than for bicyclists to lift their bikes or for horse riders to get their animals off-trail.

- When hikers meet horseback riders, the hikers should step off the downhill side of the trail unless the terrain makes this difficult or dangerous. In that case, move to the uphill side of the trail, but crouch down a bit so you do not tower over the horses' heads. Also, do not stand behind trees or brush where the horse cannot see you until it gets close—when your sudden appearance could startle trail animals. Rather, stay in clear view and talk in a normal voice to the riders. This calms the horses.

- Stay on trails and practice minimum impact. Don't cut switchbacks, take shortcuts, or make new trails. If your destination is off-trail, leave the trail in as direct a manner as possible. That is, move away from the trail in a line perpendicular to the trail. Once well clear of the trail, adjust your route to your destination.

- Obey the rules specific to the trail you are visiting. Many trails are closed to certain types of use, including hiking with dogs or riding horses.

- Avoid disturbing wildlife, especially in winter and in calving or nesting areas. Observe from a distance—even if you cannot get the picture you want from a distance, resist the urge to move close. This not only keeps you safer but also prevents the animal from having to exert itself unnecessarily fleeing from you.

- Leave all natural creatures, objects, and features as you found them for others to enjoy.
- Never roll rocks off trails or cliffs—you never know who or what is below you.

These are just a few of the ways hikers with dogs can maintain a safe and harmonious trail environment. You don't need to make these rules fit every situation, just be friendly and courteous to other people on the trail. If they have questions about your dog, try to be informative and helpful. Many of the folks unfamiliar with dogs on trails will be reassured about the friendliness and trail-worthiness of your dog if they see the animal wearing a pack or reflective vest of some sort. Indeed, I have often encountered people on the trail who have been enchanted by the fact that Parka carries her own gear. If they have dogs, they'll often ask advice on training dogs to carry a pack; if they are non-dog owners, they'll at least smile and give her a pat.

Those of us who love to hike with our dogs must be the epitome of respectful, and responsible, trail users. When other hikers encounter dog

Shadow, ready to start a week-long journey (Ken Konigsmark)

hikers behaving responsibly, they will come away with a positive impression of dogs. In this way, we also help ourselves by preventing actions that could lead to additional trail closures or restrictions for dog hikers.

In short, therefore, hikers can usually avoid problems with other trail users by always practicing the Golden Rule of Trail Etiquette: Common sense and courtesy are the order of the day.

Myths and Misunderstandings about Dogs

There are many common myths about dogs and the outdoors. Misconceptions about dogs lead to misunderstandings by people who don't own dogs and don't hike with dogs. In this book I'd like to address several of these issues.

The presence of dogs will discourage wildlife from using the area.

This claim is contrary to my experiences. Hikers with dogs generally find that if they are quiet and attentive to their dog's behavior, they frequently will see more wildlife, including deer, small mammals, and birds. Dogs will often "point" toward wildlife, or otherwise give you a heads-up to the existence of a nearby critter. Dogs were bred to assist human hunters for good reason, after all—many of their senses are far superior to ours. As long as the dog is trained not to bark, or to chase or harass wildlife, they can alert you to more wildlife sightings.

Dogs chase and injure wildlife.

This is largely a training issue, although even a domestic dog that hasn't had lessons in leaving wildlife alone will generally be extremely cautious and hesitant to chase a wild animal about which it knows nothing. Still, any dog that does chase wildlife will be an unleashed dog that fails the "good trail dog" basic skill requirements. These animals don't deserve to be on trails, but good dogs don't deserve to be lumped together with the ill-mannered beasts, either.

Dog feces spread disease to wildlife.

The wildlife biologists I've spoken with throughout the western United States couldn't identify a single case of a dog transmitting a disease to a wildlife population. There is a very slight risk that wildlife may transmit disease to dogs, however, especially tick-borne diseases, so all trail dogs should be on a tick-control system and undergo tick-checks after each outing.

Dogs spread giardia *and other waterborne illnesses.*

Dogs, like all mammals—including humans—can spread *giardia*. But this is a resource issue. People are the biggest spreaders of *giardia* and other waterborne illnesses. If you're concerned about the water, worry less about the dogs and more about the people that have contaminated the water—then filter or chemically treat every bit of water you drink in the back-country.

Dogs damage sensitive or fragile environments.

Dogs who are kept under control (on leash or under strict voice command) do less damage than the humans with whom they hike (soft pads versus heavy hiking boots). They are certainly less damaging to trails and trail resources than larger, heavier pack animals. When venturing off-trail, the same holds true—humans have more impact on fragile settings than dogs have, and in some areas, neither should be leaving the trail. That's not to say off-trail travel is out of the question. But dog-owning hikers must realize they need to evaluate the impacts of not only themselves but also their dogs when deciding to go bushwhacking.

Trails are too crowded, trailhead parking too limited, and campsite space too much in demand to let dog hikers share those resources.

This is a resource issue, not a user issue. If specific subsets of the hiking community can be banned because of limited resources, then who's next: Hikers with kids? Hikers wearing heavy lug soles?

Trail width and visibility are too restricted for safe dog use.

If two hikers can pass on the trail, then a dog and a hiker should be able to pass another hiker, too. And certainly, any trail that is open to horses—which must have room for two horses to pass—has to be wide enough for dogs to pass. In any case, good trail etiquette for dog hikers is that they and their dogs step off the trail to let other users pass first.

Gear for You and Your Dog

No hiker should venture far up a trail without being properly equipped. Starting with the feet, a good pair of boots can make the difference between a wonderful hike and a horrible death march. Keep your feet happy and you'll be happy.

You can't talk boots without talking socks. Only one rule here: Wear whatever is most comfortable. Corollary to that rule: Never wear cotton.

Doggie backpacks must fit well and be loaded so the weight is balanced to prevent muscle pain and "saddle sores."

Cotton is a wonderful fabric when your life isn't on the line—it is soft, light, and airy. But get cotton wet and it stays wet. That means blisters on your feet. Wet cotton also lacks any insulation value. In fact, get it wet and it sucks *away* body heat, leaving you susceptible to hypothermia. So leave your cotton socks, cotton underwear, and even cotton tee shirts at home. The only cotton I carry on the trail is my trusty pink bandanna (pink because nobody else I know carries pink, so I always know which is mine).

The importance of good foot care holds true for four-legged hikers, too. Dogs develop tough pads, but those pads are also susceptible to wear and abrasion. When hiking on particularly abrasive ground (such as the basalt lava fields of the south Cascades) or in areas where spiny, prickly vegetation abounds (for example, some of the desert country of eastern Washington), it makes sense to protect your dog's feet with booties. Look for those that feature good, flexible upper sections so the dog can easily bend its wrists in a natural stride. You'll also want tough, nonslip surfaces on the bottom of the booties to help the dog maintain good traction. Fit is as important for dog booties as it is for hiker boots. A too-tight bootie will cramp dog toes, resulting in numbness from lack of circulation, or pain from lack of room for the toes to spread naturally with each step. Booties that fit too loosely will rub, possibly causing blisters or raw spots on the dog's pads or toes. A well-fitting bootie should be snug enough that it doesn't flop around but offers enough room for the dog's toes to flex and spread normally when it puts weight on its feet.

Booties are also handy for romps in the snow or on ice. In the snow, dog footwear prevents snow from balling in the fur growing between the dog's toes, and on ice, it prevents ice cuts on the pads and increases traction on slippery surfaces. Be sure to check the dog's booties periodically to make sure they aren't too snug (and therefore uncomfortable) nor too loose. Remember, as conditions change and the booties flex, the fit will change as well.

Hiking with a dog also requires you to reevaluate your standard hiking gear. You'll need to make sure your tent can accommodate you and the dog comfortably. Depending on the size of the dog, you might want to let her sleep on the end of your sleeping pad, or bring a small pad specifically for the dog. After a long day on the trail, the dog will want a comfortable night's rest, too, and a lightweight, closed-cell foam pad will go a long way toward providing that comfort, as well as warmth, for the dog. A fleece-lined or insulated "jacket" for the pooch will also be appreciated by dogs, especially those used to sleeping indoors or in milder temperatures than they'll

Dogs can be trained to carry gear in their backpacks but, to avoid developmental problems, don't put packs on dogs younger than a year old.

encounter in the mountains. Dog jackets and vests can be purchased—there has been a recent boom in companies producing quality outdoor gear for dogs (see Appendix B)—or they can be made from old jackets, vests, or sleeping bags.

When hiking in areas frequented by hunters and during hunting season, a brightly colored vest is a good idea for both you and your dog. Dogs can be easily mistaken for wild animals—for instance, many times when a cougar has been reported in an area, the sighting was actually of a yellow Labrador retriever. As a general practice, you should try to avoid popular hunting areas during peak hunting seasons

Grace, at the beginning of a trip. She carries her food and warm dog vest in and carries some trash out. (Dean Cass)

to minimize the risk of accidental injury to yourself or your dog, as well as to avoid spooking game and disrupting the hunting activity in the area. But if you are hiking in the autumn, and you suspect hunters may be in the area, accidents can be nearly eliminated simply by donning your dog in a blaze-orange vest, especially at those times when the dog isn't wearing its backpack. I also recommend brightly colored backpacks for dogs. Reflective tape on the vest or pack further enhances visibility of the dog, as does a flashing red signal light on the dog pack. Contact the state Department of Fish and Wildlife for specific information about hunting seasons and locations.

You'll also want collapsible bowls to feed and water your dog. These weigh mere ounces, and by keeping a full water dish in camp, you eliminate the need for the dog to repeatedly leave camp to drink from the nearby lake or stream, thus reducing your impact on the local environment as well as on other nearby hikers.

The good news is that dogs can carry all this gear themselves, as well as their own kibble and trail treats. Dogs, like humans, can generally carry about 20 percent of their body weight on their backs. So, a fifty-pound dog can carry about ten pounds.

Dog packs come in a variety of sizes and configurations. I favor packs with removable packbags—that is, the dog wears a lightweight vest harness, and the packbags attach to this harness with Velcro straps or buckles. This way, when we stop for breaks, or if we have to cross water, I can remove the pack from Parka's back quickly and easily without having to take off the harness. Reattaching it is as simple as draping the bags over her back once more.

When loading the dog pack, make sure to keep the load balanced and centered. You should also check to make sure there are no folds or creases in the pack or harness material to cause uncomfortable rubbing or abrasion on the dog's back.

Other items you pack for your dog will vary from trip to trip and from dog to dog. But there are a few things each and every one of us should have in our packs. For instance, every hiker who ventures more than a few hundred yards away from the road should be prepared to spend the night under the stars (or under the clouds, as may be more likely in Washington). Mountain storms can whip up in a hurry, catching sunny-day hikers by surprise. What was an easy-to-follow trail during a calm, clear day can disappear into a confusing world of fog and rain—or even snow—in a windy tempest. Therefore, every member of the party should have a pack loaded with the Ten Essentials, as well as a few other items that aren't necessarily essential but would be good to have on hand in an emergency.

The Ten Essentials

1) **Extra clothing.** This means more clothing than you would wear during the worst weather of the planned outing. If you get injured or lost, you won't be moving around generating heat, so you'll need to be able to bundle up.
2) **Extra food.** Pack enough that you'll have leftovers after an uneventful trip (those leftovers will keep you fed and fueled during an emergency).
3) **Sunglasses.** For most high alpine travel, they are absolutely essential.
4) **Knife.** A blade has a multitude of uses; some come easily to mind (whittling kindling for a fire; first-aid applications), while others won't become apparent until you find you don't have a knife handy. A multitool is an even better option because the pliers

can be used in repairs of damaged packs, stoves, and other gear.

5) **First-aid kit.** Nothing elaborate needed—especially if you are unfamiliar with some of the uses. Make sure you have bandages, gauze wraps, antiseptic, some aspirin, etc. A Red Cross first-aid training course is recommended.

6) **Fire starter.** An emergency campfire provides warmth but it also has a calming effect on most people. Without it the night is cold, dark, and intimidating. With it, the night is held at arm's length. A candle or tube of fire-starting ribbon is essential for starting a fire with wet wood.

7) **Matches.** Can't start a fire without them. Pack in a waterproof container and/or buy the waterproof/windproof variety. Book matches are useless in wind or wet weather and disposable lighters are unreliable.

8) **Flashlight.** If caught after dark, you'll need it to follow the trail. If forced to spend the night, you'll need it to set up emergency camp, gather wood, etc. Make sure to include extra batteries and bulb.

9) **Map.** Carry a topographic map of the area you plan to be in and knowledge of how to read it.

10) **Compass.** Again, make sure you know how to use it.

In addition to these essentials, I add two small kit bags. One is a repair kit, containing a twenty-foot length of nylon cord, a small roll of duct tape, some one-inch webbing and extra webbing buckles (to fix broken pack straps), and a small tube of super glue. The other tiny package at the bottom of my pack is an emergency survival kit, which holds a small metal mirror, an emergency mylar blanket, a plastic whistle, and a tiny signal smoke canister—all useful for signaling to search parties whether they are on the ground or in the air.

Those are your essentials. There are other essentials for your dog.

The Ten Canine Essentials

1) **Obedience training.** Before you set foot on a trail, make sure your dog is trained and can be trusted to behave when faced with other hikers, other dogs, wildlife, and an assortment of strange scents and sights in the backcountry. If they can't behave, don't take them.

2) **Doggy backpack.** Lets the dog carry his own gear.

3) **Basic first-aid kit.** (details listed later in this chapter)

4) **Dog food and trail treats.** You should pack more food than your dog normally consumes because it will be burning more calories than normal, and if you do end up having to spend an extra night out there, you need to keep the pup fed, too. Trail treats serve the same purpose for the dog as they do for you—quick energy and a pick-me-up during a strenuous day of hiking.

5) **Water and water bowl.** Don't count on there being water along the trail for the dog. Pack enough extra water to meet all your dog's drinking needs.

6) **Leash and collar, or harness.** Even if your dog is absolutely trained to voice command and stays at heel without a leash, sometimes leashes are required by law or just by common courtesy, so you should have one handy at all times.

7) **Insect repellent.** Be aware that some animals, and some people, have strong negative reactions to DEET-based repellents. So, before leaving home, dab a little DEET-based repellent on a patch of your dog's fur to see your dog's reaction to it. Look for signs of drowsiness, lethargy, or nausea. Remember to restrict repellent applications to those places the dog can't lick—the shoulders, the back of the neck, and around the ears (staying well clear of the ears and inner ears)—which are also near the most logical places mosquitoes will be looking for exposed skin (at the eyes, nose, and inner ears) to bite.

8) **ID tags and picture identification.** Your dog should always wear ID tags, and I'd heartily recommend microchipping her as well. To do this, a veterinarian injects a tiny, encoded microchip under the skin between the dog's shoulders. If your dog ever gets lost and is picked up by animal control, or is taken to a vet's office, a quick pass over the dog's back with a hand scanner reveals the chip and allows the staff at that shelter or hospital to identify your dog and notify you. Microchipping is so prevalent now that virtually every veterinarian and animal shelter automatically scans every unknown

dog they come in contact with to check for chips. Picture identification is also helpful to have in your pack. If your dog gets
lost far from home, you can use the image to make flyers and
handbills to post in the surrounding communities.

9) **Dog booties.** These help protect the dog's feet from rough
   ground or harsh vegetation. They are also great at keeping bandages secure if the dog damages its pads.

10) **Compact roll of plastic bags and trowel.** You'll need the bags
    to clean up after your dog on popular trails. When conditions
    warrant, you can use the trowel to take care of your dog's waste.
    Just pretend you are a cat—dig a small hole several inches deep
    in the forest duff, deposit the dog waste, and fill in the hole.

See Appendix B for a list of manufacturers and dog hiking resources
for more information on specific, dog hiking gear.

Canine First Aid

Try to imagine running through a field of grass that stands at eye level.
The grass whips your face, leaving tiny cuts on your nose and barbed seeds

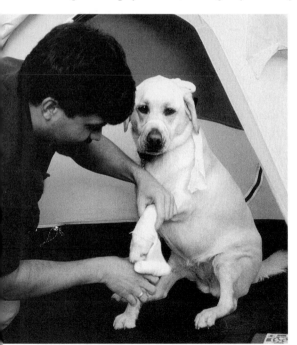

lodged in the corners of
your eyes. Now imagine
trying to pull those
painful grass seeds (also
known as foxtails) out
of your eyes without the
use of your thumbs.

That's the life of a
field dog, and despite
the problems, those trail
hounds love being out
in the woods and mead-
ows with their owners,
whether it's for a day of

*Bandages on a dog's feet
can be tricky to apply
effectively. Practice at
home to make sure you
can do it in the field.*

Pack in extra water to meet your dog's drinking needs. (Ken Konigsmark)

hunting, hiking, or just exploring the nearby state park. But those owners can make it even more enjoyable—and safe—for their pooches by being properly prepared with basic first aid for their dogs.

Dogs in the field, especially those that hit the trails with their backpacking people, face just as many, if not more, dangers to their health and well-being as do humans, so the pups' human partners should be carrying a first-aid kit tailored toward the canine needs.

Veterinarians generally agree wholeheartedly that some dogs make great outdoor companions, but even the most energetic dog needs to be taken care of before, during, and after each outing.

For instance, before heading out with your pooch, there are a few things you can do to make the trip safer and reduce the chances of having to use your first-aid kit. For starters, get your dog in trail condition. Too often, we tend to think of dogs as some kind of wonder athlete—they are ready to go at a moment's notice and they can hike all day, every day, without a problem. Sorry, folks, but dogs can be couch potatoes, too. They suffer sore muscles, charley horses, sprains, and strains just like we do. To help canines avoid muscle soreness and injury, start them on a conditioning program before you head for the hills. All dogs love morning walks, and hiking dogs (not to mention their hiking owners) will benefit greatly from a long walk in the morning before you head for work and another in the evening when you get home.

Before launching into a new exercise program for your dog, get her checked out by a vet to make sure there are no medical problems. Then start slowly. Begin with walks of ten to fifteen minutes for the first few days, and gradually add time and distance to your walks. Eventually, you can progress to covering 3 to 5 miles at a good fast walking pace; set aside at least an hour each morning and you should be able to get at least 3 miles in before breakfast. In a couple months, both you and your dog will be toned and ready for a long backpacking trip in the mountains.

Once on the trail, dogs are remarkably resilient, but there are a few common problems they endure about which humans do not have to worry. By knowing what to look for, we can keep Fido happy and healthy. One important rule to keep in mind though, before trying to administer first aid to a dog: Even the friendliest, most lovable dog can bite when it is scared or in pain, so apply a muzzle to the injured dog before treating it.

Common problems include the following:

Grass seeds. To dogs, grass seeds, especially foxtails, can be deadly. The foxtails that pierce our socks and scratch our legs can do far more damage to a dog. Because muzzle level for dogs is around our knee level—and hunting breeds typically walk with their noses even closer to the ground—foxtails can lodge in their ears, eyes, nose, and throat.

A dog that paws at its mouth, gags or drools extensively, or launches into an eating frenzy may have grass seeds lodged in the back of its mouth or in its throat.

Open the dog's mouth and, if you see a seed or other material, try to remove it with your fingers. If you cannot locate the object, feed the dog bread to try to dislodge the seed from the throat. Administer an over-the-counter cough suppressant—on routes where heavy grass cover is expected, carry a small bottle of Chloraseptic in a canine first-aid kit—to deaden the throat and make it easier for the dog to breathe. Have the dog checked by a vet as soon as possible.

Grass seeds in the nose can be even more troublesome and dangerous. The barblike protrusions on foxtails make them difficult to remove. A dog with a foxtail up its nose will be seized by a harsh fit of sneezing, and the sneezing will persist until the seed is removed. If you see the seed protruding from the nose, pull it out. If not, get your dog to the vet as soon as possible—removal of a seed far up the nose requires the use of special instruments. A foxtail seed left too long in the nose can travel into the brain and cause an abscess.

Grass seed in the ear or eyes should be removed as soon as possible as well. A dog that shakes its head violently and frequently may have a foxtail lodged inside. If you see any part of the seed, grasp it with fingers, tweezers, or small alligator forceps and pull it out. If not, get your dog to a vet as soon as possible.

Foxtails can also stick in a dog's eye and may become wedged under the third eyelid. This can cause a great deal of pain to the dog but is relatively easy to remedy. Just remove the seed. Try to flush the eye with water to wash the object out, or if you see it, use fingertip tweezers or a damp cotton-tipped swab to remove it.

Torn dewclaws and split claws. Dewclaws are the fifth "finger" on the dog's front legs. Because dogs essentially walk on their toes, the dewclaw—essentially the dogs' thumb—usually dangles uselessly several inches above the ground. The dewclaw can catch on brush, rocks, or other trail obstructions the dog has to navigate over, under, or around.

A torn dewclaw can bleed a lot but generally isn't a serious injury. First, stop the bleeding through direct pressure. Next, wrap gauze around the dewclaw and leg, then tape around that to hold the dewclaw firmly to the leg. Don't wrap it too tightly, however, or you'll constrict blood flow into the lower leg.

Dogs can also chip or split the claws on their toes. While not serious injuries, these can be painful for the dog. A bad, bleeding split may require bandaging. First, stop the bleed with a bit of styptic powder (which speeds coagulation of the blood), then bandage the wound. If the split or tear is less severe, the broken claw can often be held together with a dot of superglue. A dog bootie is valuable here to keep the injury from being made worse on the hike out.

Dehydration, heat stroke, hypothermia. Dogs are prone to all three of these, just as you are. Make sure you have enough water for both you and your dog when out hiking. If it gets hot, watch the dog for signs of heat exhaustion—lethargy, clumsiness, and heavy panting. Slow down, let the dog rest in the shade, and soak it down with water (a swim in a mountain creek or lake is the best way to beat heat exhaustion and heat stroke). You can check for dehydration on many dog breeds by pinching up a small bit of the skin along its back. The skin should snap quickly

Grace, wearing a natural flea collar, with a spare copy of the truck key attached. (Dean Cass)

back into place after you release it. If it stays peaked or creased for a moment after you pinch, the dog is dehydrated. To cool off the dog, stop immediately for a long rest and provide the pooch with plenty of water, encouraging it to drink frequently over the next hour or two. When you start hiking again, go slowly and give the dog frequent drinks from your water bottle.

Burns. When backpacking, you'll likely be cooking on a camp stove resting on the ground. If the pooch noses up to the boiling pot, it can get a severe burn quickly. Cool the burn with snow or cold water, then apply topical antibiotic where blisters are broken, and bandage lightly to keep the burn area clean. Get the dog to a vet.

Pad injury. Sharp rocks and ice can lacerate a dog's feet, but it's not only natural objects that threaten the dog. Throughout the mountains of the Cascades and Olympics, old mining claims are littered with rusty metal and glass. If Spike cuts a pad, check the wound for foreign objects—remove any bits of glass, metal, etc.—then stop the bleeding through direct pressure. Apply an antiseptic ointment and bandage the foot. A dog bootie can be used to hold the bandage in place and prevent the dog from chewing on the bandage.

Drowning. Even a water-loving Labrador can drown. Many mountain lakes are ringed with rocks that make it difficult for a dog to scramble out, and often, high country water is topped with thin ice, and dogs aren't smart enough to know the difference between solid ground and thin ice. If your dog goes in the drink and has trouble getting out, you may have to perform a rescue. Once the dog is on dry land, check its breathing. If the dog is breathing, but struggling to do so, you should try to get as much water out of its lungs as possible. First, suspend the dog by its hind legs, so it hangs upside down. While doing this, have someone close the dog's mouth and blow hard into its nose several times to force air into the lungs, displacing the water.

If the dog isn't breathing, perform CPR immediately. Lay the dog on its right side and check its pulse by placing your fingertips on the left side of the chest behind the elbow. If you find no pulse, clear the dog's airway, close its mouth, and blow into the nose until the lungs expand. Then, push over the heart four times, depressing the chest one to two inches. Repeat these two steps about fifteen times per minute for at least five minutes or until the dog regains consciousness.

Sore muscles, etc. Most vets will provide a small supply of prescription anti-inflammatory medication for a doggy first-aid kit, or you can rely on good old aspirin for the dog's aches and pains. But, while aspirin is effective, it can cause stomach ailments. To prevent this, use a buffered aspirin or one that is enteric-coated (designed to dissolve in the intestine rather than the stomach).

A Doggy First-aid Kit

Having a dog first-aid kit is essential, even if it's just the bare-bones essentials (i.e., bandages, buffered aspirin, antiseptic wash, tweezers for removing thorns and foxtails). Something is better than nothing. For a comprehensive canine first-aid kit, though, my veterinarian—a specialist in large sporting dogs who has literally written the book on field first aid for dogs—recommends that anyone heading into the wild with a canine companion carry the following essentials. Some of these are the same you would carry for yourself:

Instruments:
- Scissors/bandage scissors
- Toenail clippers
- Rectal thermometer (**NOTE:** A healthy dog should show a temperature of 101 degrees Fahrenheit when taken rectally.)

Cleansers and disinfectants:
- 3% hydrogen peroxide
- Betadine
- Canine eyewash (available at any large pet supply store)

Topical antibiotics and ointments (nonprescription):
- Calamine lotion
- Triple antibiotic ointment (bacitracin, neomycin, or polymyxin)
- Baking soda (for bee stings)
- Petroleum jelly
- Styptic powder

Medications:
- Enteric-coated or buffered aspirin
- Imodium-A-D
- Pepto-Bismol or other antacid

Dressings and bandages:
- Gauze pads (four-inches square)
- Gauze roll
- Nonstick pads
- Adhesive tape (one-inch and two-inch rolls)

Miscellaneous:
- Tweezers
- Muzzle
- Dog boots
- Any prescription medication your dog needs

For extended trips, consult your vet about any other prescription medications that may be needed in an emergency situation, including: oral antibiotics, eye medications, ear medications, emetics (to induce vomiting), pain medications and anti-inflammatories, and needle and suture for large open wounds.

Water

In the backcountry, you'll want to treat your drinking water. Wherever humans have gone, germs have gone with them, and humans have gone just about everywhere. That means that even the most pristine mountain stream may harbor microscopic nasties like *giardia* cysts, cryptosporidium, or *E. coli*. Four-legged animals also spread diseases.

Treating water can be as simple as boiling it, chemically purifying it (adding iodine tablets), or pumping it through one of the new gen-

Waterborne illnesses can strike dogs, too.

eration of water filters or purifiers. (**Note:** Pump units labeled as filters generally remove everything *but* viruses, which are too small to be filtered out. Pumps labeled as purifiers must have a chemical element—usually iodine—that kills the viruses after filtering all the other bugs out.) Never drink untreated water, or your intestines may never forgive you.

Dogs, too, are susceptible to *giardia* and other waterborne illnesses. It might be difficult to keep your pooch from drinking at stream crossings, but to minimize its exposure, make sure to give it filtered or treated water whenever possible.

Camp Care: Cleanup

When it comes time to wash up, whether it is just your hands or your dinner pots, give a thought to what you would want, or wouldn't want to find, in the water you drink. You get your drinking water from the nearby lake or stream, right? Would you want to find someone's leftover macaroni and cheese in it? Or their soap scum? Of course not, and neither do other folks, so you need to be careful with cleanup.

When washing your hands, first rinse off in plain water as much dust and dirt as you can. If you still feel the need for a soapy wash, collect a pot of water from the lake or stream and move at least 100 feet away. Apply a tiny bit of biodegradable soap on your hands, dribble on a little water, and lather up. Use a bandanna or towel to wipe away most of the soap, then rinse with the water in the pot. Follow the same procedure with your pots and pans, making sure you eat all the food first. Never dump leftover food in the water or on the ground. If you can't eat it, and you don't want to feed it to your dog, pack it into a plastic bag and store it with your other food—in other words, carry it out!

Bears

There are an estimated 30,000 to 35,000 black bears in Washington, and the big bruins can be found roaming every corner and every county in Washington. Watching bears graze through a rich huckleberry patch or seeing them flip dead logs in search of grubs can be an exciting and rewarding experience—provided, of course, you aren't in the same berry patch. The bears tend to prefer solitude to human company and will generally flee long before you have a chance to get too close. There are times, however, when bears either don't hear hikers approaching, or they are more interested in defending their food source—or their young—than they are in avoiding a confrontation.

Dogs can be both a blessing and a curse when it comes to bears. A dog on a leash, or under strict voice command, may alert you to a bear's presence and also act as a deterrent to the bear. But a dog running loose may instinctively give chase, only to find the bear turning to fight its way out of the aggressive attack. The dog, then, could do what comes naturally to it and retreat to a position of safety—namely, behind you. In this case, the bear will almost invariably follow the fleeing dog, meaning it will soon be charging straight toward your position. This is one of the best reasons for always keeping your dog on a leash.

To keep your dogs safe, always keep them on a leash. (M. David Conrad)

These instances of attack are rare, and you can further minimize the odds of an encounter with an aggressive bear by doing the following:

- Keep your dog on a leash.
- Hike in a group and hike only during daylight hours.
- Talk or sing as you hike. If bears hear you coming, they will usually avoid you.
- Be aware of the environment around you, and know how to identify "bear sign." Overturned rocks and torn-up deadwood often are the result of a bear searching for grubs. Berry bushes stripped of berries, with leaves, branches, and berries littering the ground under the bushes, show where a bear has fed. Claw marks on trees, tracks, and scat are the most common signs of a bear's recent presence.
- Stay away from abundant food sources and dead animals. Keep your dog away from carcasses. Black bears are opportunistic and will scavenge food. A bear that finds a dead deer will hang around until the meat is gone, and it will defend that food against any perceived threat.
- Leave the hair spray, cologne, scented soaps, and hand creams

at home. Using scented sprays and body lotions makes you smell like a big, tasty treat.

Speaking of food, you'll want to learn the proper method for bear-bagging your food, fragrant toiletries, and heavily scented clothing items (such as shirts with lots of sweat and/or deodorant). Unfortunately, not all hikers behave as they should in bear country, especially in camp. Bears are intelligent animals, and they are opportunistic feeders. That is, they will seek out easy meals wherever they can. That's why some bears have learned that sloppy hikers can provide good, tasty meals. These bears are smart enough to watch human camps, and look for the slobs among us. To avoid being seen as a "sloppy hiker," make sure that you follow these guidelines:

- Never eat or cook in your tent, or feed your dog there. Spilled food or even food odors can permeate the nylon material, making your tent smell, at least to a bear, like last night's dinner.
- Never clean fish within 100 feet of camp.
- Always store all food, including your dog's food and other scented items, in designated stuff sacks when preparing to hang them. (Don't use your sleeping bag stuff sack or the food odors can be transferred later to the sleeping bag, making the bear think you are a big, smelly meat roll.)
- Always suspend your food bags at least twelve feet in the air and eight to ten feet from the nearest tree trunk. At some popular backcountry camps, the land managers provide wires, complete with pulleys, to help you do this, but you should learn how to string your own rope to achieve these heights, too.
- Never try to lure wild animals closer to you with food. One notable case in Olympic National Park comes to mind. A young couple wanted to have the local chipmunks come closer to their tent so they could get pictures, so they laid down a line of M&M candies from a jumble of nearby logs to their tent entrance. They then ducked into the tent with camera ready. Soon, they heard something moving outside, snuffling up the candy. Expecting a cute little chipmunk, they got a chocolate-happy black bear. Their yells scared the bear away, but things could have turned out differently.

On the very rare occasion, hikers can do all the right things and a bear will still behave aggressively. It could be as simple as being in the wrong place at the wrong time—I found myself between a bear black sow and one of her cubs once simply because the cub had wandered downhill of the trail, while the sow was uphill of it. Fortunately, youngster was a second-year cub and momma bear was ready to toss it out on its own at any time, so she barely looked up from her huckleberry dinner as I grouped the hikers behind me into a tight cluster and hustled everyone up the trail. But the bear could have turned aggressive. If you find yourself in a similar situation, here are some guidelines to follow in an encounter:

- Respect a bear's need for personal space. Keep your dog on a leash and in close control. If you see a bear in the distance, make a wide detour around it, or if that's not possible, leave the area.
- If you encounter a bear at close range, remain calm. Do not run because this may trigger a prey-chase reaction from the bear.
- Talk in a low-pitched, calm manner to the bear to help identify yourself as a human.
- Hold your arms out from your body, and if wearing a jacket, open the front and hold it over your head so you appear to be as big as possible.
- Don't stare directly at the bear—the bear may interpret this as a direct threat or challenge.
- Slowly move upwind of the bear if you can do so without crowding the bear. The bear's strongest sense is its sense of smell, and if it can sniff you and identify you as human, it may retreat.
- Know how to interpret bear actions. A nervous bear will often rumble in its chest, clack its teeth and "pop" its jaw. It may paw the ground and swing its head violently side to side. If the bear does this, watch it closely (without staring directly at it). Continue speaking calmly in a low-pitched voice.
- A bear may bluff-charge—run at you but stop well before reaching you—to intimidate you. Resist the urge to run because that could turn the bluff into a real charge and you will *not* be able to outrun the bear—black bears can run at speeds up to 35 miles per hour through log-strewn forests.
- If you surprise a bear and it does charge from close range, lie down and play dead. A surprised bear will leave you once the perceived threat is neutralized. However, if the bear wasn't attacking because it was surprised—if it charges from a long distance, or if it has had a chance to identify you and still attacks—you should fight back.

A bear in this situation is behaving in a predatory manner (as opposed to the defensive attack of a surprised bear) and is looking at you as food. Kick, stab, or punch at the bear. If it knows you will fight back, it may leave you and search for easier prey.

- Carry a twelve-ounce (or larger) can of pepper-spray bear deterrent. The spray—a high concentration of oils from hot peppers—should fire out at least twenty or thirty feet in a broad mist. Don't use the spray unless a bear is actually charging and is in range of the spray.

Cougars

Very few hikers ever see cougars in the wild. Not only are these big cats solitary, shy animals in the woods, but there aren't very many of them: just 2500 to 3000 roam the entire state of Washington. Cougars also seem to have an inherent fear and wariness of dogs. Still, cougars and hikers do sometimes encounter one another. In these cases, the hikers should, in my opinion, count their blessings—they will likely never see a more majestic animal than a wild cougar. To make sure the encounter is a positive one, hikers must understand these cats. Cougars are shy but very curious. They will follow hikers simply to see what kind of beasts we are, but they very rarely (as in, almost never) attack adult humans. If you do encounter a cougar, remember that cougars rely on prey that cannot or will not fight back. So, as soon as you see the cat do the following:

- Do not run. Running may trigger a cougar's attack instinct.
- Stand up and face the animal. Virtually every recorded cougar attack of humans has been a predator/prey attack. If you appear as another aggressive predator rather than as prey, the cougar will back down.
- Try to appear large—wave your arms or spread a jacket above your head. The idea is to make the cougar think you are the bigger, meaner beast.
- Pick up children off the ground and hold them close.
- Do maintain eye contact with the animal. The cougar will interpret this as a show of dominance on your part.
- Do not approach the animal; back away slowly if you can safely do so.

The cougar may not buy you as a threat and may continue to display aggressive behavior, especially toward people with smaller body frames. If this is the case do the following:

- Do not turn your back or take your eyes off the cougar.
- Remain standing.
- Throw things—provided you don't have to bend over to pick them up. Throw your water bottle or camera, wave your hiking stick, and if the cat gets close enough, whack it *hard* with your hiking staff (I know of two cases where women delivered good, hard whacks across the nose of aggressive-acting cougars, and the cats immediately turned tail and ran away).
- Shout loudly.
- Fight back aggressively.

You can minimize the already slim chances of having a negative cougar encounter by doing the following:

- Keep dogs on-leash and under control. A cougar may attack a loose, solitary dog, but a leashed dog next to you makes two foes for the cougar to deal with—and cougars are too smart to take on two aggressive animals at once.
- Do not hike or jog alone (in fact, don't jog at all—joggers look like fleeing prey to a predator).
- Keep children within sight and close at all times.
- Avoid dead animals.
- Keep a clean camp.
- Be alert to the surroundings.
- Use a walking stick or hiking poles, which can be used for defense.

Remember, above all else cougars are curious animals. They may appear threatening when they are only being inquisitive. By presenting yourself as a bigger, meaner critter than the cougar, you will be able to avoid an attack (the big cats realize that there is enough easy prey that they don't have to mess with something that will fight back). Keep in mind that fewer than twenty fatal cougar attacks have occurred in the United States in the past one hundred years, whereas more than fifty people are killed, on average, by deer each year—mostly in automobile collisions with the deer.

Weather

Wild weather is a far greater threat to hikers than are wild animals. The trails of the Cascades and Olympics run through some of the most

Clouds gather over the lower Teanaway Valley, illustrating just how quickly weather can change in the mountains.

remote high country in the state. Mountain weather in general is famously unpredictable, but the Cascade Mountains stretch that unpredictability to sometimes absurd lengths. The Cascades see a lot of storms and precipitation.

The high, jagged nature of the mountains, coupled with their proximity to the Pacific Ocean, makes them magnets for every bit of moisture in the atmosphere. As the moist air comes rushing in off the Pacific, it hits the western front of the Cascades. The air is pushed up the slopes of the mountains to form clouds and condense as rain, feeding the wet rainforests that dominate the western slopes. By the time the airstream crests the Cascades and starts down the east slopes, the atmosphere has lost its moisture load, leaving the east side dry and forests filled with open stands of more drought-resistant trees.

Where east meets west—roughly marked by the Pacific Crest Trail—the wet clouds hit the dry heat, often creating thunderstorms. Hikers on the trail must be aware of this potential, because the storms can brew up at any month of the year. Storms can also come up quickly and with little warning, and a hiker stuck on a high pass as a thunderstorm develops is a likely target for a lightning bolt.

To reduce the dangers of lightning, if thunderstorms are forecast or develop while you are hiking in the mountains, the following are several steps you can take:

- Use a National Oceanic and Atmospheric Administration (NOAA) weather radio (a radio set to tune in to one of the national weather forecast frequencies) to keep abreast of the latest weather information.
- Avoid travel on mountaintops and ridge crests.
- Avoid setting up camp in narrow valleys, gullies, or ridge tops. Instead, look for campsites in broad, open valleys and meadows, keeping away from large rock formations.
- Stay well away from bodies of water.
- If your hair stands on end, or if you feel static shocks, move immediately to another location—the static electricity you feel could very well be a precursor to a lightning strike.
- If there is a shelter or building nearby, get into it. Don't take shelter under trees, however, especially in open areas.
- If there is no shelter available, and lightning is flashing, remove your pack (any metal stays or frame are natural electrical conduits) and crouch down, balancing on the balls of your feet, to reduce your surface area contact with the ground, until the lightning clears the area.

Of course, thunderstorms aren't the only weather hazards that hikers face. A sudden rain squall can depress temperatures 15 or 20 degrees in a matter of minutes. Folks dressed for hot summer hiking need to be prepared for such temperature drops and the accompanying soaking rains if they want to avoid hypothermia.

If the temperature drop is great enough, hikers can miss the rain and get hit instead by snow. I've seen snowstorms blow through the Cascades every month of the year, with as much as a foot falling on some routes in late August.

Besides fresh fallen snow, summer hikers need to be aware of snowfields left over from the previous winter's snowpack. Depending on the severity of the past winter, and the weather conditions of the spring and early summer, some mountain trails may melt out in June while others remain snow covered well into August or beyond—some years, parts of the Cascades never melt out.

In addition to treacherous footing and difficulties in routefinding, these lingering snowfields are prone to avalanches or landslides. Dogs, of course, can both trigger and be caught by avalanches. Keep your dog close.

Using this Book

No guidebook can provide all the details of a trail, nor stay current with constantly changing conditions of trails, stream crossings, access roads, and administrative rules. So, before any hike, you should call the land manager for the latest information on trail conditions—

you'll find the phone numbers in the introductory material to each hike.

You'll also find references to the Green Trails map quadrants covering the described hike, and when those are not available, the United States Geological Survey (USGS) map quadrant (7.5-minute series). Green Trails, Inc., uses the standard 7.5-minute USGS topographical maps as their starting point; but while USGS maps may not have been updated since the 1950s, the Green Trails cartographers field check trail conditions and record changes yearly. Many hikers still use the USGS maps for hiking, and they work well for locating mountains and contours because these natural features don't change much or rapidly. But the human-created features do change, and in my opinion, Green Trails does the best job of all the mapmakers at staying abreast of those changes.

Green Trails and some USGS maps are available at most outdoor retailers in the state, as well as at many U.S. Forest Service offices.

Please bear in mind that trail hiking times in this book are estimations based on my experience on the trail and the speed with which I expect the average hiker to travel with lunch and other breaks. When calculating estimated times, I start with an average speed of 2 miles per hour but vary that based on the specific trail features (steep ascents, descents, rough tread, etc.). You may find my estimates are too high or too low. I apologize in advance and again encourage you to use the estimated time given merely as a tool to help plan your hike and not as a gauge by which to measure your success or failure.

Elevation gain is the absolute feet in elevation gained or lost from the trailhead to the end of the hike. Elevation gain together with round-trip hike length helps give an indicator of the overall difficulty of the hike.

The "best hiking time" listing is another subjective tool meant to be a guide and not an absolute. Some years, the heavy winter snowpack doesn't melt off the high country until early September. In other years, the highest trails may be snowfree by the Fourth of July. Again, use this as a tool to help plan your trips, then make sure to call the land manager to get the latest information on trail conditions.

Luna, a blind Lab mix, can navigate tough trails with the help of her owner. (Carl Gronquist)

How the Trails Were Selected

Most trails on U.S. Forest Service lands, as well as those on Bureau of Land Management properties, are open to dogs (only the National Park Service bans dogs outright on trails). That means that there are literally hundreds of possible hiking routes for you and your dog in Washington. This guidebook isn't meant to be a complete source to all those trails, nor even a guide to the best of them, necessarily.

The goal with this work was to present a sampling of dog hiking routes throughout the Olympic and Cascade ranges. I sought out scenic routes that offered short day to long backpacking adventures. The single, common element is trails that are open and accessible to dogs. But when selecting places to hike with my dog, I do look for a couple of key elements. First, I try to steer clear of heavily used hiking trails— some people just plain don't like dogs, so I try to avoid encounters by avoiding the places people tend to congregate. Very few of these hikes are ones you will find to be overly crowded. That means that you won't find the popular trails lining the Interstate 90 corridor in this book.

I also look for features that will be of interest to both human and canine. For the dog's sake, I avoid routes with steep, rocky scrambles, and lean toward trails that frequently access lakes, rivers, and ponds (a hard-working dog needs an almost endless supply of water to stay hydrated and healthy). In summer months, I avoid trails where snakes are common, and in winter, I avoid trails that tend to be icy (water over the trail in summer suggests ice over the trail in winter) to avoid slips and falls by humans and dogs.

With these guidelines in mind, I gleaned eighty routes from my experiences with Parka on trails in Washington and share them here with you. But remember: This is a guidebook to get you started. Enjoy these trails, but don't limit yourself to them.

Enjoy the Trails: Get Involved

Above all else, I hope you can safely enjoy the trails in this book. If you and your dog achieve even a fraction of the enjoyment I have found with my dog, Parka, exploring the backcountry of Washington, then you will be well rewarded. These trails exist for our enjoyment and for the enjoyment of future generations. We can use them and protect them at the same time if we are careful with our actions on the land and forthright with our demands made to Congress and public agencies to continue and further the protection of our country's wild lands.

Throughout the twentieth century, wilderness lovers of all kinds helped secure protection for the lands we enjoy today. As we move into the twenty-first century we must see to it that those protections continue and that the last bits of wild lands are also preserved for the enjoyment of future generations.

Please, if you enjoy these trails, get involved. Something as simple as writing a letter to your member of Congress urging wilderness protection can make a big difference. For more information contact:

Washington Trails Association
1305 Fourth Avenue, Suite 512
Seattle, WA 98101
(206) 625-1367
www.wta.org

The Mountaineers
300 Third Avenue West
Seattle, WA 98119
(206) 284-6310
www.mountaineers.org

A Note About Safety

Safety is an important concern in all outdoor activities. No guidebook can alert you to every hazard or anticipate the limitations of every reader. Therefore, the descriptions of roads, trails, routes, and natural features in this book are not representations that a particular place or excursion will be safe for your party. When you follow any of the routes described in this book, you assume responsibility for your own safety. Under normal conditions, such excursions require the usual attention to traffic, road and trail conditions, weather, terrain, the capabilities of your party, and other factors. Because many of the lands in this book are subject to development and/or change of ownership, conditions may have changed since this book was written that make your use of some of these routes unwise. Always check for current conditions, obey posted private property signs, and avoid confrontations with property owners or managers. Keeping informed on current conditions and exercising common sense are the keys to a safe, enjoyable outing.

The Mountaineers Books

PART 2

The Trails

The great pleasure of a dog
is that you may make a fool of yourself
with him and not only will he not scold you,
but he will make a fool of himself too.

—Samuel Butler

OLYMPICS

1. Colonel Bob

Round trip: 14 miles
Hiking time: 9 hours (day hike or backpacking trip)
High point: 4510 feet
Elevation gain: 4280 feet
Best hiking time: May through November
Maps: Green Trails Quinault Lake No. 197, Grisdale No. 198
Contact: Olympic National Forest, Pacific Ranger District, Quinault office, (360) 288-2525

Starting near sea level (trailhead elevation is a mere 230 feet), the Colonel Bob Trail climbs endlessly through deep old-growth forests, small forest clearings, and alpine meadows to provide stunning views of the Quinault Lake basin from the 4510-foot summit of Colonel Bob Mountain. Hikers—those going on four legs as well as their two-legged companions—must be well prepared for the rigorous climb. While the trail can be traveled in a long day, the preferred method to enjoy this route is by backpacking in and staying overnight. There are fine, forest camps at Mulkey Shelter and again at Moonshine Flats near the summit.

To get there, from Hoquiam drive 43 miles north on U.S. Highway 101 to Lake Quinault's South Shore Road. Turn right and follow the road 6 miles to the trailhead parking area, found just south (right) of the road.

The trail begins with a gentle ascent while traversing west along the southern wall of the Quinault River valley. The deep, old forest here boasts ancient cedar and hemlock, as well as monstrous, big leaf maples. These

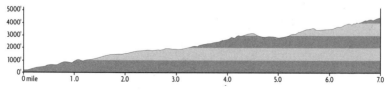

moss-laden trees support massive amounts of life within their branches. Complete microecosystems reside within the broad crotches and branch creases. Look close as you pass the big maples, and you might see families of birds, squirrels, martens, raccoons, mice, wood rats, salamanders, and more. An even closer look reveals unique plants growing in the heavy, moss-rich soil that has accumulated in the hollows and holes around the ancient trees.

Maples and alders fill the old-growth forest around Colonel Bob Mountain with tons of leaf litter each year.

After a half mile of gentle climbing, the trail turns south into Ziegler Creek Canyon and, after a short stretch of switchbacks, begins a long, moist climb south along the slope between Ziegler Creek and Wooded Peak. Keep your dog on a short leash here and watch it closely because it might alert you to elk browsing the rich forage of the rainforest around you. As the trail climbs, the forest closes in tighter, with fewer maples and far more towering hemlocks and firs. At 4 miles, you will find an old wooden shelter—one of those left by the old Civilian Conservation Corps (CCC) before World War II.

There are fine campsites around the shelter, but smart campers avoid the rustic old building. At first glance, it looks like an appealing place to toss your bed pad, but these old structures are notorious gathering grounds for woodland rodents. Namely, mice. The possibility of having little feet scampering over your sleeping body is reason enough to avoid the shelter. But, the overriding reason to sleep clear of this three-walled cabin is to eliminate the possibility of disease spreading to you or your pet. Mice are carriers of a wide array of bacteria and virus—including hantavirus—and dogs are nearly as proficient at catching mice as their feline friends back home. The last thing you want is your pooch munching on a disease-ridden rodent. Hantavirus can also be contracted by inhaling dust from mouse droppings. So pitch your tent in one of the campsites well away from the shelter.

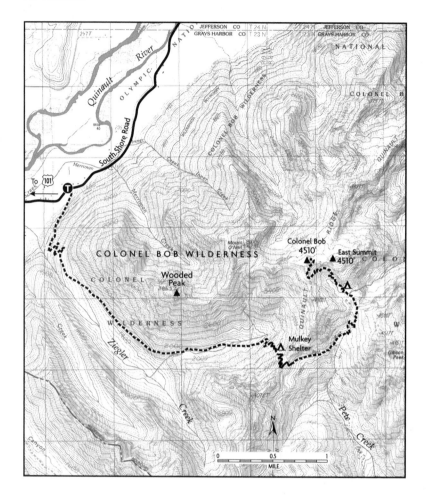

Or better yet, push on to the next camp. The trail continues to climb from Mulkey Shelter, as it swings around the ridge point to enter the upper Pete Creek Valley. At 5.5 miles, you'll intersect the Pete Creek Trail. Stay left and keep climbing. In just over 0.5 mile, you'll encounter quality campsites at Moonshine Flats camp (6.1 miles from the trailhead). Overnighters should stop, pitch camp here, then head up the last mile of trail to the summit for late afternoon views from the top of Colonel Bob. Look north onto Lake Quinault and west along the Quinault River valley to the setting sun over the Pacific. Adventurous sorts can scramble east along the meadowed crown of Colonel Bob to the East Summit—while their more contemplative companions might opt to simply sit at the primary summit and soak in the views.

2. Fletcher Canyon

Round trip: 3.5 miles
Hiking time: 3 hours
High point: 1320 feet
Elevation gain: 1029 feet
Best hiking time: May through November
Map: Green Trails Quinault Lake No. 197
Contact: Olympic National Forest, Pacific Ranger District, Quinault office, (360) 288-2525

The world-renowned temperate rainforests of the Olympic Peninsula survive mostly within the boundaries of Olympic National Park, meaning they are off limits to dogs. Yet a few remnants of the cathedral forests still remain on the national forest properties that surround the park. The deep, damp forest of Fletcher Canyon stands as a testament to the grandeur and scope of the old-growth forests that once covered nearly the entire Olympic Peninsula. The trail is located within the Colonel Bob Wilderness. You and your hound will love exploring this path into the forest primeval.

To get there, from Hoquiam drive north on U.S. Highway 101 approximately 43 miles to Lake Quinault's South Shore Road. Turn right and drive 12 miles to the trailhead, found on the south (right) side of the road. The trail leaves the South Shore Road and almost immediately begins a slow climb up the narrow canyon of Fletcher Creek. The lower stretch of trail pierces a forest rich in western red cedar and hemlock, with big leaf maples interspersed among them. Great beards of moss and lichen droop from the branches of these mighty trees, and spring mosses carpet the ground—the only bare earth you are likely to see is that of the actual trail-tread.

The trail follows the east side of Fletcher Creek upstream, yet the creek remains well below the trail much of the way. After a mile of hiking through the quiet emerald world of the rainforest, the trail becomes a bit more difficult to follow. Routine trail maintenance seems to end at this point, though the official trail continues to 2.5 miles. The narrow path

Wading in streams helps dogs to cool off. (Kelly McCaffrey)

plays hide-and-seek through the world of moss and towering trees, but savvy hikers can continue on if they merely keep the creek on their right to mile 1.75 to the point where the old, faint trail crosses Fletcher Creek. This is a good place to give up the task of tracing the diminishing trail and head back the way you came.

As you enjoy this route, keep a sharp eye on the surrounding forest. Roosevelt elk—the monarchs of these musty old for-

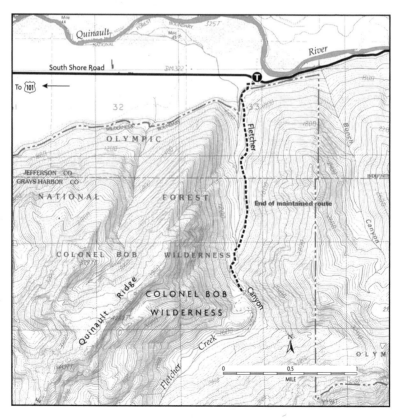

ests—call this valley home, and you're quite likely to stumble across a small herd of the big beasts. You might also see owls and marbled murrelets winging through the forest glen. Keep your dog close at hand, and pay attention to its actions—the dog's senses are much sharper than yours, so it will likely see, smell, or hear an animal before you do. Remember, though, that a good trail dog will alert you to a wild critter's presence, but never allow it to chase or bark at that animal. Barking dogs and aggressive dogs must stay at home: Harassing wildlife is a state crime and if it is an endangered or threatened species, a federal crime.

3. Leadbetter Point

Round trip: 4-plus miles
Hiking time: 2 to 5 hours
High point: 49 feet
Elevation gain: 35 feet
Best hiking time: year-round
Maps: USGS 7.5-minute series Oysterville and North Cove
Contact: Washington State Parks and Recreation, (800) 233-0321
Note: Dogs must be leashed and kept out of the National Wildlife Refuge at the northern end of peninsula.

Dogs and beaches go together nearly as well as dogs and Frisbees. Unfortunately for dog hikers, most of the wild, remote beaches of Washington are managed by the National Park Service, or are part of the National Wildlife Refuge program, and therefore off limits to dogs. You can hike with your pooch along the popular—and heavily populated—stretches of sand and dunes at Long Beach proper (hiking south from Long Beach toward Seaview is a good option because this strand of beach is closed to motorized traffic during the summer months). But to get away from the beach bums, sun worshippers, and general sand loungers, head to the northern end of the Long Beach peninsula and explore the often-forgotten Leadbetter Point State Park. This park offers great primitive beaches to explore and also unique lowland forests—the heart of the Stackpole Slough is a dense cedar swamp. There's also the marshy

world of Willapa Bay—a bird-watcher's paradise—on the eastern edge of the park.

To get to Leadbetter, from Olympia drive west on U.S. Highway 12 to Aberdeen and a junction with US 101. Turn south on US 101 and drive to Seaview and the intersection with State Route 103. Turn north onto SR 103 and drive 11.5 miles to Ocean Park. Turn east onto Bay Avenue and drive nearly a mile before turning left (north) onto Peninsula Highway/Sand Ridge Road. Continue 4 miles then turn west onto Oysterville Road, and in 0.25 mile, turn right (north) onto Stackpole Road. Continue to the park entrance, about 3 miles. Park at the first parking area.

The park has several miles of maintained trails. Head northwest out of the parking area and follow the path through the marshy forest as it curves up the sandy hill at the center of the peninsula before dropping you on the grass-covered dunes of the Pacific coast. Watch for the small, furtive black-tailed deer in this moist forest, and be aware of the resident raccoons that can grow nearly as big as a medium-sized dog. Keep Fido

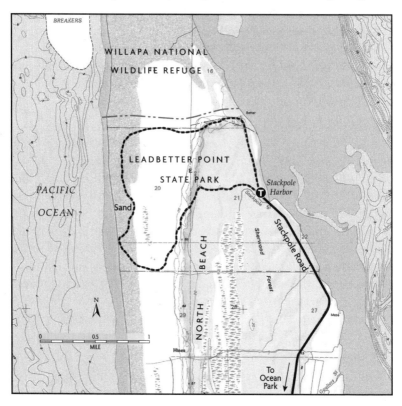

Climbing through the forest and rocks around Long Beach's Leadbetter Point

on a leash—not only is this a state park requirement, but it's the safe thing to do.

Once on the beach, head south (do not take your dog north of the trail into the Willapa National Wildlife Refuge). Here your dog can frolic in the waves or chase sticks along the sandy strand to its heart's content. Hike as far south as you'd like, noting that you'll be walking in front of private residences within a couple miles, so you'll need to avoid moving inland into the dunes until you are back within the park boundary. About a mile south of where you first enter the beach, cut inland, weaving through the clusters of dune grasses—stay high on the dunes to avoid the small boggy sloughs between some of the dunes—and find a trail angling east through the forest to return to your starting place.

Wildlife watchers take note: This park—and all of the Long Beach Peninsula and Willapa Bay area—sit right on the Pacific Flyway, the major thoroughfare for migrating waterfowl during the spring and fall. More than two hundred bird species have been seen here, so bring the binoculars and a birder's field guide so you can identify the colorful avians you see.

4. Tubal Cain Mine Meadows/ Buckhorn Lake

Round trip: 10 miles to meadows/14 miles to Buckhorn Lake
Hiking time: 6 to 7 hours (day hike or backpacking trip)
High point: 5300 feet
Elevation gain: 2000 feet
Best hiking time: June through October
Map: Green Trails Tyler Peak No. 136
Contact: Olympic National Forest, Hood Canal Ranger District,
Quilcene office, (360) 765-2200

Stride up this quiet forest trail in the spring and you'll find yourself plunging into a corridor of fragrant pink blossoms. The native rhododendron of this valley tower over and around the trail. This jungle of blooming evergreen shrubs provides a colorful setting for folks fortunate enough to visit during the spring bloom, but it also is home to an assortment of birds and animals all year round. Songbirds of all sorts as well as squirrels, raccoons, coyotes, and bobcats call the lower valley home.

Moving up the trail, you'll find the rhodies giving way to hemlock and fir forest, and then to broad, sloping meadows filled with wildflowers and grasses. In the midst of all the natural splendor, you'll find a world of human history. Remnants of a turn-of-the-century (the turn of the twentieth century, that is) ghost town straddle the trail, debris from old mining claims litter the hillsides, and a World War II–era plane wreck can be seen near the trail.

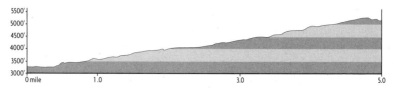

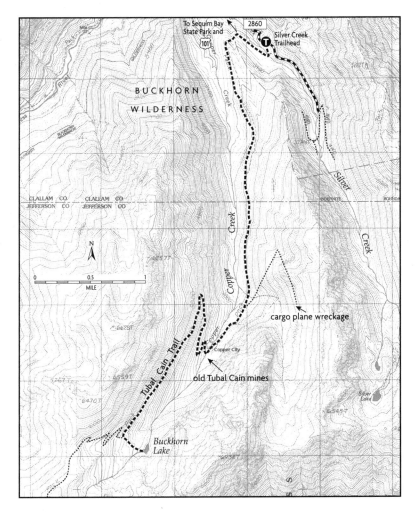

To get there, drive U.S. Highway 101 toward Sequim. Approximately 2 miles north of the Sequim Bay State Park entrance (and 1 mile southeast of Sequim), turn left (southwest) onto Palo Alto Road. Continue on Palo Alto Road as it turns into Forest Road 28. Follow FR 28 just over a mile to FR 2860. Veer right and drive 15 miles on FR 2860, about 4 miles past the Dungeness Trailhead, to the Tubal Cain Mine Trailhead near the Silver Creek Shelter.

From the trailhead, drop down to Silver Creek, passing a large three-sided wooden shelter—one of the few remaining old shelters built in the mid-part of the twentieth century for the use of backcountry rangers and

In the meadow between Tubal Cain Mine and Buckhorn Lake

fire lookouts as they traveled to their remote posts. The trail quickly leaves Silver Creek and contours around the foot of a slope to cross over to the Copper Creek valley. The trail heads south up this valley through the dense rhody jungle for the first 2 miles. As the rhododendrons taper away to tall stands of coniferous forest, look for signs of black-tailed deer—they favor the rhodies for safe, secure sleeping quarters but prefer to browse in the open forest.

At 2.5 miles from the trailhead, watch for a way trail leaving the main trail and heading uphill to the left. You'll see bits and pieces of a wrecked World War II cargo plane scattered around the trail here. The actual location of the crash site is at the end of the 1.5-mile way trail, but sightseers and scavengers have dragged and scattered hunks of the aluminum hulk down the slope. There's also an old mining shaft near the start of this way trail—feel free to peer into the dark, dank hole, but do not venture inside because the roof and walls are unstable and prone to collapses. And by all means, keep your pooch out of the hole. There are sure to be interesting scents wafting from the shaft to lure your dog in—many small animals tend to live just inside the cavern—but these shafts are potential death traps in the backcountry.

After examining the relics of human history, continue up the main trail. In another 1.5 miles, the trail drops down and crosses Copper Creek. Here, on both banks of the creek, you'll see hunks of rusty iron, bits of moldering rubber, and rotting wooden structures. Keep your dog on a short leash here because there are many places where jagged sheet metal and broken cables protrude nearly invisibly from the brush, just waiting to stab or cut a carefree dog.

These are the remains of Copper City, the small community that was built up to support the Tubal Cain mines (the primary mines are on the slope to the south of the creek). As the creek name suggests, the miners sought copper, as well as manganese and silver, though little of anything was ever found. The mines shut down by the early 1950s, and in the half-century since, anything made of wood has nearly rotted away, leaving just a few relics of rusting metal—old cast iron stoves, water heaters, barrels, etc. Most of the interesting relics have been carted off over the years, but what's left must be left in place—don't take any souvenirs or soon there won't be anything left for future generations to see of this historical site.

After viewing the ghost town, continue around Copper Creek and follow the trail as it angles up and out of the forest onto the steep north wall of the valley. At 5 miles, as the forest thins and falls away, the trail enters a vast sloping meadow of wildflowers and heather. By midsummer, these meadows are awash in color—lucky hikers who catch the peak of the bloom see meadows boasting an incredible array of blossoms. I witnessed Indian paintbrush, lupine, bear grass, tiger lilies, columbine, shooting stars, and mountain daisies (among others) all coloring the meadow one July day.

A couple long switchbacks over the next 2 miles carry you through the heart of the flower country. Turn around anywhere through this section for a day hike of 10 to 12 miles round trip. Or, if you are up to it, continue to traverse through the meadows for another 1.5 miles to a junction with a small way trail on the left. Drop 0.5 mile along this trail to Buckhorn Lake at 7 miles from the trailhead. You can camp here, or just stop for lunch while your pooch paddles around the cool waters of the small pond.

5. Silver Lakes

Round trip: 10 miles
Hiking time: 8 hours (day hike or backpacking trip)
High point: 5500 feet
Elevation gain: 2600 feet
Best hiking time: June through October
Map: Green Trails Tyler Peak No. 136
Contact: Olympic National Forest, Hood Canal Ranger District,
   Quilcene office, (360) 765-2200

Set at the end of a dead-end trail, Silver Lake is one of several out-of-the-way lakes that get fewer visitors than many other mountain lakes. But, set in a broad alpine cirque facing Mount Townsend, the blue-watered lakes lack nothing when it comes to stunning scenery and wilderness splendor. Deer and elk roam the grass-covered slopes above the lake, and marmots whistle from the rocky, talus slopes at the base of the valley walls. The lakes boast a healthy population of rainbow and golden trout (both the large upper lake and a lower, smaller lake are stocked) so skillful anglers can pluck their dinner from the cold lake waters. Nonanglers may opt to simply swim away the trail weariness before settling in for the night.

To get there, from Quilcene drive 1 mile south on U.S. Highway 101 and turn right (west) on Penny Creek Road. After 1.5 miles, turn right on Big Quilcene River Road, which becomes Forest Road 27 at the forest boundary. Continue 13.5 miles to FR 2760 and turn left (west). The hike starts at the Mount Townsend Trailhead, 0.75 mile up the road on the right.

From the trailhead, you'll immediately start uphill, climbing through a tight stand of timber for the first 0.5 mile. Beyond this stretch, though, the blissful shade of the forest is largely left behind as the trail angles up into hillside meadows and alder slopes. This next leg of the hike climbs steeply through steamy-hot, alder-clogged avalanche chutes, and there's not a drop

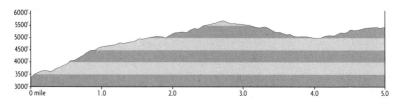

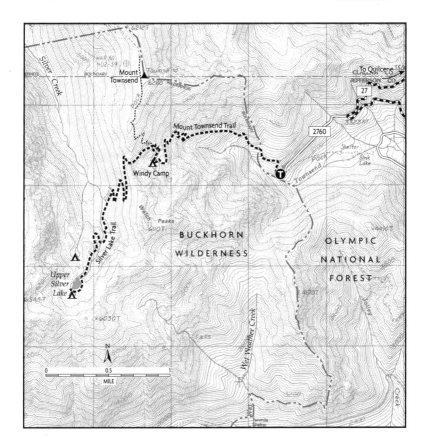

to drink along the way, so make sure you have plenty of water in your pack for both you and your dog. There are a few breaks where the tall brush gives way to fields of wildflowers, but tight greenery really dominates the local scenery—the exception being in autumn. Hike here in mid-September through October and the russet colors of fall surround the trail.

At just over 2 miles from the trailhead, the trail meanders past a small lake (well, a pond, really) and campsite. This is Windy Lake and Windy Camp. Stop here to let your hot dog cool off in the tarn before continuing on. About 0.25 mile past Windy Lake, turn left at a trail junction and begin a descent into Silver Creek Basin.

The trail drops through a modest series of switchbacks in the first mile from the trail junction before beginning a gentle traverse that continues 3 miles to Upper Silver Lake. The smaller, lower Silver Lake, which is less visited but also less scenic, can be found about 0.25 mile downvalley from the upper lake via a small way trail found near the upper lake's outflow.

At mile 5, camps on the west shore of Upper Silver Lake are the most sheltered, nestled as they are between truck-sized boulders, while the meadows on the south shore provide the best sunshine and napping places. For an additional adventure, scramble up the modest slope above these meadows to the ridge top for views southwest to Buckhorn Mountain and the Big Quilcene valley.

Bucktail deer near camp

6. Camp Mystery/Marmot Pass

Round trip: 11 miles
Hiking time: 8 hours (day hike or backpacking trip)
High point: 6100 feet
Elevation gain: 3700 feet
Best hiking time: July through October
Map: Green Trails Tyler Peak No. 136
Contact: Olympic National Forest, Hood Canal Ranger District, Quilcene office, (360) 765-2200

This hike offers an argument against those who thought that all the deep, mossy-green rainforests were on the west side of the Olympic range. The trail follows the Big Quilcene River through a deep, ancient forest filled with

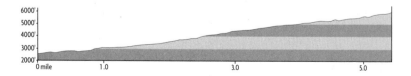

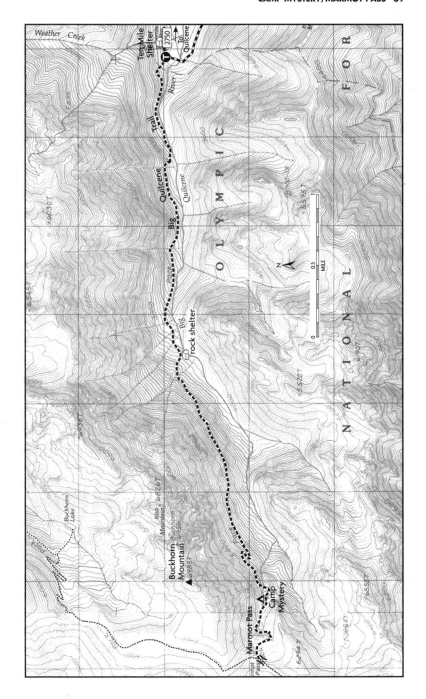

In the Buckhorn Wilderness

towering firs and hemlocks, many bearded with drooping mosses and lichens. Later, the trail climbs into drier, thinner forests and eventually reaches high into the alpine world of heather meadows and rocky peaks. Dogs will love the lower route because it dances over many small streams and frequently drops close to the main river, affording canines ample opportunities to slip into the cold waters for a refreshing dip.

To get there, from Quilcene drive 1 mile south on U.S. Highway 101 and turn right (west) on Penny Creek Road. After 1.5 miles, turn right on Big Quilcene River Road, which becomes Forest Road 27 at the forest boundary. Continue approximately 11 miles and turn left on FR 2750. The trailhead is 5 miles ahead, where the Lower Big Quilcene Trail meets the road near Ten Mile Shelter. Park here.

Keep your dog close as you start up the trail, and pay attention to him. You stand a good chance of having a wildlife encounter here because there is a large population of black-tailed deer as well as Roosevelt elk in this forest. Your dog's senses are far superior to your own, so keep an eye on your dog and he may alert you to the presence of the wild critters.

The trail climbs immediately in deep, old-growth forest and enters the Buckhorn Wilderness almost as quickly. For the next 2 miles, the trail climbs gradually, allowing you time to warm up in preparation for the steep miles ahead. In this early section, you'll cross several small feeder streams while staying close to the Quilcene River. Let your dog romp in the river to stay cool and hydrated, and make note of the good doggy swimming holes for the return trip (when Fido will be hot and ready for a refreshing dip).

At 2.5 miles, the trail passes Rock Shelter and soon leaves the river.

There is no water along the next stretch of trail, so fill your water bottles here (being sure to filter or chemically treat it).

As you leave Rock Shelter, the trail climbs out of the forest and enters the steeply sloped wildflower meadows of the alpine country. You will gain 2000 feet over the next 2 miles. As the trail climbs, the trail crosses meadows and scree slopes offering little shade—this can be a hot, exhausting climb, and it's important to monitor your dog carefully because dehydration can be lethal. Make sure your dog drinks frequently, especially if it's hot during your hike.

At 4.5 miles, you'll reach Camp Mystery and a pair of cool, sweet-water springs. The campsites here are situated among small stands of alpine fir and colorful swathes of wildflowers. If you're camping, drop your packs at your preferred camp and continue north up the trail another mile, passing under high rocky bluffs before reaching the high point of Marmot Pass at 6100 feet. Look west into the deep blue-green valley of the Dungeness River, and then turn east and look down the Big Quilcene valley you just climbed and beyond to the hazy basin of Hood Canal in the distance.

7. Mount Ellinor

Round trip: 5 miles
Hiking time: 6 hours
High point: 5900 feet
Elevation gain: 2100 feet
Best hiking time: July through October
Maps: Green Trails Mount Steel No. 167, The Brothers No. 168
Contact: Olympic National Forest, Hood Canal Ranger District, Hoodsport office, (360) 877-5254

Hikers swarm Mount Ellinor every spring as they rush to the summit for one reason—to come back down. More specifically, to come down via the long glissade route. Dog hikers will want to wait until at least

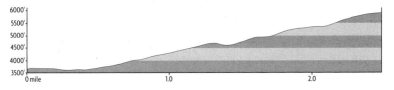

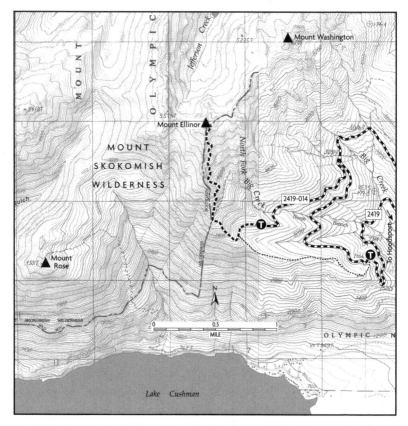

mid-July to make the descent safe for their four-legged friends (even sure-footed dogs don't have the necessary traction to stop themselves when sliding down a steep field of slushy spring snow).

Once the route is snowfree, hikers and their canine friends will find the trail steep, dry, and hot (watch your pooch for signs of dehydration and make sure she drinks frequently during the hike). But you'll also find unmatched views of the southeastern Olympics. Mount Ellinor hikers encounter fields of flowers during the summer blooming season and often see deer—and maybe even a mountain goat or two.

To get there, drive U.S. Highway 101 to Hoodsport and turn west on Lake Cushman Road/State Route 119. Continue 9 miles northwest along this route before turning right on Jorsted Creek Road/Forest Service Road 24. Drive 1.6 miles and then turn right onto Big Creek Road (FR 2419). There are two possible trailheads. On FR 2419, drive 4.9 miles to the lower one (for use when snow or mudslides block the road ahead). To access the upper trailhead, continue 1.5 miles past the lower trailhead and turn left on FR 2419-014. Follow this to its end, about 0.75 mile farther.

The trail starts straight up the ridge from the road's end. The route is steep and dry for its entire length and largely open and sundrenched, too. Plan on sweating profusely while plodding up this rough trail. The trail angles west through thin forest for 0.25 mile where it merges with the primary trail from the lower trailhead.

At mile 1 from the upper trailhead, you leave the forest behind and enter the heather meadows of the alpine zone. Here, you also find a split in the trail. The path to the right rolls on 0.5 mile to end in a broad, wildflower meadow. The dogs and kids will enjoy picnicking here. It should be noted, too, that the views from this lower meadow are nearly as good as those found at the summit.

Summit-seekers, though, should stay left at the Y-junction. The trail drives relentlessly upward through heather-speckled scree slopes and though small stands of alpine fir. At mile 2, the scree gives way to more wildflowers and ever-expanding views. The trail soon becomes a route marked by rock cairns rather than a beaten path, and the final 50 feet are a steep, hands-on rock scramble. You might want to forego this pitch, if only for your dog's sake.

At 2.5 miles reach the summit to enjoy views east to Hood Canal and

Rhododendrons line the lower trail as it weaves up the mountain.

beyond. On clear days, you'll see Mount Rainier and possibly even Mount Adams and Mount St. Helens in the distance to the east and southeast. To the south, you look directly down on Lake Cushman and the Skokomish River valley. West and north stand the peaks of the Olympic Mountain ranges.

8. Dry Creek

Round trip: up to 12 miles
Hiking time: 5 to 10 hours (depending on distance traveled)
High point: 3600 feet
Elevation gain: 2800 feet
Best hiking time: June through November
Map: Green Trails Mount Tebo No. 199
Contact: Olympic National Forest, Hood Canal Ranger District,
    Hoodsport office, (360) 877-5254

This forested valley provides plenty of opportunities to experience the forest ecosystem. Black-tailed deer and elk move through this valley, descending along the creek to the shores of Lake Cushman, while smaller critters scurry around the creek shores. Hikers have encountered raccoons, possums, beavers, weasels, martens, and coyotes, as well as cougars and bobcats, in this valley. Keep the dog close and quiet, and he'll help you see these critters as you hike this lightly used trail.

To get there, drive U.S. Highway 101 to Hoodsport and turn west on Lake Cushman Road. Drive 9 miles, then turn left on Jorsted Creek Road/Forest Road 24. Follow the road 6 miles to FR 2451 at the north end of Lake Cushman. Turn left over the North Fork Skokomish River. The trailhead is on the left, across from the lake. Hike a small dirt road past several private cabins to find the true trailhead about 0.25 mile south of where you parked.

In the late 1990s, volunteer crews from Washington Trails Association restored this largely forgotten trail to hiking condition. The trail skirts the western shore of Lake Cushman southward for a mile before turning west

up Dry Creek Canyon. The initial mile along the lake provides an excellent opportunity to see shore birds and migratory waterfowl—not to mention opportunities for your dog to dive in for a refreshing swim before (and after) the canyon hike.

As the trail starts up Dry Creek valley, the forest closes in and the views disappear. The woods here are largely second-growth forests, but there are scads of birds dipping through trees and an array of wildlife in the woods, too. The trail continues up the valley, crossing Dry Creek at about 3 miles, before reaching a low pass below Dry Mountain at about 6 miles. This is the place to turn around (if not before) because the trail ends 0.5 mile farther at a logging road. Thanks to the clearcutting done in the 1980s, there are decent views from the pass, back to Lake Cushman and the summits of Mounts Ellinor and Washington to the north.

Dry Creek is sometimes wet, but even in the rain, it's a fine route to walk the dog.

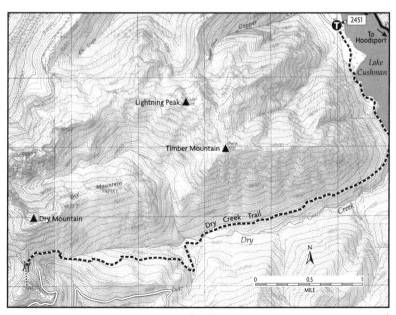

NORTH CASCADES

9. Skyline Divide

Round trip: 6 miles
Hiking time: 4-plus hours
High point: 6215 feet
Elevation gain: 2000 feet
Best hiking time: late July through early October
Map: Green Trails Mount Baker No. 13
Contact: Mt. Baker–Snoqualmie National Forest, Glacier Public
Service Center, (360) 599-2714

This route represents some of the best combinations of trail features you'll find in the Pacific Northwest. You get to explore high alpine country, but you also get much of the climbing over with during the drive to the trailhead. You experience pristine old forests and sprawling alpine meadows. The local scenery is blessed with a plethora of flora and fauna, and the distant views are filled with stunning peaks and glacier-covered volcanoes. And the trail is short enough that you can enjoy sunrise and/or sunset from the route during a simple day hike if you want. The one thing this route doesn't have is a lot of water—pack plenty for you and your dog.

To get there, drive north on Interstate 5 to Bellingham and exit 255 (Mount Baker). Turn east onto State Route 542 (Mount Baker Highway) and continue 31 miles to the town of Glacier. Continue another mile to

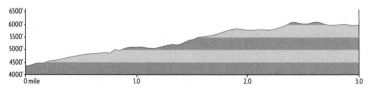

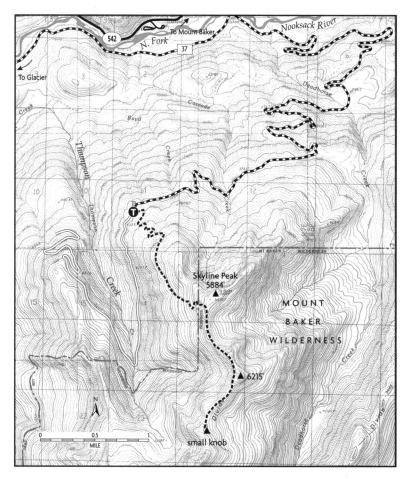

Glacier Creek Road/Forest Road 39. Turn right (south) and take an immediate left on Deadhorse Road/FR 37. Drive 13 occasionally steep, narrow miles to the trailhead, which has parking for about two dozen vehicles.

The trail starts fairly high (elevation 4300 feet) but still gains 2000 feet over its 3-mile length. It isn't muscle-popping steep, but it does climb enough to put some pain in the thighs and sweat on the brow. The first 2 miles of trail angle upward through a low forest of subalpine firs and small meadows with occasional peeks out for views toward Mounts Baker and Shuksan. At 2 miles, the trail leaves the timber behind and slopes southward into a vast ridgetop meadow (5800 feet) with endless views. Visit in early summer and you'll likely find lingering patches of snow. If

One of the meadows of Skyline Divide

your pooch is anything like mine, she'll appreciate a game of fetch-the-snowball on the bigger patches, because it not only lets her romp and play, but cools her off at the same time.

As the trail continues upward through the fields of wildflowers, the views grow ever more expansive. The glacier-clad slopes of Mount Baker slide higher and Mount Shuksan punctuates the southeastern horizon. Look west and you can see out over the San Juan Islands and along the Strait of Juan de Fuca. Note the gray-green massif of Vancouver Island to the north of the Strait and the shimmering peaks of the Olympic range to the south. Turning and looking north along the route you've just climbed, you'll see British Columbia. And all around you stretch fields of wildflowers.

As good as this stretch of trail is, if you keep hiking, it keeps getting better. Finally, at 3 miles from the trailhead, you'll top out on a small knob of rock, at 5900 feet. From here, Mount Baker looks close enough to touch—or at least close enough that you might catch a whiff of sulfur wafting out of the summit crater. Enjoy the views here, or stay for an afternoon nap in the warm sunshine. Stay until late afternoon, and enjoy the colorful alpenglow on Mount Baker.

Turn around at this point and enjoy the hike back down. Even though you'll be retracing your steps, you'll enjoy all new views as you head north, now looking across into Canada rather than up to Mount Baker. Late August is typically the time to come to enjoy the peak of the wildflower bloom, but late September has even more to offer. By early autumn, the crowds of hikers have thinned out, the clouds of flies have died out, and the fall colors have come out. The green heather, the red leaves of the low-bush blueberries, and the scattered gold and russet colors of the vine maples and slide alder provide a wonderful display of autumn splendor.

A final reminder: There is no water source along this trail, so carry enough to keep you and your dog safely hydrated.

10. Damfino Lakes

Round trip: 2 miles to lakes, 7 miles to Excelsior Mountain
Hiking time: 4 to 5 hours
High point: 5700 feet
Elevation gain: 1500 feet
Best hiking time: late July through early October
Map: Green Trails Mount Baker No. 13
Contact: Mt. Baker–Snoqualmie National Forest, Glacier Public Service Center, (360) 599-2714

A pair of sparkling alpine tarns, surrounded by bright granite and rich huckleberries, awaits you on this route. But for those with the energy and desire, the picturesque lakes are just the beginning of the wonders

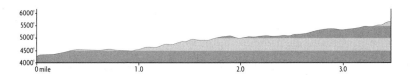

Happy dog after a day hike (Dean Cass)

found on this alpine ramble. Stunning views of the craggy peaks of the North Cascades can be found farther along the trail, and from the top of Excelsior Pass, hikers can bask in the delightful views of Mount Baker far across the Nooksack Valley.

To get there, drive north on Interstate 5 to Bellingham and exit 255 (Mount Baker). Turn east onto State Route 542 (Mount Baker Highway) and continue 31 miles to the town of Glacier. Continue another 1.5 miles and turn left onto Canyon Creek Road (Forest Road 31) at Douglas Fir Campground. Continue 15.3 miles up FR 31 to the trailhead parking area.

The trailhead sits amidst the wreckage of an old clearcut at 4200 feet elevation but the trail falls into forest from the get-go. Immediately, the path begins a gentle climb for 0.75 mile through cool, shaded woods before reaching a junction with the Canyon Ridge Trail. To the left, that faint trail heads west along the ridge crest, paralleling the road you drove to the trailhead. Your course steers right, traversing east toward Excelsior Mountain.

At 1 mile, find the two jewels of Damfino. These pocket-sized lakes offer wonderful camping opportunities—the short hiking distance and gentle ascent make them ideal camping spots for novice backpackers, families with young children, or hikers traveling with short-legged or elderly dogs. For day hikers, the lakes provide a great place to stop for a breather while your dog paddles through the pools. Visit in late August to partake of the local fruit—rich, sun-ripened huckleberries that grow around the lake basin. Note that the best campsites are found near the smaller of the two lakes—they are more scenic and more remote.

To continue your journey, return to the trail and amble east through the woods another easy mile before climbing a steep pitch to the start of the alpine meadow country. The trail continues to climb through fields of heather and flowers another 0.5 mile before cresting the saddle of

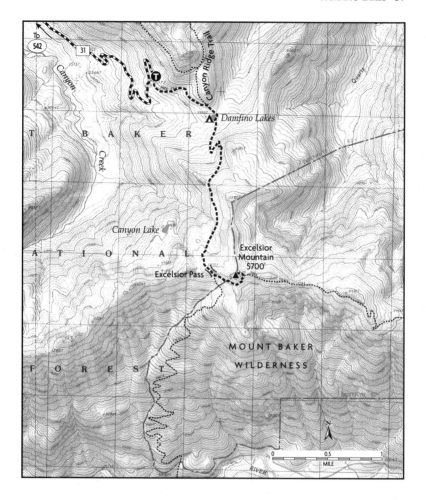

Excelsior Pass at 5350 feet. Good views can be had from here, but for truly outstanding scenery, you and your dog must cinch your pack straps and keep climbing. At the trail junction near the top of the pass, turning back here makes for a 6-mile round trip hike. Or stay left to traverse around the flank of Excelsior Mountain, enjoying the wildflowers around your ankles and the mountains sprawled on the horizon. At the end of the 0.5-mile walk from the pass, find a small way trail on the left leading to the 5700-foot summit of the mountain. It's an easy walking scramble through the rocky meadows to the top, and the rewards at the summit are priceless.

To the south, you can count the glaciers on the face of Mount Baker, and then add in the rivers of ice on Mount Shuksan to the southeast. Turn and look over into the mountains of the Great White North (Canada). Return the way you came, with a late-day stop at the lakes to camp, or at least to capture some evening photos of alpenglow on Mount Baker before heading home.

11. Tomyhoi Lake

Round trip: 10 miles
Hiking time: 7 hours
High point: 5400 feet
Elevation gain: 1600 feet
Best hiking time: late July through early October
Map: Green Trails Mount Shuksan No. 14
Contact: Mt. Baker–Snoqualmie National Forest, Glacier Public Service Center, (360) 599-2714

Tomyhoi is a broad, deep lake filling a broad, deep glacier valley high in the Mount Baker Wilderness. The lake offers views of the ice-capped summits of Tomyhoi Peak, Mount Larrabee, Yellow Aster Butte, and Goat Mountain. There are views of Mount Shuksan, Mount Baker, and the border peaks—Canada resides less than 3 miles north of the lake. Wildlife lovers will appreciate the bounty of this basin. Tomyhoi Lake harbors a few lunker trout and its shorelines are inhabited by deer, black bear, and assorted woodland critters, while the bluffs above the lake shelter small herds of wooly mountain goats.

To get there, drive north on Interstate 5 to Bellingham and exit 255 (Mount Baker). Turn east onto State Route 542 (Mount Baker Highway) and continue 31 miles to the town of Glacier. Continue another 13.5 miles to the Department of Transportation sheds on the north side of the highway. Just beyond them turn left on Forest Road 3065 (follow the signs to Tomyhoi Trail/Twin Lakes). Follow the road 4.5 miles to the trailhead on the left.

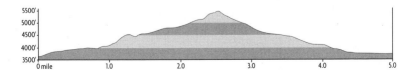

Autumn colors the foliage along the lake.

While the lake is nearly at the same elevation as the trailhead, a high mountain pass stands between them, meaning hikers face a sweat-inducing climb both coming and going. From the trailhead, 3600 feet, the trail angles north into the forest and starts climbing immediately and steeply. The path switches back and forth through forest and meadow for more than 1.5 miles to a trail junction. Stop here and give Fido a good dosing of water from the small ponds and rivulets that trickle through the meadows—the next mile climbs through open, sun-drenched meadows and dehydration is a real threat to you and your pooch.

From the junction, stay right on the main trail and keep climbing. In late summer, this stretch of trail pierces a colorful slope of wildflower blooms. In early summer, the slope may be littered with lingering snowfields. At just over mile 2 near timberline, the pitch of the trail tapers off and the route rolls into the saddle of Gold Run Pass (5400 feet). Stop here for a breather and another long drink of water while enjoying the views.

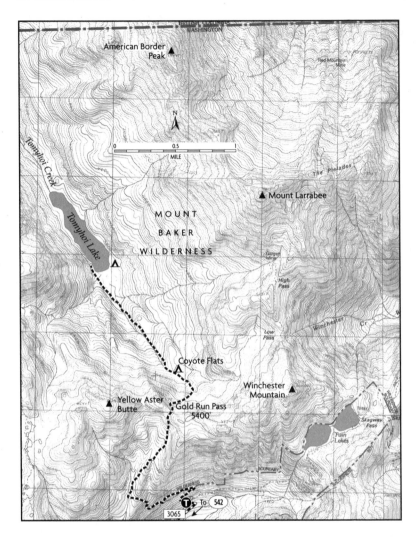

Look back to Mounts Baker and Shuksan and forward down to the lake basin.

The trail drops north from the pass and reaches the first camps along the trail in just a mile more at Coyote Flats, about 3.7 miles from the trailhead. As nice as these campsites appear, however, you'll do yourself a favor by pushing on to reach Tomyhoi Lake at 5 miles. There are fine campsites at the head of the lake and around its shoreline.

12. Welcome Pass

Round trip: 6 miles
Hiking time: 5 hours
High point: 5200 feet
Elevation gain: 3000 feet
Best hiking time: July through early October
Map: Green Trails Mount Shuksan No. 14
Contact: Mt. Baker–Snoqualmie National Forest, Glacier Public
  Service Center, (360) 599-2714

Welcome Pass could have earned that name because this high point on the trail was such a welcome sight for the first folks to head up this trail. The trail begins in deep old forests at a low 2200-feet elevation and climbs steeply and relentlessly all the way to the view-rich pass, gaining an average of 1000 feet with every mile of trail. And because the first mile is mild and gentle, the rest are even more ruthlessly steep. The trail turns through so many switchbacks that you're in danger of meeting yourself coming as you plod up through the tight corners. Before heading up this thigh-bursting trail, make sure you and your pup are well conditioned for the climb, and then make sure you have several quarts of water in your pack to keep the both of you well hydrated along the way.

Hearing the rigors of the route, you might wonder why you'd hike here. Perhaps for the exercise, but more likely, because of the variety of terrain and quality of the views found at Welcome Pass.

To get there, drive north on Interstate 5 to Bellingham and exit 255 (Mount Baker). Turn east onto State Route 542 (Mount Baker Highway) and continue 31 miles to the town of Glacier. Continue another 11.5 miles before turning left (north) onto a poorly marked road (Forest Road 3060)—if you reach the Department of Transportation sheds along the highway, you've gone a mile or so too far. Turn left on FR 3060 and follow it north to its end, about 0.75 mile, and park.

The Welcome Pass Trail starts out on an old logging road, meandering

Small ponds — a.k.a. tarns — dot the ridges of the high North Cascade range.

through cool, old forests. For the first mile, the trail gains a modest 400 feet. As the roadbed fades into true trail-tread though, the route turns steep and the forest thins, first with small glades showing between the trees, then opening onto broader meadows. After that first mile of meandering course, the trail adopts a rigorous routine of climb, turn, climb, turn, climb, turn. By some counts, there are more than sixty-five switchbacks in the next 2 miles. Fortunately, as the trail climbs, the views and the scenery improve. Every step forward brings you into more flower meadows with more panoramic views.

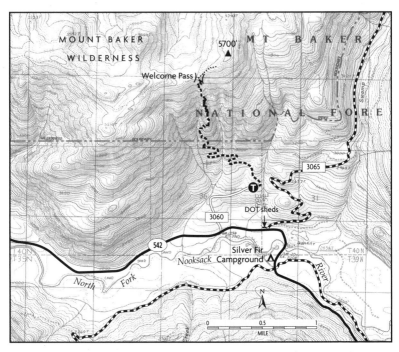

As you near the welcome embrace of Welcome Pass 3 miles from the trailhead, you have a decision to make. You can stop at the pass to enjoy a long lunch, with the panorama of Mount Baker, Mount Shuksan, and the Nooksack River valley sprawled before you before descending back down the trail. Or you can rest briefly at the pass before scrambling farther upward, to the top of an unnamed knob (5700 feet) to the northeast. Because the views from the pass are as good as any you'll find higher up, do yourself and your dog a favor and skip that 0.5-mile excursion. Once you've digested the views and recovered your breath and energy, return the way you came. But watch your step—the steepness of the trail makes the descent a bit slippery at times. Take your time.

13. East Bank Baker Lake

Round trip: 8 to 28 miles
Hiking time: 4 hours to 4 days
High point: 1000 feet
Elevation gain: 300 feet
Best hiking time: May through June and September through November
Map: Green Trails Lake Shannon No. 46
Contact: Mt. Baker–Snoqualmie National Forest, Mount Baker
    Ranger Station, (360) 856-5700

While the trail does parallel the east bank of Baker Lake, this isn't a true lakeshore trail. It is an old-growth forest hike, with occasional side excursions to the lake. Because it stays under the forest canopy most of the way, it lacks distant panoramic views and stunning alpine scenery. But that's okay. There are plenty of other trails with those features. What this trail offers is immersion into an ecosystem that has become rare and precious—the Cascades old-growth forest. The trail rolls under massive hulks of ancient Douglas firs, western hemlocks, and western red cedars. The trees are hung with long curtains of lichen, and the ground between the trees boasts a deep shag carpet of moss.

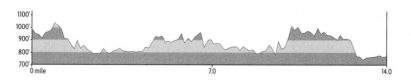

Small bay off Baker Lake

Day hikers can stroll up the trail as far as they please before turning around, and backpackers can spend many nights exploring the quiet solitude of this cathedral forest. Because the trail stays at a low elevation—below 1000 feet— along its length, the route is generally snowfree year-round and therefore is one of the few mountain trails that can be hiked in the early spring and late autumn. Spring is the time to visit, while other hikers are still waiting for the snow to melt up high.

To get there, from Mount Vernon drive north on Interstate 5 to exit 230 (Anacortes/Burlington). Turn east on State Route 20 (North Cascades Highway) and continue about 16 miles to Baker Lake–Grandy Road (Forest Road 11). Turn left (north), and at 14 miles turn right on FR 1106, signed for Baker Lake/Koma Kulshan Campground. In about 1 mile, turn right over the Puget Sound Energy Dam. On the far side of the dam, turn left on FR 1107. The trailhead is on the left, about 0.75 mile down the road.

From the trailhead the path swings north into the forest and traverses a gentle slope well above the lake. At 1.8 miles, a side trail leads 0.25 mile west (left) onto a small peninsula in the lake. This makes a great place to stop for a rest, while letting the pooch splash along the lakeshore. If you

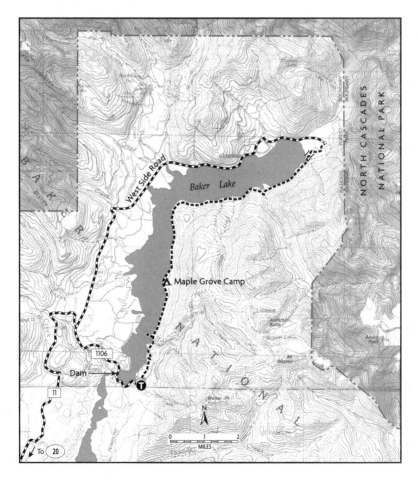

want a short hike, you can turn around here. But because the trail is so smooth and easy, you should push on past this peninsula rest stop.

From the junction with the peninsula trail, head back up the slope, leaving the lake several hundred yards below, and continue to explore the ancient forest for another 2 miles. At 4 miles from the trailhead, find Maple Grove Camp. Hikers, horse packers, and paddle-sport enthusiasts who have steered their kayaks and canoes up the lake share this campsite. Indeed, Baker Lake is a popular backcountry-paddling destination. An array of camps line both sides of the lake for canoeists and kayakers who ply the waters in their sleek crafts.

Maple Grove Camp is also the preferred turnaround point for most day hikers. Backpackers can continue much farther on this woodland pathway. The trail rolls in time to the northern end and head of the lake, where it crosses the Baker River on a new footbridge and connects with the Baker River Trail, as well as roads on the lake's west side. (The Baker River Trail soon enters North Cascades National Park, where dogs are not allowed.) The completed trail allows a one-way shuttle hike of about 14 miles between the East Bank and Baker River Trailheads.

14. Watson Lakes/Anderson Butte

Round trip: 5 miles to lakes; 6 miles to butte
Hiking time: 5 hours
High point: 4900 feet (5720 feet to butte)
Elevation gain: 600 feet (1100 to butte)
Best hiking time: June through November
Map: Green Trails Lake Shannon No. 46
Contact: Mt. Baker–Snoqualmie National Forest, Mount Baker Ranger Station, (360) 856-5700

East Bank Baker Lake Trail (Hike 13) offers an adventure in ancient forests, but for an alpine experience, you can head a few miles east of the lake and

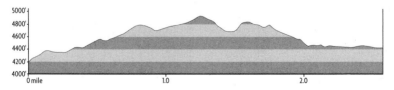

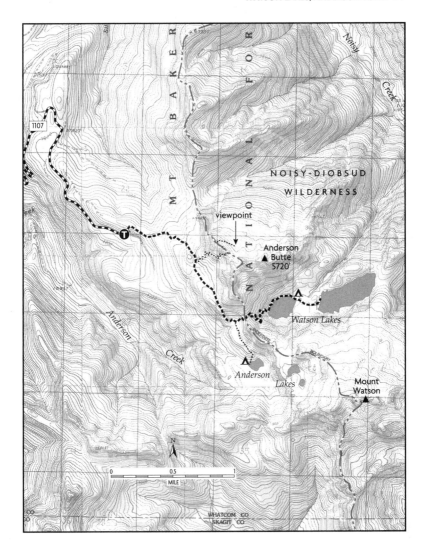

hop the line into the Noisy-Diobsud Wilderness Area. A trio of destinations can be sampled in a day, all from the same trailhead. Head for Watson Lakes, a pair of sparkling blue gems set in granite, for great camping and picnicking in an alpine environment. Take a side trip to the summit of Anderson Butte for stunning vistas and a lesson in forest history—Anderson Butte was once capped by a fire lookout tower. For quiet camping, drop down to the small pools of Anderson Lakes, a trio of ponds that are nearly as scenic as the Watson sisters but far less visited by hikers.

A tumbling stream graces the route's upper section.

This route has a lot to offer. It starts high and stays high, so hikers don't have to struggle up steep switchbacks. It gets you to the destinations (regardless of which of the three you choose) quickly, so hikers of all abilities can enjoy them. And it offers destinations of supreme beauty and wilderness splendor.

To get there, from Mount Vernon drive north on Interstate 5 to exit 230 (Anacortes/ Burlington). Turn east on State Route 20 (North Cascades Highway) and continue about 16 miles to Baker Lake–Grandy Road (Forest Road 11). Turn left (north), and at 14 miles turn right on FR 1106, signed for Baker Lake/ Koma Kulshan Campground. In about 1 mile, turn right over the Puget Sound Energy dam. On the far side of the dam, turn left on FR 1107. Proceed about 10 miles to the trailhead parking area.

From the trailhead, head into the forest and climb the moderately steep trail for nearly a mile. As the path leaves the trees at a little over a mile to enter a long, broad meadow, find a small way trail on the left. This is the path that leads to the top of a viewpoint near Anderson Butte (5720 feet). It's just 0.5 mile to the top, with a gain of some 800 feet. If you have the time and energy, it's worth the sweat to make the short jaunt to the top. You'll find incredible views of Baker Lake, Mount Shuksan, and the whole expanse of the Noisy-Diobsud Wilderness. You might consider saving the butte trip for the return from the lakes, however; the late-day light makes for dramatic photographs.

If Watson Lakes are your destination, keep to the main path (stay right) at the junction with the butte trail, and angle southeast, continuing to climb through the meadows. Less than 0.5 mile past the trail junction, you'll crest a low ridge (4900 feet) in the middle of the meadow and start a steep descent for another 0.5 mile. At this point, about 2 miles from the trailhead, the route splits. To the left, the trail climbs a low rise before descending into the Watson Lakes basin. The trail ends near the small upper lake, but way trails lead around its perimeter to the larger lake to the east. Here, at 2.5 miles, find a place to picnic, camp, or just rest while your dog snuffles through the rocks at water's edge.

To get to Anderson Lakes, go right where the route splits to head to Watson Lakes. Drop steeply into the lakes basin, reaching the first pond in about 0.5 mile.

15. East Creek to Mebee Pass

Round trip: 16 miles
Hiking time: 2 days
High point: 6500 feet
Elevation gain: 4000 feet
Best hiking time: July through September
Map: Green Trails Mount Logan No. 49
Contact: Okanogan National Forest, Methow Valley Ranger District, Visitor Information Center, (509) 996-4000

Pure and simple, this is one for the dog to enjoy. Oh sure, you also will appreciate the deep old forest that fills the East Creek valley and the many views of the rushing creek as it tumbles through rocky slots and over tangles of logs. You'll enjoy the assortment of wildlife that roams this woodland oasis—deer, coyotes, mink, river otters, weasels, bobcats, cougars, black bears, and lynx live in the deep valleys of the North Cascades. Overhead you might see flickers, woodpeckers, grosbeaks, nuthatches, crows, ravens, owls, hawks, and eagles. Dippers flit through the creek valleys, and trout dart through the creek waters. At the end of the valley, as the trail climbs to the high pass on the ridge crest, you'll find open meadows of wildflowers and vistas that include panoramic views of craggy mountains in every direction.

But as much as this sounds like a place for you to explore, it is really a

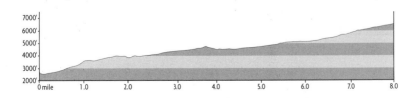

trail-dog paradise. There's a soft forest path to romp along and a cold creek, with frequent deep pools, in which to splash and play. There are several side creeks over which to jump and leap. And there's an array of interesting odors to sniff and follow. Many of these show the presence of wild critters; and although a good trail dog knows not to chase or bark at wildlife, she can take pleasure from picking up the animals' scents and letting her two-legged companion know that the creatures are near.

To get there, drive east on State Route 20 (North Cascades Highway) for 72 miles to Colonial Creek Campground and then approximately 15 miles more to the East Creek Trailhead, found on the left (northeast) side of the road. The trail begins on the far side of the bridge over Canyon Creek. **NOTE:** State Route 20 is closed in winter.

The trail begins with a steep, steady climb over the first 1.5 miles,

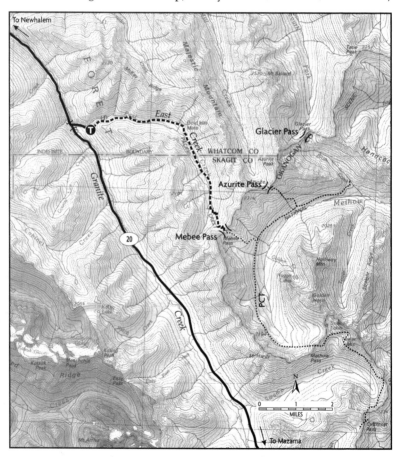

Autumn color on the creek

gaining nearly 1500 feet in that distance. The trail stays in old, fir forests as it climbs into the East Creek valley and crosses the creek. From this point, the trail stays near the creek, while still deep in forest. The trail crosses several side creeks over the next mile—most of these are easily crossed on stepping stones and small footlogs. At 4 miles, reach a trail junction. Stay right and continue up the East Creek valley as it angles southeast. The trail hugs the north bank of the creek for the next few miles before turning to the east flank of the valley and climbing a steep mile of switchbacks, leaving the forests behind as it ascends into open heather meadows around Mebee Pass at 8 miles. Another couple miles and the trail connects to the Pacific Crest Trail. Backpackers can drop their packs at one of several potential campsites along the upper reaches of East Creek before heading for the pass—or else you can make a dry camp near the pass. But your dog is going to need plenty of water to prevent problems associated with dehydration, so dry camps should be avoided.

16. Cutthroat Pass

Round trip: 10 miles
Hiking time: 6 hours
High point: 6800 feet
Elevation gain: 2000 feet
Best hiking time: July through September
Map: Green Trails Washington Pass No. 50
Contact: Okanogan National Forest, Methow Valley Ranger District,
Visitor Information Center, (509) 996-4000

Your dog will appreciate the dry pine forests for the assortment of scents that waft through the woods. You will appreciate the picturesque nature of the larch-studded alpine meadows that await you along the Porcupine Creek valley. Hitting the trail in late summer, you will see the meadows awash in color as wildflowers rush to bloom in the couple short months of summer that exist between the melting out of last year's snow and the falling of new snow. Hit the trail in early autumn—late September is the prime time—and you'll find the flower blooms long gone, but the plant's leaves are brilliant orange and crimson, and the thousands of larch trees are deep gold. Be aware that once the snowpack has melted away (midsummer) the water sources are widely spaced, so you'll need to carry an extra liter or two of agua for Fido.

To get there, drive the North Cascades Highway (State Route 20) to Rainy Pass and park in the large trailhead parking lot at the pass.

The Cutthroat Pass Trail is part of the Pacific Crest Trail. Begin by finding the trailhead near the horse ramp at the west end of the parking lot. The trail curves north through a thin pine and fir forest, climbing gradually in the first mile as it rounds a ridge on the flank of Cutthroat Peak.

The forest begins to open up as the trail climbs into the Porcupine Creek basin and meadows show themselves, first on the slope opposite the trail, then around the trail itself. In a couple miles, the trail crosses Porcupine Creek and climbs into the east-facing meadows on the slopes above it. This is where the views expand beyond the wonderful local scenery. Looking

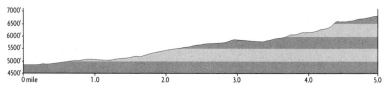

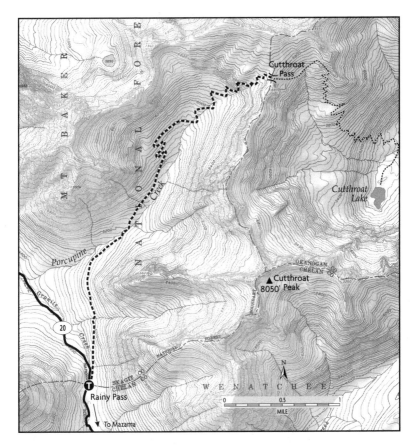

back to the southeast, you'll see the ragged, rocky top of 8050-foot Cutthroat Peak. Larches and aspen give a golden hue to the slopes below the
rocky summit from about mid-September to mid-October.

Within 0.5 mile of the creek crossing, the trail climbs a bit more steeply,
swinging through a few long switchbacks to reach the 6000-foot level.
Now it's nothing but wildflower meadows and glorious views as you
traverse the slope at this elevation for the next mile. Keep pup on a short
leash and watch his reactions—he may alert you to nearby wildlife that
you might otherwise miss.

At 4 miles, the trail begins to climb at the head of the Porcupine Creek
valley. A long series of switchbacks ascends the final 800 feet up the
headwall of the valley, finally cresting the ridge at 6800 feet at the narrow saddle of Cutthroat Pass at 5 miles.

Now that your account is cleared, you are rewarded with a big bonus:

Larch along Pacific Crest Trail near Cutthroat Pass

striking views as towering rock summits protrude into the sky in every direction. Pulling your eyes downward, the views are equally grand. Far below Cutthroat Pass, on the north slope of Cutthroat Peak, is the blue gem of Cutthroat Lake, and on all the slopes around you there are vast meadows of wildflowers. Look closely and you might see deer, mountain goats, black bears, coyotes, marmots, pikas, golden eagles, red-tailed hawks, merlins, ospreys, or even peregrine falcons.

The Pacific Crest Trail continues north toward Canada, but day hikers should turn around at the pass and enjoy the thrills of hiking down through those glorious meadows.

17. Cutthroat Lake

Round trip: 4 miles
Hiking time: 3 hours
High point: 5000 feet
Elevation gain: 500 feet
Best hiking time: July through September
Map: Green Trails Washington Pass No. 50
Contact: Okanogan National Forest, Methow Valley Ranger District, Visitor Information Center, (509) 996-4000

I've heard no explanation for the violent nature of the names given to this area's prominent features. Indeed, this beautiful area is big enough and scenic enough for all to enjoy, meaning there's no real justification for the name for this hike's featured route. Cutthroat Lake, at the head of Cutthroat Creek, lies in a deep cirque below Cutthroat Peak and can be accessed from Cutthroat Campground or Cutthroat Pass.

Despite the name, this trail offers a blissful alpine experience for you and your canine companion. Heading up the little, pretty creek valley, the trail swings into the scenic lake basin nestled below the craggy granite walls of an 8000-foot peak. You'll appreciate the views; your dog will appreciate the plethora of places to play and scents to sniff.

To get there, drive the North Cascades Highway (State Route 20) about 5 miles beyond Rainy and Washington Passes to Cutthroat Creek Road (Forest Road 400). Turn left (west) and drive 1 mile to the road's end and the trailhead at Cutthroat Campground.

The trail begins with a leg-warming climb of a couple hundred feet right off the bat before swinging west to traverse the valley wall well above

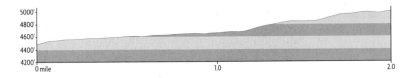

Cutthroat Lake below the Cascade Crest

the creek level. The trail stays in the thin pine and fir forest high above
the waterway for the first 1.5 miles before angling down to cross the creek.
At 1.7 miles, find a small trail leading south (left) off the main trail. Follow this 0.25 mile as it climbs a little over 100 feet to the oval jewel that

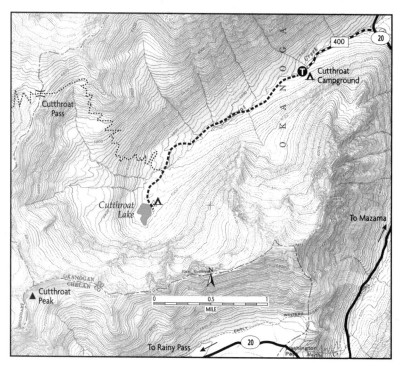

is Cutthroat Lake. Fine campsites can be found around the perimeter of the lake, but the best are on the north side, providing stunning views up the vertical wall of Cutthroat Peak to the southwest.

If you are looking for a longer hike, after a leisurely rest in the lake basin, return to the main trail, and turn left to continue climbing the Cutthroat Creek valley. The trail crosses the creek again just past the trail junction, then winds 3.5 miles—gaining 2000 feet—up to Cutthroat Pass on the Pacific Crest Trail. This option adds 7 miles to the round trip total.

18. Blue Lake

Round trip: 4.5 miles
Hiking time: 4 hours
High point: 6300 feet
Elevation gain: 1100 feet
Best hiking time: July through September
Map: Green Trails Washington Pass No. 50
Contact: Okanogan National Forest, Methow Valley Ranger District, Visitor Information Center, (509) 996-4000

The granite spires of the Washington Pass area—Early Winters, Liberty Bell, Silver Star Mountain, Cutthroat Peak, Whistler Mountain—are world famous, and they are all visible from this short trail. Indeed, the views of the mountain-spiked horizon captivate hikers on the trail into Blue Lake basin. But it's the beauty of the lake itself that captures your eye once you reach the cool pool of water set against the glittering white granite at the base of Liberty Bell Mountain.

To get there, drive the North Cascades Highway (State Route 20) about 2 miles east of Rainy Pass and turn into the parking area on the south side of the highway. **NOTE:** If you reach the summit of Washington Pass on SR 20, you've traveled about a mile too far east.

The noise of the highway follows you into the forest, but the beauty of the thin larch-studded woodland helps you push the noise from your mind—imagine it as the rushing wind in the valley behind you—as you

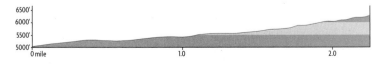

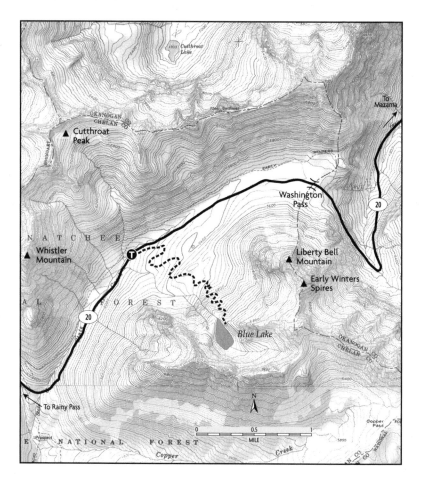

climb the gentle switchbacks up the flank of Liberty Bell. The trail passes through frequent forest glades filled with small, delicate wildflowers, between forests of subalpine firs, larches, and pines.

The clearings along the trail provide plenty of viewpoints from which to take in the jagged summits of Whistler Mountain and Cutthroat Peak to the north and the tall towers of the Early Winters Spires above you on the south side of Liberty Bell. But it's at trail's end, 2.2 miles from the trailhead, that the true views really shine. Standing beside the sapphire blue waters of the lake, you can look up at the spires and the crags and cracks on the sides of Liberty Bell. You can look across the valley to Cutthroat and Whistler. And, should you tire of the mountain views, spend time exploring the local beauty around the lake. Come August, heather

The trail climbs a high ridge through the fog.

meadows awash with colorful wildflower blooms surround the lake.

Your dog can romp along the lakeshore or paddle through frigid waters if she is a waterdog. The lake is typically too cold for most humans to enjoy as a swimming hole, but there is a healthy population of trout (stocked) in the lake, so alpine anglers might be able to pull a pan-sized fish from the pool before heading back down the scenic trail.

19. Remmel Lake

Round trip: 33 miles
Hiking time: 2 to 3 days
High point: 6870 feet
Elevation gain: 3400 feet
Best hiking time: July through October
Map: Green Trails Coleman Peak No. 20
Contact: Okanogan National Forest, Methow Valley Ranger District, Visitor Information Center, (509) 996-4000

The Pasayten Wilderness offers endless options for long walks with the dog. This remote and pristine protected area contains the wildest, most remote backcountry in all of Washington. Hikers are likely to find little company on the trails other than their immediate companions and the hosts of wild-

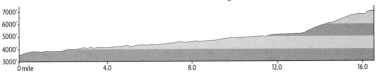

Paintbrush and lupine along the rock-lined trail

life, including an army of mammals such as deer, bear, elk, moose, bobcats, cougars, and coyotes, and the endangered woodland caribou and lynx. Both black bear and the endangered grizzly live here, though the latter exists in very limited numbers—by most estimates, fewer than twenty individuals total.

But the plethora of wildlife available for viewing is just one of the great things about the area. This trail to Remmel Lake and the Pasayten Wilderness in general provide hikers with a variety of scenery to absorb and recreational opportunities to enjoy. Large native trout dart through the region's rivers and lakes, ready and eager to latch onto a fisherman's fly. Nonanglers (including canines) can enjoy cooling off in the deep pools of the rivers or the crystal waters of the lakes. And late season hikers will soon realize that the best fall colors in the state can be found in the heart of the Pasayten.

To get there, from State Route 20 in Winthrop, turn north onto the Chewuch River Road (Forest Road 51) and drive north 30 miles (the road changes to FR 5160 about 15 miles from Winthrop near the Crystal Trailhead) to the road's end at Thirtymile Camp and Trailhead.

The Pasayten, with its long and looping trails, is a popular place with hard-core horse packers and this trail is no exception. Unless you get here early in the spring before too many iron-shod hooves have chewed the trail, you'll be stomping through powdery dust as you start up the Chewuch River Trail from the trailhead. The first few miles are the worst because they get the heaviest traffic—be sure to avail your dog of plenty of water during frequent water stops to keep his tongue free of the persistent dust.

The trail meanders gently through open, airy pine forests for 3 miles below Thirtymile Peak before reaching the first real views along the route—Chewuch Falls. Just past this pretty cascade, the valley narrows and the forest closes in a bit as the trail continues to climb gradually to

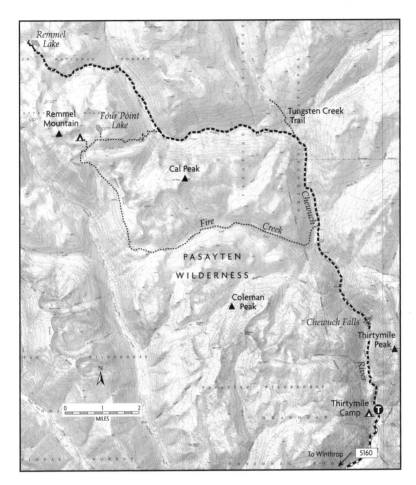

Pocket Lake. This marshy pool, about 5.5 miles from the trailhead, is more a mosquito incubator than a true lake and should be considered only as an emergency camping location. A better plan, especially given the gentle rise of the trail, is to continue up the river valley another 3 miles to the junction with the Tungsten Creek Trail. You can find decent camps near the river all along this stretch of trail. You've gained just over 1000 feet on the 8.5 miles from the trailhead to the Tungsten Creek junction.

The river valley hooks west from Tungsten Creek but stays fairly gentle in its pitch. In another 4 miles, gaining another meager 600 feet, at mile 12.5 you'll pass a side trail leading northwest to Four Point Lake on the flank of Remmel Mountain. At this trail junction, the Chewuch River—and our trail along its banks—turns north once more and begins a steadier, steeper climb. The pine forests give way more frequently to meadows from this point onward. Two miles from the Four Point Lake Trail junction (14.5 miles from the trailhead), the trail leaves the Chewuch River and begins an ascent of the Remmel Creek Valley. In the next 2 miles, you'll gain nearly 1000 feet, but that modest elevation increase brings you into a completely different ecosystem. You'll find yourself strolling through broad meadows more often than not, with wonderful views of the craggy summits of the ridges lining the river valley. The final miles lead through forest parklands and the meadow-ringed Remmel Lake at 16.5 miles. From these open fields around the lake, you can look up on Remmel Mountain, Cathedral Peak, and Andrews Peak.

NOTE: Dogs unaccustomed to horses should be leashed at all times on this trail because the route is a favorite with horse packers. The plethora of wildlife means that dogs prone to chasing critters must be leashed at all times, too. **REMEMBER:** Harassment of wildlife is illegal and it's also irresponsible behavior by dog owners.

20. Horseshoe Basin/ Louden Lake

Round trip: 14 miles
Hiking time: 8 hours (day hike or backpacking trip)
High point: 7200 feet
Elevation gain: 1200 feet
Best hiking time: July through early October
Map: Green Trails Horseshoe Basin No. 21
Contact: Okanogan National Forest, Tonasket Ranger District,
   (509) 486-2186

Sure, you can make this route in the Pasayten Wilderness into a long day hike, but the question is, why would you want to? The relatively easy hike into this high, alpine meadow country makes it possible for back-packers to get in, set up camp, then spend time rambling through the

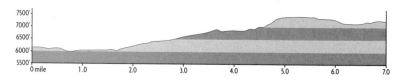

Spike and Koko looking down on Louden Lake and Horseshoe Basin.
(Ken Konigsmark)

endless fields of flowers, soaking in the sun-drenched meadows and taking in the sprawling vistas all around the basin. Horseshoe Basin stretches from Haig Mountain to Arnold Peak, with nearly all of it open meadow country between 7000 and 8000 feet in elevation. Deer, elk, and even a few rogue moose roam these natural pasture lands. Bring binoculars to watch those big beasts as well as the smaller critters that thrive here, such as marmots, snowshoe hares, bobcats, Canada lynx, weasels, badgers, and more. If you're sure your dog will return to you rather than follow the fascinating scents of these beasts, you might bring a Frisbee, or find a stout stick, and play endless games of fetch with Fido in these huge fields.

To get there, from Tonasket, at the junction of State Route 20 and U.S. Highway 97, drive north on US 97 to Ellisforde and turn west, following Forest Road 9425 to the community of Loomis. Continue on FR 9425 about 1.5 miles north of Loomis and turn west onto FR 39 (Touts-Coulee Road). Drive east on FR 39 for 16 miles, passing the North Fork Campground (about 11 miles) before turning right (north) onto FR 39-500 (Iron Goat Road). Continue to the end of this road, about 7 miles, to the Iron Gate Trailhead.

The trail descends gently for the first 0.5 mile, angling initially through tight lodgepole and white pine forests. The route enters the wilderness area mere yards from the road's end and follows an abandoned roadway to an old shepherds camp (Iron Gate Camp) at a four-way trail junction at 0.75 mile. The roadway was used by shepherds driving flocks into the high country and miners accessing their claims in days gone by. Continue straight ahead as the trail slowly climbs along the slope above Clutch Creek. The trail stays well above the creek, and there is no dependable source of water here—the small creeks feeding into Clutch Creek are seasonal. Water

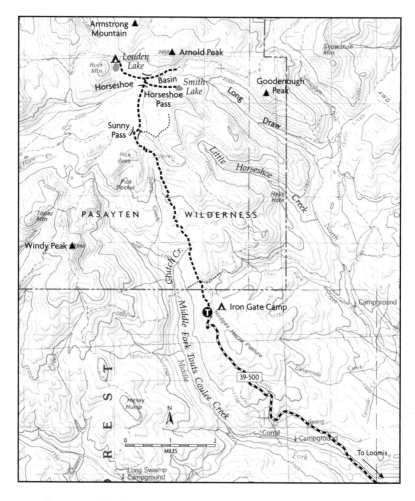

must be carried for both human and canine hikers.

As the trail angles gently upward, the pine forests start to open, first with broad glades and broken canopies, then with increasingly large clearings and meadows between the stands of trees. At 5 miles from the trailhead, the forest falls away as meadows stretch before you. In another 0.25 mile of climbing, you'll cross Sunny Pass (7200 feet elevation) and enter into the true heart of the Horseshoe Basin meadows. From the pass, the fields of grass and wildflowers stretch north to Armstrong Mountain, west to Haig Mountain, and east to Arnold Peak.

Enjoy the views from the pass, then continue north as the trail slides downward, descending a meager 200 feet in 1.5 miles to Horseshoe Pass and a split in the trail. A small side trail on the right leads east 0.75 mile to Smith Lake on the edge of the Horseshoe Mountains. The middle trail leads northeast through the meadows to the flank of Arnold Peak. Staying left, the trail glides west to just over 7 miles from the trailhead to reach Louden Lake at the base of Rock Mountain. Great camps can be found in the meadows surrounding Louden; however, in this fragile alpine meadow country, you must be very diligent about practicing Leave No Trace principles and even extend them by keeping your camp 400 or 500 feet from the lake rather than the recommended 100 feet setback. Campers will find endless enjoyment in ranging out through the meadows of Horseshoe Basin, exploring all the little coves and forest stands that fill the area.

NOTE: Skill with a map and compass is vital for safe off-trail explorations in the Pasayten or anywhere. Be sure you have solid backcountry navigation skills before setting off cross-country because the meadows can be hard to distinguish one from the other once you leave the security of the trail. Also, be sure to keep Pooch close at hand because a far-ranging dog may not hear your return commands and could become lost or injured. In other words, keep a leash on the dog unless she will unquestioningly stay within a few yards of you at all times.

21. Scatter Lake

Round trip: 9 miles
Hiking time: 8 hours
High point: 7050 feet
Elevation gain: 3900 feet
Best hiking time: July through early October
Map: Green Trails Stehekin No. 82
Contact: Okanogan National Forest, Methow Valley Ranger District, Visitor Information Center, (509) 996-4000

You'll want your dog on a short leash here—if only so he can help pull you up this thigh-burner of a trail. The trail angles upward steeply,

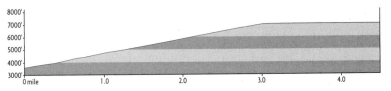

maintaining nearly a 20 percent grade for the first 3.5 miles (i.e., ascending more than 1100 feet per mile). Adding to the pleasantness of the trail, the route stands out on a sun-baked hillside; so on a midsummer day not only will your quads be screaming in agony but you'll be drenched in sweat, too. People who prefer to avoid these types of painful approaches might wonder what could possibly prompt hikers to subject themselves to such agonizing grinds up the sides of mountains. To learn the answer, you merely have to hike this steep trail; for at its end is one of the most serenely beautiful lake basins in all of the Cascades.

The snow-freshened waters of Scatter Lake fill a granite-lined basin on the flank of Abernathy Peak. The lake basin is nestled deep in

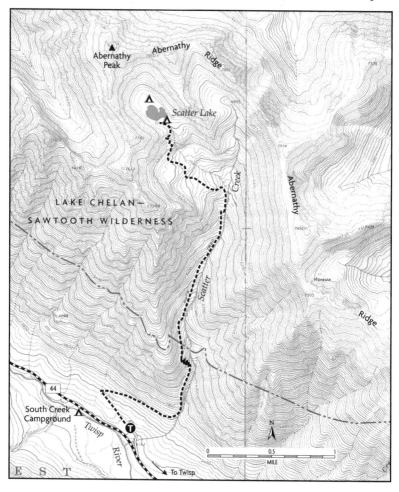

Heather and berry bushes along the lake basin

a three-sided cirque and the lake is edged with towering larch trees, which glow brilliant green in early summer and shimmer luminescent gold in autumn. These majestic deciduous conifers, standing in colorful meadows of heather and low-bush blueberries, give the basin a nearly magical feel. You'll love the scenic splendor of the lake—not to mention the outstanding views of the surrounding peaks—and your dog will love hiking at your side to this wonderful swimming pool.

To get there, from State Route 20 in Twisp, turn west onto the Twisp River Road (Forest Road 44) and drive 22 miles to the trailhead, found on the north side of the road near the South Creek Campground.

Before you start, make sure you've filled all available water bottles—both you and your dog are going to need plenty of fluids on this trail. From the trailhead, wander up the rough old roadbed, which serves as a trail for 0.25 mile. At that point, the route narrows to a proper path and begins the long, steep climb. The first mile cuts back and forth through widely spaced switchbacks before angling into the narrow Scatter Creek canyon. More switchbacks bring hikers closer and closer to the plunging waters of the creek, until finally, at 2.5 miles, the water is reached, providing a place for the pup to really drink his fill while you rest and mop up sweat.

Make sure you've fully recovered your breath and drank your fill before continuing, because the next mile is ruthlessly steep as the trail follows the straight-line approach of the creek. No more switchbacks. Instead, the trail cuts steeply up-canyon by sticking to the west bank of the creek.

At 3.5 miles, the pitch yields a bit as the trail angles west away from the main branch of the creek and cuts upward along the creek that drains Scatter Lake. The modest climb over the next 0.5 mile brings you to a large camping area near the base of a crashing waterfall. This camp is popular with horse packers but also perfect for backpackers—just stay clear of the areas where horses have been picketed. From this campsite, the trail turns nasty again for the last 0.5 mile as it climbs out of the trees, crosses above the falls, and rolls through sprawling meadows to reach the banks of the small lake at 4.5 miles. There are several good campsites around the lake. Those on the southeast side have the best views of Abernathy Peak, but the ones in the broad meadows on the northwest side of the lake (at the base of Abernathy) get the best morning light.

22. Boulder River

Round trip: 9 miles
Hiking time: 6 hours
High point: 1600 feet
Elevation gain: 600 feet
Best hiking time: March through December
Maps: Green Trails Oso No. 77, Granite Falls No. 109
Contact: Mt. Baker–Snoqualmie National Forest, Darrington Ranger Station, (360) 436-1155

Like many of the trails in the lower reaches of the Cascades, Boulder River Trail begins in dense second-growth forests that sprang up (unaided) after the area was logged decades ago. But unlike most other low trails, this one quickly leaves the tight stands of alder and spindly hemlock and fir to enter an ecosystem all too rare in today's North Cascades—lowland old-growth

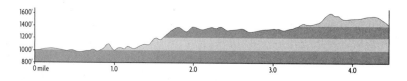

Hiker resting on large moss-covered rock

forest. Along the way, the trail passes within view of a stunning horsetail waterfall, follows a pretty river, and brings you into an area rich in native flora and fauna. The cool, shaded trail makes this a great place to hike in the heat of summer—your dog will certainly appreciate a day of cool, damp hiking. But, because the trail rarely climbs higher than 1600 feet, the route is snowfree most of the year and can be hiked in late fall through spring, when other, higher elevation trails in the Cascades are closed by heavy snowpacks.

To get there, drive Interstate 5 to exit 208 (Silvana/Arlington). Turn east onto State Route 530 and continue 19.5 miles before turning right (south) onto French Creek Road (Forest Road 2010). Drive 3.8 miles to the trailhead at the end of the road.

The trail begins along an old railroad grade. At one point just 0.25 mile from the trailhead, you'll find yourself on a long section of railbed supported by a massive stone wall on the side of a steep slope. In less than a mile, you'll enter the Boulder River Wilderness Area. This early section of trail leading up to the wilderness passes through second-growth forest full of alder trees. Alders are fast growing but are very susceptible to wind damage, as can be seen if you hike this trail in midwinter through early spring. The trail is frequently littered with blown-down alders in these months, though volunteer trail crews from Washington Trails Association work year-round to keep the route clear.

As the trail enters the wilderness, the tightly packed, alder forest suddenly falls away as massive western hemlocks, western red cedars, and

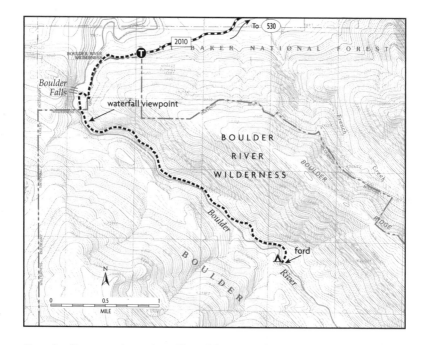

Douglas firs come into view. This old-growth forest, protected by wilderness designation, is one of the largest remaining blocks of pristine forest below 2000 feet in the northern Cascades.

The trail climbs modestly its entire length. About 1.25 miles from the trailhead, the path stoops down to a viewpoint overlooking the Boulder River. The river is pretty enough but the real draw here lies across the narrow river where a thundering waterfall (Boulder Falls) fans across the cliff that makes up the opposite bank of the river. A couple logs have been laid along the trail here as makeshift benches for hikers to stop and rest while enjoying the spectacular view of the falls.

Moving beyond this point, the river drops out of sight and sound of the trail for the next few miles. Instead of riparian views, the trail now provides a close-up study of the old-growth forest. Keep your dog on a short leash and watch his ears and eyes carefully—he will alert you to any critters that might be moving through the valley. Petite black-tailed deer live here, as do the infamous northern spotted owls. There are also great horned owls and many small songbirds living in this rich ecosystem.

The trail eventually angles back to the riverside at 4.5 miles and abruptly ends at the water's edge. At one time, the route crossed the river via a broad ford and continued up the opposite valley wall to an old lookout site at the top of Three Fingers to the southeast. Today that trail is abandoned and the few scattered remnants of it aren't worth seeking. Better to turn around at the riverside—or, if you are backpacking, set up camp at the broad campsite adjacent to the old ford.

23. Round Lake

Round trip: 11 miles
Hiking time: 8 hours
High point: 5500 feet
Elevation gain: 3600 feet
Best hiking time: July through October
Map: Green Trails Sloan Peak No. 111
Contact: Mt. Baker–Snoqualmie National Forest, Darrington Ranger Station, (360) 436-1155

Though steep, this trail provides hikers plenty of places to stop and rest while surveying the stunning views of the surrounding peaks found here on the western boundary of the Glacier Peak Wilderness. Day hikers can cut a tough mile off the trail by halting at the ridge overlooking the lake, while backpackers will find outstanding places to pitch camp and enjoy a night of stargazing alongside a broad, blue-watered lake. If day hiking along the route, it is important to carry enough water for the entire round-trip journey because there are no permanent water sources along the trail (except the lake—but for day hikers it is a steep descent to the basin). Your dog will need more water than normal, too, because the open forest canopy allows a lot of heating to occur along the route. **Remember:** Even mild dehydration can be deadly for dogs.

To get there, from Darrington and State Route 530, drive south on the Mountain Loop Highway about 16 miles and turn left (east) onto Forest Road 49 (North Fork Sauk River Road). Drive 3 miles to the trailhead, found on the left (north) side of the road.

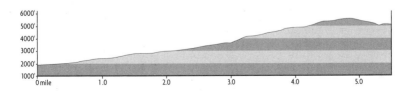

Beargrass blooms along the trail

Walking out of the trailhead parking area onto the trail, you'll duck under the forest canopy and follow a soft path on a gentle incline for 0.5 mile, allowing you time to adjust your pack and work the kinks out of your joints before the real work begins. The trail turns steep, entering a long series of tight switchbacks through open forest for the next several miles. This section of trail will wear you down, but along the way, you'll find the trail crossing plenty of forest glades, which present views south to glacier-flanked Sloan Peak and rocky-topped Bedal Peak. Just past 3 miles from the trailhead, the path levels briefly as it crosses Bingley Gap in the saddle between Spring Mountain and the many summits of Lost Creek Ridge. If the climb to here proved tougher than you thought, Bingley Gap makes a fine turnaround for day hikers.

The trail continues past the gap, though, rolling another 2 miles along the ridgeline with occasionally great views of the Sauk River valley and the peaks beyond. At 5 miles out, the trail reaches another saddle, this time on the ridge overlooking Round Lake. This is the destination for day hikers. From here, there are great vistas to the west, south, and east, with Round Lake nestled in a rocky basin below the ridge to the north.

Campers will find a small trail dropping almost due north from this point, descending 500 feet in just 0.5 mile to reach the lakeshore at 5.5 miles. This steep, rocky trail requires care and caution to descend—don't attempt this trail with a leashed dog who likes to pull because you risk being pulled off balance for a nasty tumble. Once at the lake, you'll find primo campsites among the heather meadows surrounding the lake.

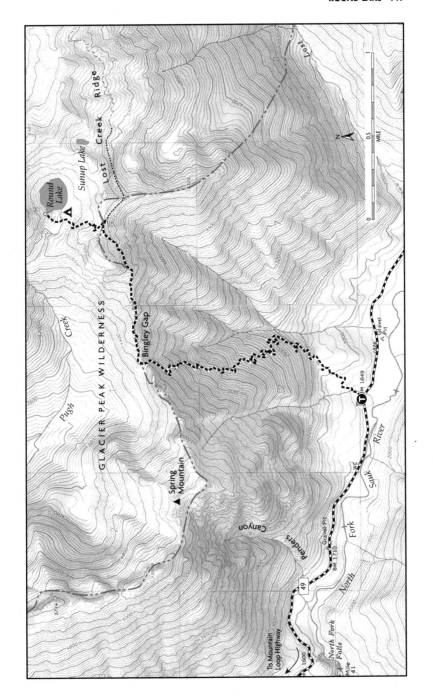

24. Poodle Dog Pass/Silver Lake

Round trip: 11 miles
Hiking time: 8 hours (day hike or backpacking trip)
High point: 4400 feet
Elevation gain: 2000 feet
Best hiking time: July through early November
Maps: Green Trails Sloan Peak No. 111, Monte Cristo No. 143
Contact: Mt. Baker–Snoqualmie National Forest, Darrington Ranger
 Station, (360) 436-1155

You can enjoy an almost leisurely stroll along the initial 4 miles of this wonderful route as it follows the well-graded old dirt road from Barlow Pass to the historic mining town of Monte Cristo. Indeed, perhaps even miniature poodles could enjoy this picturesque walk. The road, still used by the few folks who retain rights to the mining claims and cabins in the old ghost town, passes through lush, old forest alongside the South Fork Sauk River. From the town, though, the route gets more difficult. No more strolling through forest glades here. After viewing the old railroad turnstile and other rusting hulks of mining equipment around the town, you'll start a long, steep slog up a series of switchbacks that will leave you huffing, puffing, and sweating buckets. Be aware, too, that July is the peak month for mosquitoes here most years, and the soggy forest tends to breed swarms of the nasty little biters. The breezes found in the pass, though, sweep away the worst of the little nasties, and by late summer, the bugs are mostly past their prime.

To get there, from Granite Falls drive east on the Mountain Loop Highway for 12 miles to the Verlot Public Service Center and continue another 19.5 miles to Barlow Pass. Parking is on the left side of the highway. The trail begins on the right (south) side of the highway, on a gated dirt road.

From the large parking area, cross the Mountain Loop Highway at the very pinnacle of Barlow Pass and walk around the steel gate that bars vehicle access to the small dirt road leading south from the pass. For

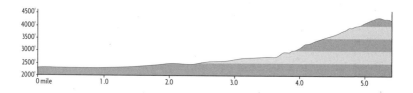

View of Monte Cristo Valley from Poodle Dog Pass

the next several miles, you'll follow this road. Be aware that mountain bikers enjoy riding this portion of the route; keep your dog under control so she doesn't tangle with spinning wheels. The road crosses the South Fork Sauk River at 1.5 miles, and it's worth stopping for a break alongside the pretty river at this point. Let the dog splash through the shallow pools, while you enjoy the sparkling sunlight glistening off the quartz-speckled summits of Foggy, Del Campo, and Silvertip Peaks, as well as the other Monte Cristo peaks.

At 4 miles from Barlow Pass, the road crosses a small wooden bridge and leads to a cluster of old cabins and shacks—this is Monte Cristo, a town founded by miners searching for silver and other precious metals. The

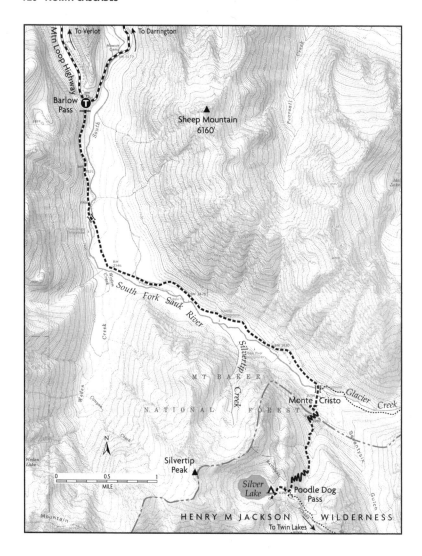

mountains didn't yield much wealth, and much of the town was continually hammered by winter avalanches, hastening the abandonment of the settlement. Poke around as you please and enjoy the history left on the ground, but please steer clear of those cabins clearly still in use and respect all areas marked as private property. Pampered poodles and other pooches should call it quits here, making due with the gentle 8-mile round trip to Monte Cristo. Tough trail dogs, though, should push on to Poodle Dog Pass (note that I have found no reference to explain the name).

To find the trail to Poodle Dog Pass: after crossing the bridge over the Sauk, look for the pathway, well signed, on the right. The trail from this point on is classic Cascade single-track trail. That is, it is steep, rutted, and lined with rolling rocks and toe-grabbing roots nearly all the way to Poodle Dog Pass. From Monte Cristo (2800 feet) the trail climbs 1.7 miles, gaining 1600 feet along the way to cross the saddle of Poodle Dog Pass at 4400-feet elevation.

Silver Lake can be seen shining in the low basin off to the right (west) as you reach the pass. A short 0.25-mile trail leads down to the lake. There are a few campsites on the south side of the ice-cold pond, and great views of Silvertip Peak tower above the lake to the north.

Silver Lake makes a great day-hike destination and a modest backpacking camp. If you have the stamina and the desire, though, you might consider turning south from Poodle Dog Pass another steep and rough 2.7 miles up and over the Twin Peaks Ridge. There you'll find Twin Lakes with excellent camps amid beautiful heather meadows, all in the shadow of the steep granite cliffs of Columbia Peak.

25. Phelps Creek/Spider Meadows

Round trip: 14 miles
Hiking time: 8 hours (day hike or backpacking trip)
High point: 5500 feet
Elevation gain: 2000 feet
Best hiking time: July through October
Map: Green Trails Holden No. 113
Contact: Wenatchee National Forest, Lake Wenatchee Ranger District, (509) 763-3103

Ever wonder what a glacier-carved valley looks like? Wonder no more, because the Phelps Creek valley is a classic U-shaped valley that was scraped, shaped, and buffed by an ancient river of slowly flowing ice. The broad dished-out bottom of this valley cradles vast wildflower meadows

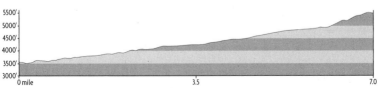

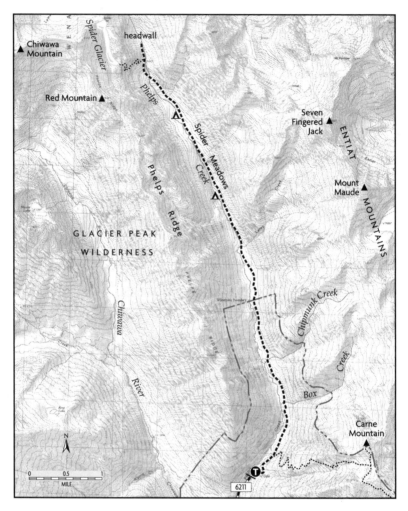

nestled below sky-scraping ridges topped with rocky crags and spires. Through it all meanders the milky blue waters of Phelps Creek as it drains off the slowly melting ice of Spider Glacier high above the valley floor. And if the views of the stunning landscape aren't enough to entice you to visit this incredible basin, consider this: the sprawling fields of flowers and grasses feed large numbers of ungulates, from deer to mountain sheep. There are coyotes prowling the trees and meadows, hunting for the plentiful ground squirrels, snowshoe hares, and marmots. Bobcats pad silently about in search of the same prey. Overhead, golden eagles soar on the lifting thermal currents, as do red-tailed and Cooper's hawks, merlins, and kestrels. There are even a few falcons in these valleys.

To get there, drive U.S. Highway 2 to Coles Corner, about 20 miles east of Stevens Pass summit. Turn north onto the Lake Wenatchee Road (State Route 207), crossing the Wenatchee River Bridge, and staying right at the road split onto the Chiwawa Loop Road for 1.5 miles. Turn left onto the Chiwawa River Road (Forest Road 62) and continue 22 miles to the Phelps Creek Road (FR 6211). Turn right and drive 2 miles to the trailhead at the gate. Do not block the gate because some mine-claim owners continue to use the road beyond the gate.

The hike begins with a road walk—the one drawback to this trail. It seems there are still active placer mines along the Chiwawa River and the miners (hobbyists, really, who have manipulated the system to allow them to maintain permanents camps up this pristine valley) have retained the right to drive on this otherwise-closed road. Let the dog romp beside you on this broad track and let him enjoy the proximity of the river to drink from frequently and paddle away the heat of the trail.

A quarter mile up the rolling road, you'll pass a side trail leading to Carne Mountain summit, and in the next 2 miles, you'll pass trails leading up Box Creek and Chipmunk Creek, where the two-track road begins to bleed away to a single-track trail. At 2.75 miles, you'll cross the boundary into the Glacier Peak Wilderness and leave the miners and their road behind for good.

These first few miles of the route are carved out of the dry pine and fir forest of the eastern Cascade foothills, but as the trail moves into the wilderness, the forest opens more and more frequently onto small clearings and then increasingly broad meadows. Just past 5 miles into the hike, you'll suddenly find yourself stepping out of the trees into the lower reaches of the long, sprawling fields of Spider Meadows near the 4700-foot elevation.

Indeed, the trail continues another 2 miles, crossing Phelps Creek about a mile after entering the meadow near an old miners cabin. The trail pushes on another mile to end at 7 miles, and hikers can ramble to their heart's content through the nearby meadows.

Almost as soon as you enter the lower end of the meadow, spectacular vistas of the surrounding peaks spring into the view. Phelps Ridge and Red Mountain tower over the western side of the valley. The Entiat Mountains, from Mount Maude and Seven Fingered Jack to Dumbbell Mountain, stretch along the eastern skyline. To the north, at the head of the valley, stands a towering rock wall cradling a small sliver of ice—Spider Glacier—below the summit of Chiwawa Mountain.

Backpacker exploring in upper meadow

You can find good campsites in these lower fields and more farther up the meadow. At 6 miles the trail crosses Phelps Creek, about a mile after entering the meadow, and passes an old miners cabin.

Less than 0.5 mile after the creek crossing, the trail splits, with the left fork climbing more than 1000 feet along a steep, dry route used by miners in days gone by to attain the terminal end of Spider Glacier. This is the trail for gung-ho, highly motivated hikers and their dogs with boundless energy and zest for adventure. But even the most enthusiastic hiker will want to avoid the ice sheet itself. Even experienced mountaineers find the ice unstable and unpredictable.

A better option for a careful hiker and dog is to stay right and follow

Phelps Creek into more meadows nestled on the upper flanks of the main valley. This route leads to incredible camping options with unmatched views and veritable lawns of wildflowers. The trail ends at the headwall of Phelps Creek valley below Dumbbell Mountain.

Whether you pick a camp high in the valley for views down the long meadows to the mountains at the far end, or a camp low in the meadows for views up the valley to the craggy peaks above the headwall, find a site set well back from any water to help keep the water unpolluted. Try to place your tent against a backdrop of trees so it doesn't stand out and mar the view for other valley visitors.

26. Chelan Lakeshore Trail

One-way trip: 18 miles (requires boat pick-up and drop-off)
Hiking time: 2 to 3 days (generally, an additional travel day is needed for the return boat ride and long drive home)
High point: 1700 feet
Elevation gain: 800 feet
Best hiking time: March through November
Maps: Green Trails Stehekin No. 82, Lucerne No. 114, Prince Creek No. 115
Contact: Wenatchee National Forest, Chelan Ranger District, (509) 682-2576
Warning: This trail crosses rattlesnake country. Dogs must be kept on leash at all times when rattlesnakes are active (warm summer and early fall months) to reduce the risk of snakebite. This trail is best visited in spring and autumn when the vipers are less active. But at all times, be aware that rattlesnakes may be encountered and know the proper actions to take in the event of snakebite.

The Chelan Lakeshore Trail works best as a one-way trip, with the start and end points accessed by the *Lady of the Lake* ferry. The trail is actually hikeable nearly year-round, but the best times to hit this lakeside route

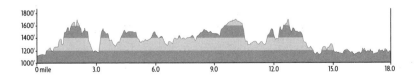

Two- and four-legged hikers should enjoy the area, but they both need to be cautious of the rattlesnakes common to Lake Chelan's hot sun-blasted rocks. (Kelly McCaffrey)

are during the shoulder seasons—that is, spring and fall. In spring, the trail is snowfree and hikeable when other mountain trails are buried under a deep snowpack. Autumn provides hikers a chance to experience the splendor of the northern Cascades clad in the colorful tapestry of fall foliage. Summer can be (okay, always is) hot and dry, but hot in this part of the country seldom gets much above 100 degrees Fahrenheit. That heat can seem sweltering, but it is just hot enough to drive off the hordes of hikers and the swarms of bugs. And, no matter how hot it gets, there is always a huge, deep lake only minutes (often, only seconds) away from the trail. If doing the trail in summer, you should hike in shorts you don't mind dunking, and plan on frequent dips to keep both you and your dog cool and comfortable.

The trail follows the shoreline, sometimes dipping close enough to allow you to chuck sticks into the waves for the dog, and at other times rolling high up on the slope above to views of the broad valley-bottom lake and the surrounding mountains. The trail weaves through deep old-growth pine and fir forests, cuts through sweeping grassy meadows, and slices across the sides of steep banks and bluffs. Look for deer and elk as they migrate along the shore, enjoying the forage and plentiful water. Enjoy the abundance of wildflowers, some of which start blooming in spring while others pop throughout the summer. There is bear grass, trillium, skunk cabbage, lilies—glacier, avalanche, and tiger are a few of the lily varieties—columbine, scarlet gilia, and endless other varieties to enjoy. Watch for otters, weasels, badgers, coyotes, cougars, and bobcats. Listen for the songs of tweety birds, the shrieks of raptors (eagles, hawks, ospreys, turkey vultures, and falcons), and the rattles of snakes. Yes, this is rattlesnake country, and that means special, specific attention for your dog. Keep

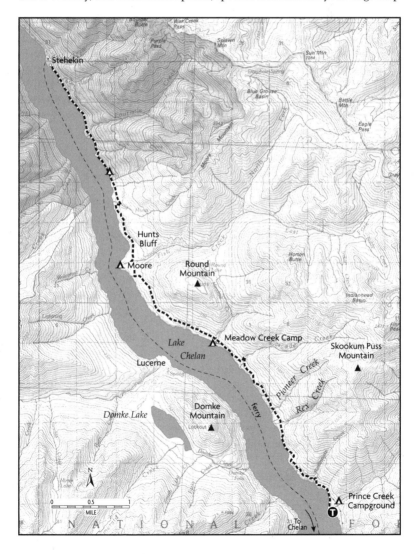

Bowzer on the leash at all times from late spring through late fall when the vipers are commonly active on this trail. Human hikers know enough to be cautious when they hear the rattle, but dogs—unfamiliar with snakes—tend to be curious, which more often than not leads to snakebites. By keeping the pooch on a short leash, you can keep him away from the reptiles. Still, you must be well aware of the proper procedures for dealing with snakebites, whether it is the dog or you that gets bit. (See Appendix B for recommended readings on canine first aid.)

To get there, from Chelan, catch the water taxi up Lake Chelan to the Prince Creek Campground or Stehekin. The Lake Chelan Boat Company operates the ferries; call (509) 682-2224 to request a current schedule of times and fares. Dogs are allowed on the ferries, but they must be secured in a dog crate. You may bring your own, or rent one from the boat company. The trail can be hiked from the north or the south, though hiking from south to north is recommended because it provides more views of the mountains of the North Cascades. For the southern trailhead, hop off the boat at Prince Creek. If instead hiking north to south, you'll need to make arrangements to ensure the boat stops at Prince Creek to pick you up on your return.

From Prince Creek Campground, hop over the creek and start north along the trail. You'll hug the shoreline pretty closely for the first few miles, dipping inland only to cross Rattlesnake Creek before swinging back down to the lakeside. This section—from Prince Creek to Meadow Creek at 7 miles—passes through forests and small clearings, with good views across the lake to Domke Mountain, and beyond to Emerald Peak and Pinnacle Mountain.

A few miles north of Prince Creek, the trail climbs high on the flank of Skookum Puss Mountain to cross the bench between Rex and Pioneer Creeks more than 800 feet above the lake. The trail then angles back down toward the lake, staying well above the waterline for the 3 more miles as the trail rolls across open fields of flowers and cool stands of pine forest before reaching Meadow Creek Camp at mile 7, which offers a good place to bed down. A rustic wooden cabin is available for campers, but smart dogs will avoid this mouse-laden shack and stick to their tent.

From Meadow Creek, the trail alternates between cool forests and open sun-drenched glades as it cuts across the slope above the lake. You'll find fewer water views along the 3 miles between Meadow Creek Camp and Moore Point, but you can cover this gentle section quickly and stop for a rest at Moore Point—a short side trail drops you on the beach at the large maintained campground here.

Cutting north across the neck of Moore Point (a small, blunt peninsula), the trail climbs the modest heights of Hunts Bluff (a gain of some 600 feet) and then drops back down to the lakeshore. From here, the trail rolls 6 miles north to Stehekin, passing another campground along the way.

27. Eagle Lakes

Round trip: 12 miles
Hiking time: 2 to 3 days
High point: 7200 feet
Elevation gain: 2900 feet
Best hiking time: late June through October
Map: Green Trails Prince Creek No. 115
Contact: Okanogan National Forest, Methow Valley Ranger District, Visitor Information Center, (509) 996-4000

You'll have a tired dog after this outing, but chances are he'll do better than you along the way. The trail climbs steadily right from the start, carved into the steep side of a long ridge running down from Mount Bigelow. As the trail climbs, the forest, open and airy to begin with, thins and eventually disappears as meadows take over and the trail climbs to the upper reaches of Sawtooth Ridge. The sprawling network of interlocked meadows—separated by stands of timber, fins of rock, and broad, blue lakes—provides wonderful opportunities to ramble through knee-deep fields of flowers while soaking in views of the North Cascades.

To get there, from Twisp off State Route 20, drive south on SR 153 about 15 miles to the junction with North Fork Gold Creek Road (County Road 1029) and turn right (west). Drive about 5 miles, staying right at the road junction near the forest boundary where the road becomes Forest Road 4340. At 7 miles from SR 153, turn left onto FR 4340-300, a

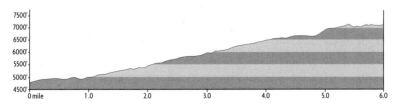

Tumbling creek and shooting stars

narrow dirt road leading off to the northwest. Drive 5 miles to the end of the road and park at the trailhead.

The trail angles upward from the road, though it maintains a mercifully gentle grade for most of the first 0.5 mile as it traverses the forest into the Crater Creek valley. Soon after crossing the creek, the trail splits. The right branch climbs Crater Creek for a long amble to Crater Lakes (another fine hike in its own right) while our route goes left and climbs the steep snout of the ridge separating Crater Creek from Martin Creek. The trail weaves upward through a few switchbacks, passing another trail junction on the left (this side trail leads to Martin Lakes); and at 4.5 miles, reaches the third junction at 6600-feet elevation in heather fields. A tiny, way trail drops away to the left, descending a little more than 100 feet in a third of a mile to reach Lower Eagle Lake. There are fine campsites here, and if a lot of other folks are on the trail, this might be the best opportunity for solitude on this route.

The main trail continues past this trail junction, climbing through increasingly scenic flower fields to the 7000-foot level. Soak in the views of the surrounding peaks, then at nearly 5.5 miles, turn right onto another side trail climbing another 150 feet in elevation to 6 miles and the broad, scenic waters of Upper Eagle Lake at the foot of Mount Bigelow. Meadows and larch-studded forests surround this jewel of a lake. Plenty of campgrounds can be found here, too, though they tend to draw the biggest crowds.

And crowds do come here. This trail is popular with hikers and horse packers, and it is also open to motorized trail users, though the steep, rocky

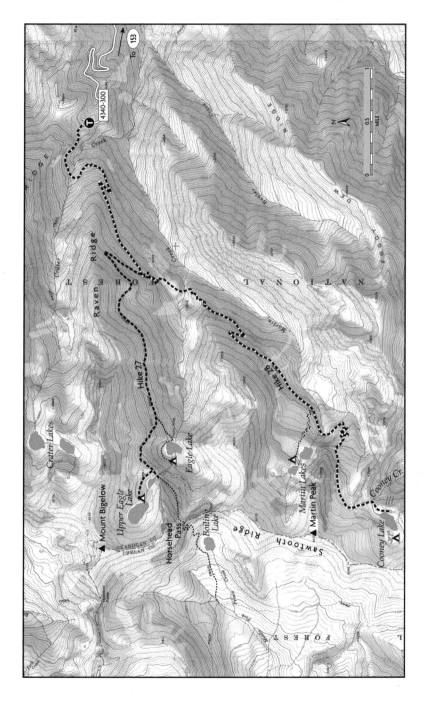

nature of the trail keeps the majority of the speed seekers away. Still, you might find yourself encountering a puttering dirtbike anywhere along the trail, so keep an eye on Spot and make sure he is under control at all times.

For additional mileage or perhaps an afternoon stroll after setting up camp, continue up the main trail 0.5 mile past the upper lake trail junction, you'll cross Horsehead Pass at 7590 feet. Here you'll find views west to Old Maid Mountain and other unnamed peaks of the Sawtooth Wilderness. You can look north and south along the craggy line of Sawtooth Ridge and peer down on Boiling Lake.

28. Cooney Lake/Martin Lakes

Round trip: 17 miles to Cooney, 15 to Martin
Hiking time: 2 to 3 days
High point: 7240 feet
Elevation gain: 2500 feet
Best hiking time: late June through October
Map: Green Trails Prince Creek No. 115
Contact: Okanogan National Forest, Methow Valley Ranger District, Visitor Information Center, (509) 996-4000
See map page 131.

Want to give your dog something to howl about? How about a trail that leads to an assortment of lakes while following a pretty valley through open pine forests and rolling alpine meadows. Any dog that likes a dip at the end of the day will appreciate the plethora of lakes in which to paddle, and even water-phobic hounds will appreciate the meadows in which to romp. The trail shares a trailhead and the first 2.5 miles with the Eagle Lakes Trail (Hike 27), and the crowds that often fill the lower trail diminish after the split, drawn off to the ever-popular Eagle Lakes basin.

To get there, from Twisp drive south on State Route 153 about 15 miles

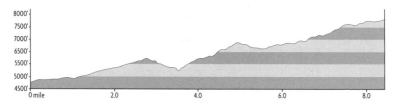

At Cooney Lake (Ken Konigsmark)

to the junction with North Fork Gold Creek Road (County Road 1029) and turn right (west). Drive about 5 miles, staying right at the road junction near the forest boundary, where the narrow road becomes Forest Road 4340. At 7 miles from SR 153, turn left onto FR 4340-300, a narrow dirt road leading off to the northwest. Drive 5 miles to the end of the road and park at the trailhead.

The trail follows a gentle grade for most of the first 0.5 mile as it traverses a small slope leading into the Crater Creek Valley. Soon after crossing Crater Creek, the trail splits, with the trail to Cooney and Martin Lakes going left. From here, the trail climbs steeply as it traverses the nose of the ridge separating Crater Creek from Martin Creek. The trail weaves upward through a few switchbacks to reach another trail junction at 2.5 miles. To the right is the Eagle Lakes Trail (Hike 27). Stay left and drop a few hundred feet in the next mile to cross Eagle Creek, letting the dog bury her dusty muzzle in the water for a well-deserved drink, before starting up once more to continue the traverse of the slope above Martin Creek.

The next few miles climb steadily, sometimes through short series of switchbacks, sometimes along long, climbing traverses, to a trail junction at the 6400-foot level about 6.5 miles from the trailhead. Over most of this last section, you'll be hiking through open forests with intermittent clearings and meadows.

Standing at the trail junction, you have a choice. To the right lies a steep climb to the twin pools of Martin Lakes. These ponds are beautiful alpine tarns surrounded by larch-studded forests and meadow-studded mountains. The trail to Martin Lakes climbs 350 feet in a rough 0.5 mile to the lower lake and another 0.25 mile to the small upper lake. There are good campsites at each.

If you go left at the trail junction, you have a longer hike in front of you. In the next 2 miles, you'll climb a long series of switchbacks then traverse through the steep meadows at the end of the Martin Creek valley before crossing a small saddle and entering the Cooney Lake Basin at 7200 feet, about 8.5 miles from the trailhead. Cooney Lake, surrounded by brilliant meadows of flowers and heather, offers great camping and awesome views of Martin Peak and the other unnamed summits along the crest of Sawtooth Ridge.

Be aware that this trail is a multiuse trail, open to hikers, horseback riders, mountain bikers, and motorcyclists. Keep your dog close and under firm leash command at all times.

29. Sunrise Lake/Foggy Dew

Round trip: 13 miles
Hiking time: 8 hours (day hike or backpacking trip)
High point: 7240 feet
Elevation gain: 2500 feet
Best hiking time: late June through October
Map: Green Trails Prince Creek No. 115
Contact: Okanogan National Forest, Methow Valley Ranger District, Visitor Information Center, (509) 996-4000

You don't have to be Irish to enjoy Foggy Dew. Sure, Foggy Dew may be one of the best-known fighting songs of the Irish (the tune was penned by Father P. O'Neill in tribute to the men who fought and died in the Easter Uprising of 1916 in Dublin), but Foggy Dew Trail is a tribute to peace and serenity. This quiet forest trail scrambles over rocks and through meadows alongside the tumbling waters of Foggy Dew Creek

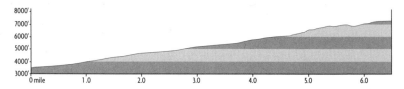

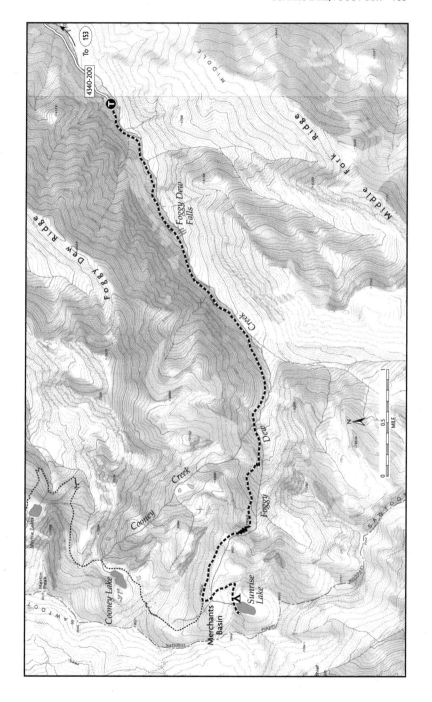

Field of paintbrush near Sunrise Lake

before turning and ascending into the bright green meadows surrounding Sunrise Lake. Adding to the quiet nature of this route is the fact that, unlike some other more popular trails in the area, the Foggy Dew Trail is off-limits to motorcycles.

The creek valley may have been named not for the acclaimed Irish song but for the morning mist that rises off the chilled waters of the creek in late summer.

To get there, from Twisp drive south on State Route 153 about 15 miles to the junction with North Fork Gold Creek Road (County Road 1029) and turn right (west). Drive about 5 miles, staying right at the road junction near the forest boundary, where the road becomes Forest Road 4340. At 5.5 miles, turn left onto FR 4340-200, a narrow dirt road leading off to the northwest. Drive to the end of the road and park at the trailhead.

The trail begins in dense forest alongside the Foggy Dew Creek. Let the pup splash and play in the water when the trail comes to creekside because eventually the trail turns steep, hot, and dusty, and a wet-saturated dog will be better able to deal with a workout in the sun. For more than 4 miles, the trail parallels the creek, climbing steadily but gradually through the forest. Keep an eye out for deer and, late in the summer, for huckleberry-hungry black bears. Yes, there are plenty of berry bushes growing in this forest valley. Pluck a few for you and your dog as you hike.

At 2.5 miles from the trailhead, the first trail highlight is found: Foggy Dew Falls. This pretty cascade is worth a picture or two (or three or four if you want to make sure you get a good shot and angle). Just over a mile past the falls, the trail slides upward away from the creek, crossing Cooney Creek at 4 miles. From here, it's a steep, dusty mile to a junction with a side trail connecting Foggy Dew to Cooney Lake/Martin Lakes Trail (Hike 28).

To head toward Sunrise Lake, stay left at the junction. After about a third of a mile, get a tight grip on the leash and let your dog pull you up a (thankfully) short series of steep, rocky switchbacks. As you climb out of the last of the hairpin turns, you'll find the trail returns to a more moderate angle of ascent and the thinning forests fall away to reveal the sprawling meadows of Merchants Basin.

Six miles from the trailhead, in the middle of the Merchants Basin wild-flower fields (around 6800 feet elevation), find a small way trail leading south (left) to Sunrise Lake. A long 0.5 mile gets you to the shores of the picturesque tarn at 7240 feet. There are one or two suitable tent sites around the lake basin and plenty more down in Merchants Basin. Those who have time to kill during an extended stay can follow the main trail from Merchants Basin west to the crest of Sawtooth Ridge for impressive views of the Lake Chelan/Sawtooth Wilderness and its many jagged peaks and deep gray-green valleys.

30. Pear Lake

Round trip: 12 miles
Hiking time: 8 hours (day hike or backpacking trip)
High point: 5200 feet
Elevation gain: 1400 feet
Best hiking time: mid-July through early autumn
Map: Green Trails Benchmark No. 144
Contact: Wenatchee National Forest, Lake Wenatchee Ranger District, (509) 763-3103

This route abounds with delightful treats for you and your hound. While Fido splashes through the waters of the resident lakes and ponds, you can soak in the sun-brightened views of the local peaks and meadows. The trail to Pear Lake (and its neighboring tarns) may be done as a day hike (the route is relatively gentle and gradually graded), but it makes a great backpacking

Blue-watered lake on the ridge top

destination with plenty of options for out-of-camp explorations.

To get there, from Lake Wenatchee, drive west on the Little Wenatchee River Road (Forest Road 6500) and, near the Riverside Campground, turn left (south) onto FR 6701, which follows the south bank of the river upstream. In about 6 miles, turn left onto FR 6701-400 (**Note:** The Green Trails map incorrectly shows this as FR 500). The trailhead is at the end of this road.

As you leave the trailhead, you'll traverse a tree-covered slope on the flank of Shoofly Mountain and stay fairly level for a mile. Your dog might be alert and attentive here—keep an eye on her because she'll likely be the first to sense or see any of the resident deer that browse through this forested basin.

After a mile, the trail turns steep as it enters a long series of switchbacks before drifting north to the meadows under the summit of Fall Mountain. You'll cross a shallow saddle at 5200 feet. Pause for a breather here, about 3 miles from the trailhead, and soak in the views of Shoofly and Fortune Mountain, with the Lake Creek valley between. Early in the summer, you might find a few pockets of snow—if it's a hot day, you might play a game of catch with Bowser. By tossing him a few snowballs, you not only give him some playtime but you cool him off as well.

From Fall Mountain, descend through meadows back into the trees, passing Top Lake before joining with the Pacific Crest Trail (PCT), and then reaching Pear Lake at 6 miles (elevation, 4800 feet). There are fine campsites near this meadow-lined lake. A short scamper through a small heather-filled saddle under Fortune Mountain leads to Peach Lake at the same elevation.

Once camp is established, enjoy exploring the region later in the afternoon or even in coming days (if you plan an extended stay). From Pear Lake, follow the PCT south through Wenatchee Pass and climb up onto the long, open ridge leading to Grizzly Peak. It's just 4 miles from the lake to the peak, but the views along the way are endless. The trail stays on the crest of the Cascades for those miles, offering stunning views to the east and west.

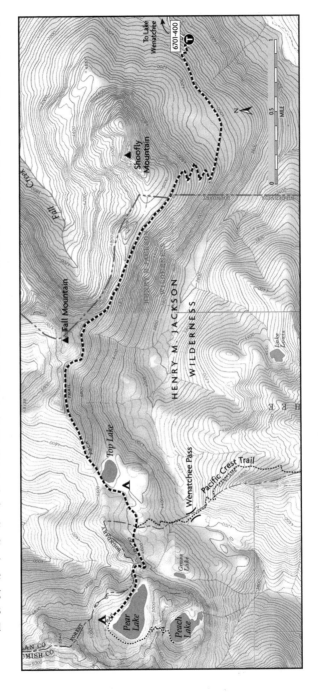

CENTRAL CASCADES

31. Surprise and Glacier Lakes

Round trip: 11 miles
Hiking time: 7 hours (day hike or backpacking trip)
High point: 5200 feet
Elevation gain: 3000 feet
Best hiking time: mid-July through early October
Map: Green Trails Stevens Pass No. 176
Contact: Mt. Baker–Snoqualmie National Forest, Skykomish Ranger Station, (360) 677-2414

The cool forest trail and the lakes at trail's end are the ideal recipe for a happy dog hike. The shaded woodland trail keeps the pooch cool and hydrated, while the meadow-lined lakes at the end of the path provide a place to swim, scamper, and play. Human hikers will enjoy this route, too. The deep, mossy forest is cool and refreshing, and a pair of clear lakes at the base of a pair of jagged peaks provide stunning visual joy at trail's end. Adding to the pleasure for all hikers—the four-legged as well as two-legged variety—are the broad wildflower meadows. What's more, I've yet to see a hiker who could resist the impulse to grin and chuckle at the antics of the pesky camp-robber jays and whistling marmots, both of which are commonly encountered on this trail. Even dogs seem to enjoy

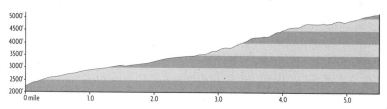

Above Glacier Lake at Surprise Gap (Ken Konigsmark)

the flitting and flinching antics of the jays—Parka will sit for hours and watch the birds dip and dive around camp. She has learned to stay still and watch them hop to within feet of her snout in pursuit of dropped kibble. And if you want to baffle your dog, let one of the resident gray jays drop down to land on your hand as you hold out a tidbit of bagel or tortilla—the canine can't understand how you can let the bird touch you without issuing at least a warning "Rrrruff!".

Dogs that are more than curious must be actively restrained by a leash at all times because chasing or harassing wildlife—including the lumbering marmots and flittering jays—is illegal and unacceptable. Even if your trail dog is simply excited about the possibility of playing with these new friends, keep her restrained because the beasts of the wild don't understand the difference between deadly pursuit and simple play.

The persistent presence of the gray jays is a testament to the fact that Surprise Lake has been discovered by the masses, but the pretty lake is worth sharing. Solitude-seekers can always push on to the next

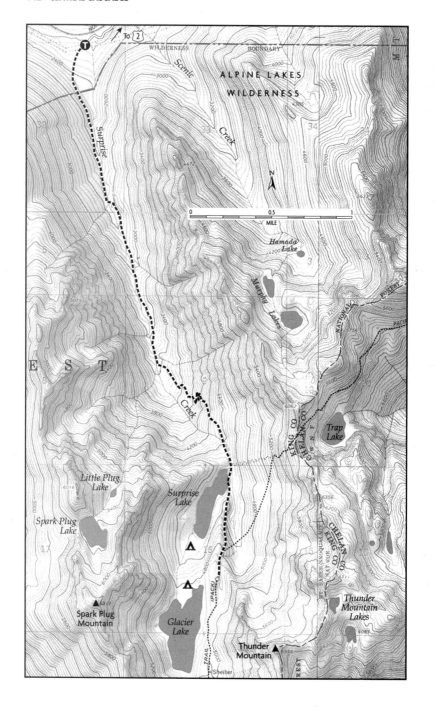

lake—Glacier—along the trail, or scramble up into the rocky mead-ows above the pools to find a quiet nook in which to picnic.

To get there, from Skykomish drive east on U.S. Highway 2 about 10 miles to the town of Scenic and turn right (south) onto a dirt road lo-cated just before the highway dips under a railroad trestle. At the next opportunity, turn right onto another dusty dirt road, and follow it to its end. The trailhead is the wide spot at the road end, marked with a ge-neric trail sign (a hiker silhouette).

The trail climbs away from the dusty trailhead and enters a clean, cool forest of ancient Douglas firs, hemlocks, and cedars. The trail parallels Surprise Creek for the next 4 miles, staying within the shady cover of the forest. The creek is often close enough to let the dog drink deeply from its cold waters, and it is always within hearing distance. From the sound of it, you'll know that the water is crashing over a series of falls and through narrow rock chutes, and frequent views of the creek prove your hearing is dead-on. Countless waterfalls—some little more than white-water rap-ids, others tumbling cascades—can be seen as you trudge up the trail. Keep your dog on a leash when he enters the creek because the last thing you want is to have him slip away over a slime-slick waterfall.

The trail steepens in the last mile before the lake and crosses several sun-baked clearings, ensuring that you'll be hot and sweaty when you reach the shores of Surprise Lake at 4.5 miles. The rock-lined lake couldn't have been designed better for swimming—the rocky bottom keeps the water sparklingly clear, and the numerous boulders rising from the lake surface and lining the lakeshore make ideal sun beds. After a hot hike up a steep trail, there's nothing more refreshing than a plunge into a cold lake, especially when you can drag yourself out and recline on a flat rock that has been warmed by the morning sun.

Most day hikers (and a lot of backpackers) will stop at Surprise. The lake basin offers stunning views of Surprise Mountain above. To escape the crowds and give you a chance to share a quiet, solitary camp with your canine, however, move south (after a long rest to soak in the beauty of the Surprise basin, of course) along the trail for another 0.7 mile to reach the Pacific Crest Trail (PCT). Continuing south on the PCT for another 0.25 mile gets you to Glacier Lake. Besides fewer people, Glacier offers better views because it is nestled above tree line on the bench between Surprise, Thun-der, and Spark Plug Mountains. Acres of heather meadows surround Glacier Lake, and marmots continually whistle at the revelers around the lake.

32. Chain Lakes

Round trip: 22 miles
Hiking time: 2 days minimum
High point: 5790 feet
Elevation gain: 3700 feet
Best hiking time: mid-July through early October
Map: Green Trails Stevens Pass No. 176
Contact: Wenatchee National Forest, Leavenworth Ranger District,
(509) 548-6977

Don't let the dog roam too far ahead on this trail—he could run all the way to Mexico without leaving the path. That's right, Mexico. The Pacific Crest Trail (PCT) runs 2600 miles from Canada to Mexico along the spine of the Cascades, and this hike uses a chunk of that grand interstate trail to get you and your pooch into some of the most awesome, high country of the Cascades. You may not believe that right off the bat—the trail begins by climbing the slopes of a developed ski area—but as you leave the resort behind you'll climb into high alpine meadows and pass some of the most beautiful wilderness lakes you'll find anywhere. Keep yourself and your pup well hydrated as you trek along. The route is high and sun-parched much of the way, though the scatter of lakes, tarns, and tumbling creeks means that your dog, at least, should be well watered along the way. You'll have to remember that you, too, need to drink in more than the views along this glorious high-country route.

To get there, from Skykomish drive east on U.S. Highway 2 to Stevens Pass summit and turn right (south) into a large parking lot just east of the ski area lodges and U.S. Forest Service cabins.

The PCT climbs south along the edge of the ski runs, climbing a series of switchbacks through the woods and open slopes between the lifts until it passes under one high ski lift and crests a rocky ridge (5100 feet) at the 1.5-mile mark. From here, the trail descends gradually through a talus slope and, at 1.75 miles, cuts under a string of high-tension

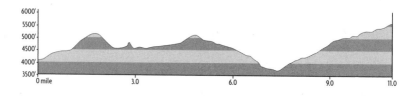

powerlines and crosses a narrow, dirt service road alongside the wires.

After the service road, the PCT leaves the developed area behind and at about 2.5 miles from the trailhead, enters the Alpine Lakes Wilderness. The trail traverses through fields of flowers with wondrous views east to Jim Hill Mountain and Nason Ridge before descending a few hundred feet to the picturesque basin of Lake Susan Jane at 3.5 miles (elevation, 4600 feet). Nestled in a rocky cirque below the high, unnamed ridge, this tiny lake is the picture that forms in many hikers' minds when they think of alpine lakes. Framed by cliffs and meadows, the lake offers views down the deep Mill Creek valley and across to Big Summit Chief Mountain. A few fine campsites ring the lake, but they get heavy pressure in midsummer. Believe it or not, there are prettier, more remote lakes ahead. So let the dog drink his fill—maybe toss him a stick or two to retrieve from the cold water—then continue on south.

The trail slants back up to the 5000-foot level in the next 0.5 mile, cresting out in rock-lined meadows near a trail junction at the 4-mile mark above the sparkling waters of Lake Josephine. Leave the PCT here by

Along the Chain Creek valley trail

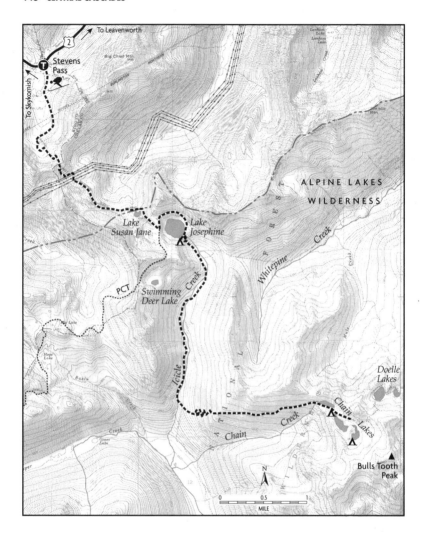

turning left (east) and descend along the Icicle Creek Trail as it loops around the north shore of scenic Lake Josephine before dropping sharply into the timbered valley of Icicle Creek.

Three miles after leaving the PCT, at mile 7, you reach another trail junction at 3800 feet. Turn left once more and begin a long, plodding climb up a series of tight switchbacks. As you break out of the trees now and then, you'll find glorious views into the deep valley of Icicle Creek and into the heart of the Alpine Lakes Wilderness. After 2.5 miles more of climbing—after the long pitch in the switchbacks, the trail continues on a steep traverse, steadily gaining elevation—the trail levels out as it comes to the first of the links in the Chain Lakes Basin. This first pond is rocklined and scenic but lacks any campsite. Move on to the second pond, found just past the first, and you'll find more meadows spreading out before you. The next two small lakes at 11 miles are merely small blue ponds dotting the sweeping green fields of heather and wildflowers on the flanks of Bulls Tooth Peak. Let your dog splash and play in the ponds, roll in the grasses, and retrieve a stick or two as you pick out the best campsite from the assortment that's available around the basin.

33. Twin Falls

Round trip: 3 miles
Hiking time: 2 hours
High point: 1000 feet
Elevation gain: 500 feet
Best hiking time: year-round
Map: Green Trails Bandera No. 206
Contact: Washington State Parks, (800) 233-0321
Note: Dogs must be leashed on this trail.

Twin Falls Natural Area was preserved as part of a mitigation plan that allowed the development of a small hydro-electrical project on the South Fork Snoqualmie River. That project is largely a series of underground pipes and facilities that the public doesn't see or hear, and as part of the development agreement, the hydro company has to maintain a steady flow of water to the river, keeping the falls falling. The public lost a little of the mighty flow of water (the falls aren't as dramatic as they once were, as old timers will tell you) but got a state park that holds a last remnant of the once-expansive stands of low-land old-growth forest that covered the Cascade foothills. The pretty little trail that weaves through the state-owned, natural area presents you with up-close and personal contact with massive old-growth trees, gives you access to the sparkling river, and offers

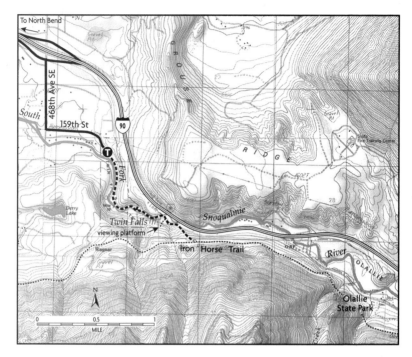

up stunning views of the thundering waterfalls—both the towering 150-foot lower falls and the stair-stepped upper falls.

To get there, from Seattle drive east on Interstate 90 to exit 34 (Edgewick Road). Turn south on 468th Avenue Southeast and drive 0.5 mile. Immediately before the South Fork Snoqualmie River Bridge, turn left (east) on Southeast 159th Street and drive 0.5 mile to the trailhead parking lot at the road's end.

This relatively easy walk through the cool forest offers hikers of all abilities an extraordinary chance to experience the glory of the northwest forest and river ecosystem. The gently graded trail and modest length makes the trail enjoyable for hikers young and old. Short-legged hounds and toddling children can enjoy this modest trek—just keep them on a leash (a leash—or at least a restraining hand—isn't a bad idea for the kids, either, when you step out onto the falls overlook platforms). The trail is also ideal for winter visits because in most years it sits well below snow level.

The first mile of trail is almost flat, great for kids and basset hounds. The route follows the clear, cold South Fork Snoqualmie River. Before moving on up the trail, let your youngster toss sticks for your Labrador to retrieve from the river's deep pools. As you hike, take note of the massive trees and the long beards of moss draped from their limbs—looking suspiciously like a rainforest. Guess what? It *is* a rainforest. This area, at the base of the Cascades, gets a ton of rain each year. Every storm front that piles into the Cascades dumps some of its water weight here before sliding up and over the mountains. The result is an annual rainfall average of more than 90 inches—twice that which the Seattle-area receives.

Raccoon along the river bank

After the initial .025 mile of gentle trail, the route begins a modest climb, gaining some 500 feet in the next .75 mile. Stop often to catch your breath and enjoy the forest—look for nurse logs (fallen trees from which sprout new saplings)—before continuing onward and upward. At about 1.25 miles out from the trailhead, you'll find a small side trail leading off to the right. Descend a short distance to a sturdy wooden platform perched on the side of a cliff. From this deck (while keeping one hand on your dog's leash, one hand on your kid's hand, and one hand on the handrail?), enjoy stunning views of the lower part of the Twin Falls of the South Fork Snoqualmie River. This 150-foot cascade is especially dramatic in spring when the snowmelt-swollen river plunges through the narrow rocky gorge and shoots over the vertical rock wall to crash into a deep splash pool below.

After soaking in this view (and if the wind is right, you will soak in the falls' spray, too), return to the trail and continue your hike. In a few hundred yards, you'll cross a broad wooden bridge. From the center of this bridge, look upstream and enjoy the view of the upper falls, a series of short drops looking a lot like a white-water staircase.

A half mile past this bridge the trail ends at a junction with the Iron Horse Trail—the cross-state railtrail. Turn around here and return to the trailhead the way you came.

34. Big Creek Falls (Taylor River)

Round trip: 10 miles
Hiking time: 5 hours
High point: 1750 feet
Elevation gain: 700 feet
Best hiking time: year-round
Maps: Green Trails Mount Si No. 174, Skykomish No. 175
Contact: Mt. Baker–Snoqualmie National Forest, Snoqualmie Ranger District, North Bend office, (425) 888-1421

It seems impossible: Finding quiet solitude on a backcountry trail leading through ancient cathedral forests and past magnificent waterfalls less than a hour from Seattle. Yet the Taylor River Trail offers just that. While nearby Mount Si bristles with sweating hikers and out-of-control hounds, and the Middle Fork Snoqualmie Trail hosts hordes of outdoor enthusiasts, the Taylor River Trail—an old road that's been reclaimed by the forest—goes largely unnoticed and unused. It's a dog-hiker's paradise because it lets human and canine walk side by side much of the way up a broad trail through lush old forest.

As you hike, search out some of the mammoth old stumps that dot the hills above and below the trails. On many, you'll find deep notches cut every couple feet up their sides, laid out in a stair-step pattern around the perimeter. These are springboard notches. The loggers who worked these forests earned their day's wages. They had to reach far up the trunks of the massive trees to find a narrower section to pull their cross-cut saws through. To get up off the ground, the loggers chopped deep notches in the tree, then inserted long boards. They then stepped up on the board, which tended to bounce like a diving board, and proceeded to chop another notch, for another springboard, so they could get that much higher on the tree.

Other relics of human history grace the trail as well, but be sure to give equal attention to the natural history elements. In addition to the magnificent trees, the forest is home to an assortment of bird species.

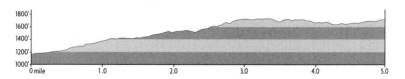

Big Creek Falls

Keep the dog close and watch his eyes and ears: he'll alert you to the presence of critters. I've seen black-tailed deer, pine martens, raccoons, and black bear in the area. Woodpeckers, nuthatches, flickers, jays, and swallows are a few of the avian residents flitting through the trees. Grouse are also common—just listen for their distinctive "whump, whump, whump" call as you stride up the trail. If the birds are bashful, watch the ground. Underfoot, you might find tree frogs, toads, alligator lizards, and salamanders.

To get there, from Seattle drive east on Interstate 90 to exit 34 (Edgewick Road). Turn north onto the Middle Fork Snoqualmie Road (Forest Road 56) and continue 12.5 miles to the Taylor River Road (FR 5620) (just past the new Middle Fork Trailhead parking area). Turn left onto the Taylor River Road and drive to its end, about 0.5 mile. A wide parking area is found at the road's end.

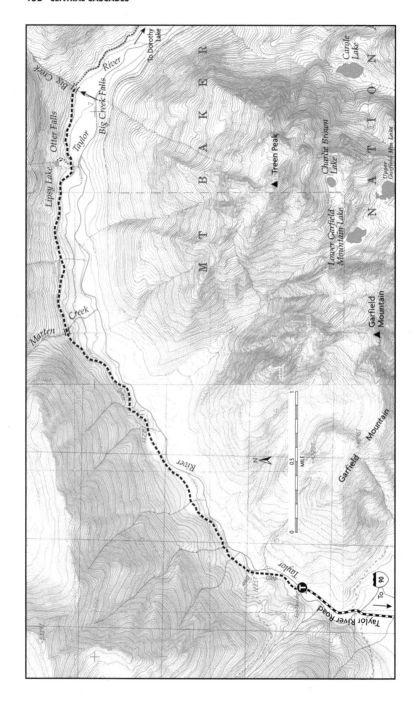

The trail weaves up the valley, following the old roadbed through the dense, old forest. The trail crosses an old bridge structure at Marten Creek, about 3 miles up the track. Modern planking has been added to the bridge deck to ensure safe crossing. But once across, peer under the bridge to gain an appreciation of the type of timber harvested from this area. Huge cedar logs serve as the spanners that support the bridge.

From here, the trail rolls gently on to the Big Creek Bridge at about 5 miles from the trailhead. This structure appears to be out of place here. The wide, concrete bridge belongs on a highway not a backcountry trail, but it is a remnant of the old road and a developer's dream—a dream that fortunately died before it was brought to fruition. The wide road planned for the headwaters of the Taylor River Valley never progressed much beyond logging road status, and even logging has now largely disappeared, leaving this a primitive trail, open to mountain bikes but not off-road vehicles.

The Big Creek Bridge may be the first thing to grab your attention when you reach the creek, but it fades into the background as soon as you step onto its deck. Big Creek Falls tumbles off the hillside on the north side of the bridge.

The creek slides over a series of granite steps and down smooth granite faces to create a sparkling tapestry of watery jewels. A deep plunge pool lies at the foot of the falls, just below the bridge itself.

The Big Creek Bridge makes an ideal lunch stop—the sun streams down onto the bridge deck and the concrete curbing along the edges of the deck serve as fine benches.

Adventurous hikers can push on up the valley, reaching Snoqualmie and Dorothy Lakes in another few miles. If you opt to turn around here, though, be sure to pause on your way back down for a side trip to Otter Falls. As you head back down the trail, watch for a small sign and a cairn (pile of rocks) about 0.25 mile west from Big Creek. Here a side trail leads north through the woods for a few hundred yards, ending at a wide, but shallow, pool of water at the base of a huge vertical granite slab. A ribbon of water slides down the smooth gray rock face to splash into the pool. This is Lipsy Lake and Otter Falls. In a normal snow year, the falls sparkle and crash as the melting snowpack feeds the creek, but even in a low-water year the falls are pretty, especially reflected in the calm waters of Lipsy, and especially when viewed in the quiet solitude that reigns along this valley trail.

35. Dingford Creek to Hester Lake

Round trip: 11 miles
Hiking time: 7 hours (day hike or backpacking trip)
High point: 3900 feet
Elevation gain: 2600 feet
Best hiking time: April through November
Map: Green Trails Skykomish No. 175
Contact: Mt. Baker–Snoqualmie National Forest, Snoqualmie Ranger
    District, North Bend office, (425) 888-1421

Make sure the dog kennel is well secured in the truck and give your dog an extra blanket or rug to pad the bumps during the drive to the trailhead. The Middle Fork Road has a well-earned reputation for being ruthlessly rough on vehicles and passengers. But those who survive the drive find that a few bumps are a small price to pay for the wonderful hiking found in the Dingford Creek valley. Indeed, the road and its nasty reputation tend to keep the crowds away, providing an excellent chance for hikers to find solitude on a trail within an hour of Seattle. And what a trail it is. The route pierces the old-growth forest in the valley as it enters the Alpine Lakes Wilderness and leads to glorious examples of the wilderness's namesake lakes. Hester Lake sprawls below Mount Price, and this trail offers short scrambles to Little Hester Lake and the scenic ridges around the basin.

To get there, from Seattle drive east on Interstate 90 to exit 34 (Edgewick Road). Follow Edgewick Road north to the junction with the Middle Fork Snoqualmie Road (Forest Road 56). Follow this road east about 18 miles (it becomes FR 5620) to the Dingford Creek Trailhead.

Dingford Creek Trail climbs from the banks of the Middle Fork Snoqualmie River paralleling the namesake creek for 3 miles. The hike climbs steeply for the first mile through a long series of switchbacks. At the top of the last switchback, the trail ducks into the Alpine Lakes Wilderness Area

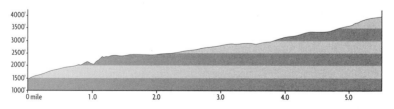

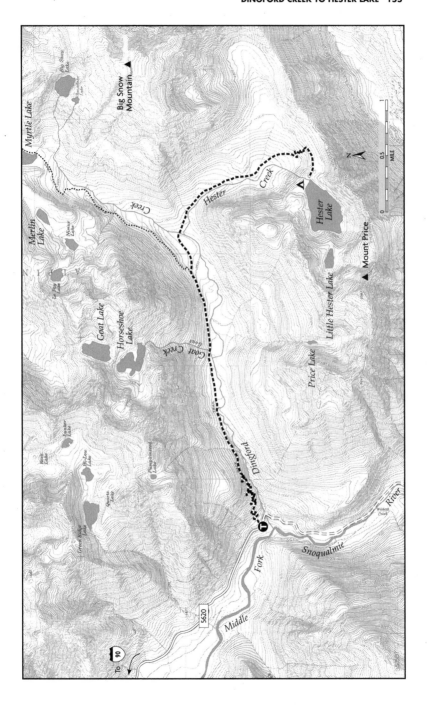

Revegetation work on a popular lakeshore

and the pitch levels out a bit. The surrounding forest, which is young second growth near the trailhead, slowly returns to native old-growth status as the trail penetrates deeper into the wilderness. At 3.5 miles, the trail—and the creek—splits. To the left, the trail continues due north another 2.5 miles to Myrtle Lake, while the right fork heads due south to Hester Lake in just 2 miles. Both lakes are enjoyable, and both hold pan-sized trout. Myrtle, however, has prettier surroundings, nestled as it is in a deep rocky cirque. Of course, Hester has the jagged peak of Mount Price looming above it.

Choosing between the two lakes may boil down to trail conditions. Typically, the spur to Myrtle is rougher, steeper, and muddier, while Hester's access trail is shorter, drier, and less steep. Parka recommends Hester because it is broader and deeper, proving to be the nicer of the two lakes for dog paddling.

36. Williams Lake

Round trip: 15 miles
Hiking time: 2 days
High point: 4600 feet
Elevation gain: 1600 feet
Best hiking time: late June through October
Maps: Green Trails Skykomish No. 175, Stevens Pass No. 176
Contact: Mt. Baker–Snoqualmie National Forest, Snoqualmie Ranger District, North Bend office, (425) 888-1421

Although this trail is generally snowfree by mid-June and can be hiked throughout the summer, the Williams Lake Basin may well be one of the top three best alpine lakes for autumn color. With the plethora of huckleberries, vine maples, and slide alder, as well as sloping lakeside meadows of heather and low-bush blueberries, this basin comes alive with color every year around mid-September, making it a prime candidate for autumn hiking. And this "shoulder season" between the end of summer hiking and the start of winter skiing offers a great deal to the hiker who can tolerate the cold nighttime temperatures and frequently wet weather. By early September, most of the biting flies and mosquitoes are dead or dying, leaving you free to hike DEET-free. The trails are also less crowded as the fair-weather hikers hang up their boots for the season.

But whether visited in summer or fall, Williams Lake is a joy for two- and four-legged hikers. This 15-mile round-trip hike leads up the Middle Fork Snoqualmie River valley to its headwaters. The long walk up the valley features views of steep hillsides garishly decorated with colorful clumps of vine maple and slide alder. Williams Lake is a deep blue pond nestled in the shadow of Big Summit Chief Mountain.

To get there, from Seattle drive east on Interstate 90 to exit 34 (Edgewick Road). Follow Edgewick Road north to the junction with the Middle Fork Snoqualmie Road (Forest Road 56). Follow this road east, passing Dingford Creek at about 18 miles (it becomes FR 5620), and

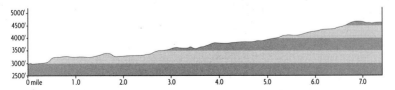

Big Summit Chief Mountain towers over the lake.

continue east another 6.5 miles to the trailhead at the end of the road. Note that the last few miles are extremely rough and may be impassable to passenger vehicles, requiring a few extra miles (how many depends on road conditions) of hiking.

From the road end, the trail leads up the north side of the river valley, angling steadily but not too steeply upward as you hike east into the heart of the Alpine Lakes Wilderness. The trail crosses several small side creeks and drops alongside the Snoqualmie River frequently enough that the dog can get wet to stay cool. The trail meanders in and out of forest, sliding through meadows, beneath alder-clogged avalanche chutes, and over small creeks and gullies. This varied terrain and gentle climbing goes on for nearly 6.5 miles until the trail reaches a stunning little valley-bottom meadow dotted with small ponds and laced with wandering streams.

Cross a stout wooden bridge and bear left onto a trail leading north away from these pretty little meadows. You'll find fine campsites here.

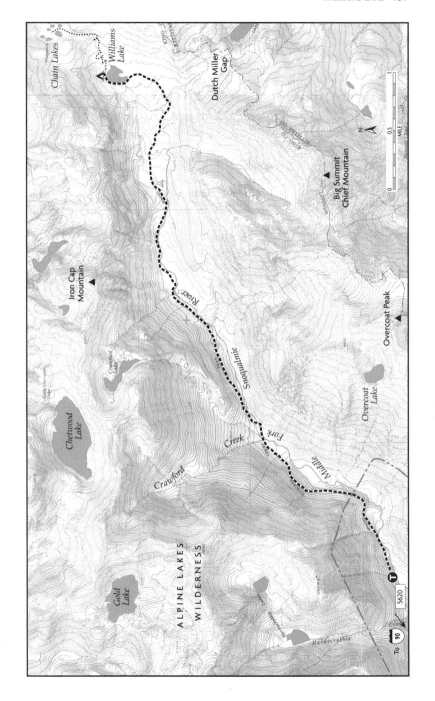

The path climbs through forest for 1 mile to roll onto the huckleberry-filled shores of Williams Lake. Hit this lake in autumn and you'll find its northern shore emblazoned with red-leafed bushes of huckleberries separated by green and umber clumps of heather. Looking south across the shimmering blue waters of the lake, you'll see brilliant gold and orange vine maple along the opposite shores. Far behind this autumn splendor towers the craggy rock monolith of Big Summit Chief Mountain.

The best camps are on the north side of the lake, near the base of the talus slope. Light sleepers should bring earplugs, though, because the resident population of pikas bark out a chorus of shrill "eeps" and "eehhs" all afternoon, evening, and into the night. Adventurous hikers can scramble up an old miners trail to Chain Lakes, a bit more than a mile from Williams. The trail passes an old mine shaft well marked by the pile of tailings, and more shafts and mining debris are found in the Chain Lakes basin.

37. Kendall ~~Kat~~ DOGwalk

Round trip: 11 miles
Hiking time: 7 hours (day hike or backpacking trip)
High point: 5760
Elevation gain: 2700 feet
Best hiking time: July through October
Map: Green Trails Snoqualmie Pass No. 207
Contact: Wenatchee National Forest, Cle Elum Ranger District, (509) 674-4411

Forget the "Katwalk" name—it's inappropriate. Cats don't belong on trails, even precarious perches such as this. No, like the rest of the 2600-mile Pacific Crest Trail (PCT), which runs from Mexico to Canada, this section is purely a dog's trail.

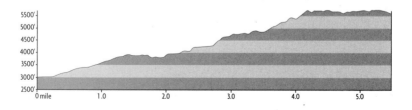

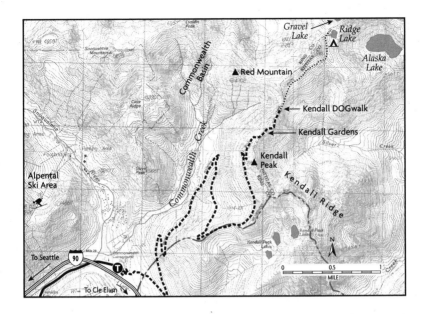

The Kendall Katwalk (make that DOGwalk) was carved into the side of a granite cliff to add a degree of truthfulness to the name Pacific *Crest* Trail. This path along the spine of Kendall Peak offers a remarkable hiking experience—striding on a narrow shelf hundreds of feet in the air. In terms of hiking, though, the Katwalk isn't really narrow. There's plenty of room for hikers, with dogs, to pass one another (there is room for two strings of packhorses to pass if needed). The Katwalk is a good 4 or 5 feet wide as it stretches across a vertical cliff face on the ridge between Kendall Peak and Red Mountain. The trail, blasted into the cliff face by dynamite crews who hung suspended from ropes, is perfectly safe once the winter's snow has completely melted off. If there is any lingering snow on the Katwalk, though, don't attempt to cross it—the Katwalk is not the place to slip and fall on a snow patch.

To get there, drive Interstate 90 to exit 52 (Snoqualmie Pass West). At the bottom of the exit ramp, turn left (north), cross under the freeway and, in about 100 yards, turn right onto a dirt road leading into the PCT Trailhead parking area. You'll be following the PCT for the duration of this hike.

Leash your dog before you start up the trail. Regardless of how well behaved the pooch, and how strong his commitment to your verbal commands, you should keep the dog on-leash on this route, if only

*Kendall Katwalk (make that **DOG**walk) leads across the face of Kendall Peak.*

because the trail is popular and odds are high that you will encounter multiple hiking (and horse-riding) parties during your hike.

The trail climbs into the trees above the parking lot and then makes a long, lazy sweep east before rounding a hairpin turn to return west across the lower end of an avalanche slope. The jumble of trees piled around the trail illustrates how powerful a little snow can be when it starts to slide down a hill. The trail stays in the trees for the first few miles, passing a side trail to Commonwealth Basin at 2.5 miles. There is no water along the route until the lakes at the far end of the Katwalk so make sure to stop and water the dog frequently whenever you can—the exposed nature of the route will leave you and your dog hot and dehydrated if you are not careful.

Just past the Commonwealth Basin junction, the trail drives upward into a series of long switchbacks. The forest thins as the trail gains elevation, and about 3.5 miles into the hike, the forest starts to break up as small clearings and meadows appear. Soon, the trail angles across the open meadows below Kendall Ridge. Red Mountain fills the skyline ahead while steeply sloped wildflowers color the ground around your feet. These wildflower fields—known to some as Kendall Gardens—continue as the trail crests the ridge and angles north through a jumble of boulders on the ridge top. Finally at 5.5 miles, the Gardens narrow to a mere path, and the path suddenly disappears onto a broad shelf on the east face of the ridge. This is the Katwalk. Keep a firm hand on the leash, and make sure your dog doesn't spook and pull you off the trail. The timid can turn back on the near side, but most hikers prefer to cross the Katwalk before heading back to the Gardens for a leisurely lunch and return hike to the trailhead.

Those who want to spend the night can continue another 2 miles on relatively level trail to a pair of lakes that border the trail just below Alaska Mountain. The best campsites are found just south of Ridge Lake, but Gravel Lake (on the north side of the trail) also has a few good camping locations.

38. Tinkham Peak/Silver Peak Loop

Round trip: 8 miles
Hiking time: 6 hours
High point: 5605 feet
Elevation gain: 2600 feet
Best hiking time: July through October
Map: Green Trails Snoqualmie Pass No. 207
Contact: Wenatchee National Forest, Cle Elum Ranger District, (509) 674-4411

If your dog is a scent hound, get a good grip on his leash before starting up this loop route. The forest and dense underbrush along the lower sections of the route are perfect cover for a host of critters, from raccoons and possums to bobcats, coyotes, badgers, weasels, martens, mink, and more. The plethora of passing wildlife scents hitting the keen nose of a hound may make the dog crazy with the desire to explore those endless smells. If your pooch is a typical trail dog, though, and only has a passing interest in the smells of his wild relatives, then you merely need to keep the dog close and

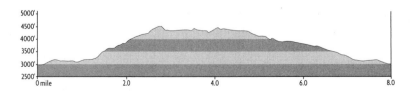

The flank of Silver Peak

watch for his reactions to be able to spot some of the nearby creatures.

Wildlife viewing can be a fickle business, though. Fortunately, the route offers far more than the opportunity for wildlife encounters. Pretty alpine meadows await you on the flanks of rocky Tinkham Peak, sparkling little alpine tarns dot the ridgeline, and glorious views from the grassy summit of Silver Peak spread out like a picnic buffet before your feet. It's a veritable feast for the eyes as you look south to the Norse Peak Wilderness, north to the Alpine Lakes Wilderness, northwest through the gap of Snoqualmie Pass to Granite Mountain, and east into the slowly dropping peaks of the Cascades foothills.

To get there, from Seattle drive east on Interstate 90 to exit 54 (Hyak). At the bottom of the ramp, check your odometer and turn right, followed by a left onto a gravel road leading into a broad parking lot at the base of

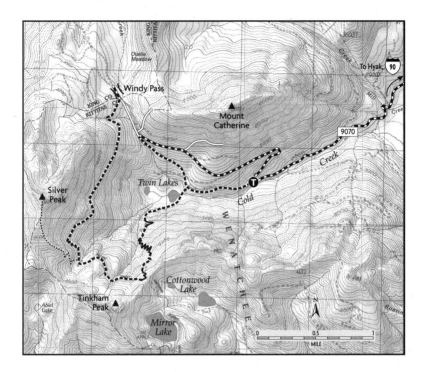

Hyak Ski Area. Stay left as you cross the parking lot and find a road, signed Hyak Estates Drive, leading east out of the center of the parking lot. Continue east through a series of vacation homes and public works buildings. The road soon turns to gravel and becomes Forest Road 9070. Continue up the road to a hairpin turn to the right, found about 3.5 miles from the interstate ramp (where you were asked to check you mileage, remember?). The remnant of an old road provides parking at the apex of the tight corner, or you can move farther up on the straightaway above or below the corner to park along the road. Your trail, the Cold Creek Trail, begins at the corner.

The trail angles off into a tight bramble of slide alder, fireweed, and lupine before climbing slowly into a stand of second-growth forest. The trail stays mostly in shady forest for the next mile as it climbs gradually to Twin Lakes. This heavily forested lake basin sports a couple small campsites; but the lakes are easily reached from the road, and are prone to being heavily littered and possibly occupied by campers more interested in creating their own version of "wild life" than they are in seeing the resident wildlife. Move on quickly past the lakes (besides the mess, the forested lakes are great mosquito breeding sites) as the trail turns left and climbs a long, steep slope toward Tinkham Peak. The first 0.5 mile past the lakes leads into a steeply-angled tangle of devil's club and stinging nettles. The trail stays above the worst of the pricking weeds, but it's a good idea to resist reaching out for handholds along this trail. Watch for wildlife here—lots of small mammals use the cover of the devil's club as shelter from predators, and the tangle of prickly brush swarms with flitting and twittering birds.

At 2.5 miles from the trailhead, the route has climbed to a junction with the Pacific Crest Trail (PCT) below Tinkham Peak. The PCT drops south (left) a mile to reach Mirror Lake, but you should go right and traverse through small meadows and past tiny tarns for a little more than 0.5 mile to reach a climber's path leading to the summit of Silver Peak. The side trail can be difficult to spot—watch for a path leading into the thin forest clearings as the PCT turns almost due north. The 1-mile scramble to the top of the mountain requires some routefinding skills, as it climbs nearly a mile through stands of forest and rocky meadows to the 5605-foot summit. The upper slopes of the peak are carpeted with colorful wildflowers, and the views are wonderful from the top. But dogs that don't want to take that walk will have just as much fun sticking with the main trail. It, too, offers great views, with the rocky crags of Tinkham Peak visible from this side of the valley bowl you're circling, and across the basin, with Mount Catherine standing tall on the horizon.

Beyond the Silver Peak side trail junction, the PCT continues north to Windy Pass, 5.3 miles from the trailhead (7.3 with the summit trip). The last 0.5 mile of the route to Windy Pass slices through a relatively fresh clearcut—the replanted trees are barely taller than most (two-legged) hikers. These types of clearcuts are great habitat for deer because there is plenty of food (the lack of a closed canopy of tree branches means there's lots of sun reaching the ground plants, bringing them into lush growth) and lots of cover for protection. Look closely at the surrounding young forest and you might spot a herd of deer.

At Windy Pass, the PCT strikes a dirt road. Turn right onto this road and hike 0.5 mile to the trail dropping off the right side of the road. The trail descends the steep slope on a long traverse. The path is brushy— few trees to shade and restrict the low-growing bushes—for the first 0.5 mile before dropping into trees to roll down at mile 7 to Twin Lakes and the junction with the Cold Creek Trail, which leads you back to the trailhead in 1 mile.

39. Margaret Lake/Lake Lillian

Round trip: 6 miles to Margaret, 10 to Lillian
Hiking time: 4 to 6 hours (day hike or backpacking trip)
High point: 5200 feet
Elevation gain: 1300 feet
Best hiking time: June through October
Map: Green Trails Snoqualmie Pass No. 207
Contact: Wenatchee National Forest, Cle Elum Ranger District,
(509) 674-4411

Who wants to hike in old clearcuts? When they are packed with huckle-berries, I do! Besides, the old clearcuts found on the lower portion of this route peter out quickly as you climb the ridge and enter old stands of forest before cresting the ridge and dropping into the picturesque lake basins.

To get there, from Snoqualmie Pass drive east on Interstate 90 to exit 54 (Hyak) and turn left (north) at the bottom of the exit ramp. On the north side of the freeway, turn right onto Gold Creek Road (Forest Road 4832), and drive east, paralleling the interstate briefly before it angles upward. At 3.9 miles from the freeway off-ramp, turn left onto FR 4934 and in 0.25 mile, look for the parking lot on the left.

The hike begins on the road. Head up the gravel road leading past the parking lot and in 0.25 mile veer left onto a small dirt road. Hike around an old cable gate and climb the dirt road as it slants steeply upward into an old clearcut. Don't let the ugly connotations of that name fool you, however. This field of stumps has been reclaimed by the native flora and, between the stumps, acres of huckleberries colored by an array of wildflowers stand tall over the berry-rich bushes. Bear grass, lupine, paint-brush, tiger lilies, fireweed, and more grace these slopes.

The road peters out in 0.5 mile and the narrow trail weaves upward, providing great views south over Keechelus Lake and back up toward Snoqualmie Pass. As you near the ridge, Mount Rainier comes into view far to the south, too. About 1.5 miles from the trailhead, the trail enters forest and at 2.5 miles, reaches a junction near the ridgeline. Turn right

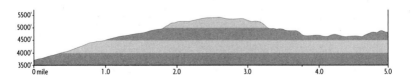

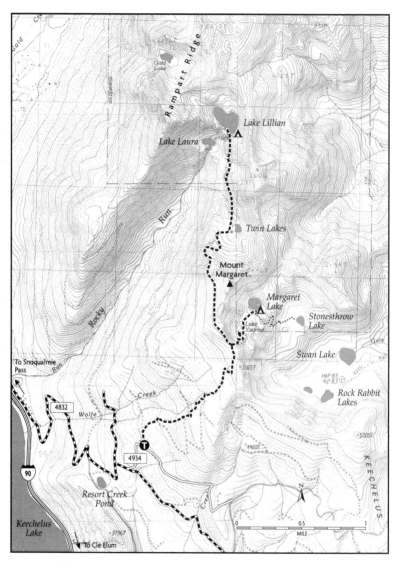

to cross the ridge and descend into Margaret Lake or left to follow the ridge around Mount Margaret to Lake Lillian.

Heading to Margaret Lake, the trail drops a steep 0.5 mile into the rocky cirque. The blue-watered gem, though, is worth the rugged climb as it sparkles in its granite setting like a sapphire on a silver band. Campsites ring the lake, and on the ridge below the pool you can see other small jewels glittering in the sun—Stonesthrow, Swan, and Rock Rabbit Lakes perch precariously on the slope under Mount Margaret. There are plenty of rocks on which to recline while your dog paddles after sticks and rocks in the cold waters of Margaret during a leisurely lunch.

The route to Lillian stretches along the steep, rough ridgeline for a couple miles past

Shadow and Morven Balmidiano above Lake Lillian (Ken Konigsmark)

the junction, at times forcing human hikers to act like their dogs and go on all fours. A steep descent drops you into the Twin Lakes basin on the flank of Mount Margaret, and a long, rocky traverse leads to Lake Lillian at trail's end. Great campsites can be found at either lake.

40. French Cabin Creek

Round trip: 5.6 miles (7 miles with side trips)
Hiking time: 4 hours
High point: 4900 feet
Elevation gain: 1100 feet
Best hiking time: June through October
Map: Green Trails Kachess Lake No. 208
Contact: Wenatchee National Forest, Cle Elum Ranger District, (509) 674-4411

This easy day hike offers you and the dog a chance to stroll through open pine forests, cross sprawling fields of flowers, and bask in the glorious

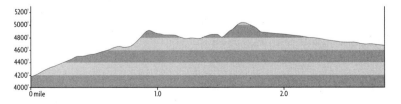

The dry routes of the eastern Cascades require carrying in extra water to prevent canine dehydration.

views of surrounding alpine peaks. There are potential campsites among the meadows of French Cabin Basin and Silver Creek Basin, but they are largely dry unless you visit early in the year when there are still snow-drifts to tap for meltwater. That lack of water means carrying extra water for the canine, too, making camping a truly heavyweight deal. Better to go with a day pack and enjoy the fabulous alpine environments on a leisurely day-long ramble.

To get there, take exit 80 (Roslyn/Salmon la Sac) off Interstate 90 and head north on the Salmon la Sac Road (State Route 903) about 15 miles, passing through Roslyn and past Cle Elum Lake. Just beyond the upper end of the lake, turn left onto French Cabin Road (Forest Road 4308). Drive 6.5 miles up FR 4308 to a small dirt road, FR 4308-122 (marked

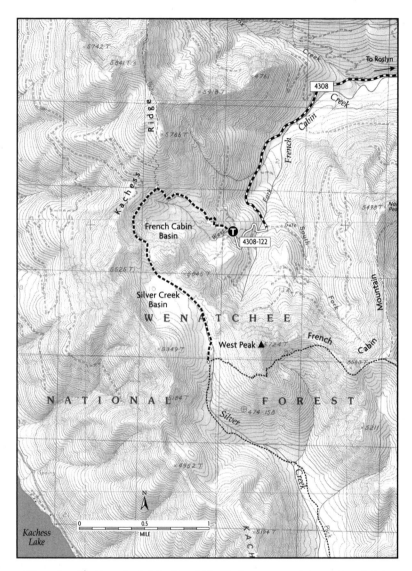

with a sign for French Cabin Creek Trail). Turn onto this road and drive 0.5 mile to the road end. The trail begins here. Note that FR 4308-122 is narrow and rough. Those driving low-clearance passenger cars should park at the bottom of the road and walk the 0.5 mile to the trailhead.

The trail starts with a steady climb up a steep, badly eroded trail through the forest. For nearly a mile, the route stays under the overhanging branches, providing relief from the sun, but no views and little local scenery to enjoy (occasional forest glades along the way do provide glimpses of tiny forest flowers, like avalanche and glacier lilies).

At 1 mile, the trail breaks out onto a clearing with views up to the spires of French Cabin Mountain. In another 0.25 mile, the scattered clumps of trees and meadows give way to a small section of clearcut as the trail hooks out into a section of private timberland. Just inside the clearcut, the trail splits. Stay left and descend briefly before climbing once more to reach a high pass (5000 feet) separating the forest and meadows of French Cabin Basin from the sprawling meadows of Silver Creek Basin. Stop and enjoy the views of the flower fields before you drop steeply into Silver Creek meadows. For nearly a mile, you'll climb gently as you wander through grass and knee-high wildflowers in the sun-drenched meadows below French Cabin Mountain. Let the dog romp in the hearty grass meadows, but keep him close in the more fragile flower fields.

At 2.8 miles from the trailhead, you'll find another trail junction. Heading left here leads you up to the flank of West Peak for great views of the Kachess Ridge and French Cabin Peaks. Turn around and head back the way you came before the trail starts to descend the other side.

41. Thorp Mountain

Round trip: 7 miles
Hiking time: 4 hours
High point: 5854 feet
Elevation gain: 1800 feet
Best hiking time: July through October
Map: Green Trails Kachess Lake No. 208
Contact: Wenatchee National Forest, Cle Elum Ranger District, (509) 674-4411

It's a short hike but one to tax the strength of two- and four-legged hikers. But the strenuous climb earns you great rewards. The top of Thorp

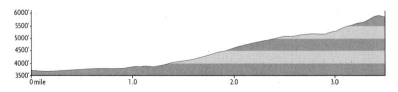

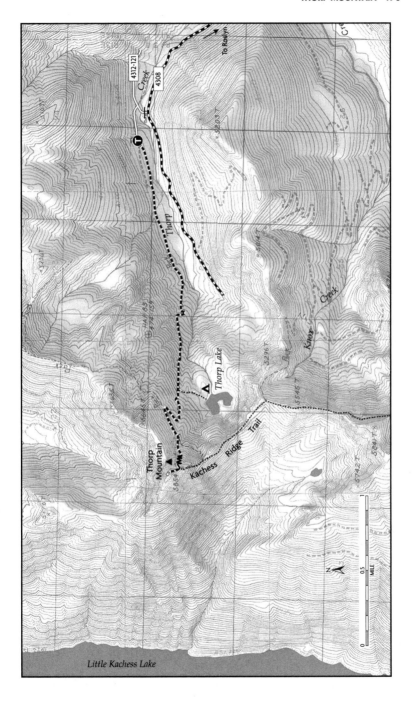

On Thorp Mountain (Ken Konigsmark)

Mountain sports a rustic old fire lookout cabin, and anywhere these watch stations were constructed you'll find outstanding views in every direction. Thorp is no different—from the heather-carpeted top of the peak you can scan the horizon in every direction, picking out peaks and valleys throughout the Alpine Lakes Wilderness but also down into the south Cascades (Mount Rainier can be seen on clear days). The ridges rolling away from the mountain sport colorful, flower meadows, and the blue pool of Kachess Lake sparkles in the deep valley at the foot of the mountain.

To get there, take exit 80 (Roslyn/Salmon la Sac) off Interstate 90 and head north on the Salmon la Sac Road (State Route 903) about 15 miles, passing through Roslyn and past Cle Elum Lake. Just past the upper end of the lake, turn left onto French Cabin Road (FR 4308). Drive 3.25 miles up FR 4308 to FR 4312 on the right. Go right and drive 1.5 miles to another road junction, with FR 4312-121. This road is typically gated, so park here (do not block the gate), and walk around the gate 0.25 mile to a bridge over Thorp Creek. Cross the creek and turn left. The true trail starts 0.25 mile up this road on the left.

The trail climbs steadily but modestly as it parallels the tumbling Thorp Creek. Keep the dog on a leash and your eyes wide open and you might spot lots of wildlife along the lower trail, especially as the path leaves the stands of forest and pops briefly into old, overgrown clearcuts. These transition zones are popular places for deer to hang out, because they provide good cover (the forest) as well as close proximity to good browse (the clearcuts).

About 1.5 miles from the gate, the trail starts to climb more steeply, angling upward away from the creek. As it gains elevation, the forest thins, providing more and more sun breaks and viewpoints. At nearly 3 miles, a small side trail drops 0.5 mile to Thorp Lake. If time permits, this makes a nice side trip on the return. But on the way up, bypass this trail and continue climbing as the trail sweeps upward around the headwall of the Thorp Valley.

At 3 miles, another junction is reached, this time with the Kachess Ridge Trail. Stay left as it angles east around the flank of Thorp Mountain, and in less than 0.25 mile, go right to climb the steep scramble trail to the top of the mountain, elevation 5854 feet, and its awesome views.

42. Pete Lake

Round trip: 9 miles
Hiking time: 6 hours
High point: 2980 feet
Elevation gain: 200 feet
Best hiking time: May through November
Map: Green Trails Kachess Lake No. 208
Contact: Wenatchee National Forest, Cle Elum Ranger District, (509) 674-4411

With little elevation gain, plenty of scenery and a broad, sun-warmed forest lake at the end of the valley, this hike makes a great warm-up outing for you and your dog. Do it as a respectably long day hike or a gentle backpacking trip to shake out the kinks while practicing camping with the canine.

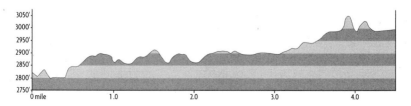

Parka lounging in camp at Pete Lake

Adventurous hikers can modify the route by adding excursions up to more remote and scenic lakes, over high alpine ridges, and to the summits of towering peaks along the nearby Pacific Crest Trail.

To get there, take exit 80 (Roslyn/Salmon la Sac) off Interstate 90 and head north on the Salmon la Sac Road about 15 miles, passing through Roslyn and past Cle Elum Lake. Turn left (west) onto Forest Road 46 and drive 5 miles to Cooper Lake. Turn right onto FR 4616, crossing Cooper River, and continue 1 mile past the upper loops of the campground to the trailhead at the end of the road near the upper end of the lake.

The trail follows the broad Cooper River valley upstream all the way to the lake. The trail begins in deep forest, with close views of the river during the early stretch. Watch for activity in the deeper pools as beavers make every effort to turn the river into a series of interconnected ponds. Just be sure to keep the dog away from the river, though, because beaver dams pose a problem for dogs—it's far too easy for a canine's leg to plunge through the weave of sticks and branches that form the dams, resulting in a leg fracture. Fortunately, the trail stays upslope from the creek so dogs aren't easily tempted into the hazard-laden waters.

The valley is blanketed with thick, old-growth forest and the occasional river meadow but few distant views. The lack of vistas, though, means you can focus on close-in scenery. Lush foliage and forest wildflowers line the trail. All that vegetation means good feeding for wildlife. Keep your dog leashed and close at hand, and watch her—especially if she is a hunting breed—for any indication that there may be wildlife nearby. Rabbits, weasels, fishers, and martens scurry around the bushes. Black-tailed deer roam in great numbers through the area; and bobcats, coyotes, and cougars prowl around the lairs of those vegetarian beasts.

The trail weaves through forest, and as it nears the lake, it passes an old, massive rock slide around the 3-mile mark. The slide covers the south

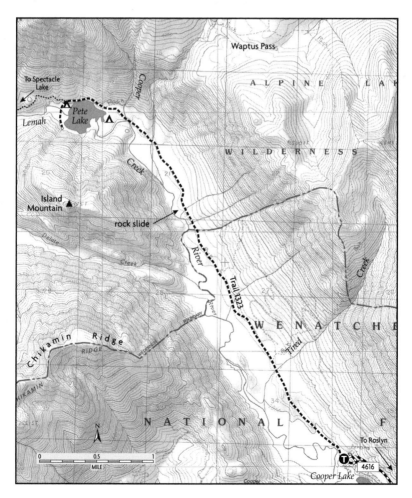

side of the valley. The trail skirts the worst of the rubble but provides good views of the pile of rock and displaced earth.

Pete Lake fills a broad basin near the upper end of the valley. The eastern shore of the lake offers good views of Big Summit Chief Mountain to the west and the surrounding ridges. The lake boasts a healthy population of rainbow trout—if you can keep your dog out of the water, you might be lucky enough to pull a pan-sized fish out of the lake for a dinner treat. Good campsites line the lake, with the best found on the west end.

Hikers who want further adventures can continue an additional 5 miles to Spectacle Lake (elevation, 4239 feet).

43. Waptus and Spade Lakes

Round trip: 16 miles to Waptus, 27 miles to Spade
Hiking time: 2 to 4 days
High point: 3000 feet (5200 feet at Spade)
Elevation gain: 600 feet (2800 feet to Spade)
Best hiking time: mid-July through early autumn
Maps: Green Trails Kachess Lake No. 208, Stevens Pass No. 176
Contact: Wenatchee National Forest, Cle Elum Ranger District,
    (509) 674-4411

Awaiting you on this trail is a modest hike up a spectacular river valley; a vast, beautiful alpine lake; and a strenuous trek up and over a high, meadow-lined mountain ridge to another, more spectacular lake. Those travelers looking for an easy outing can stop at the sprawling Waptus Lake, which fills the valley-bottom for more than a mile. More adventurous hikers can push on up the steep route to the remote and scenic Spade Lake below the summit of Mount Daniel. Both lakes are stunning, but Spade rewards the extra effort required to reach it with glorious alpine meadows and unmatched views. Waptus, meanwhile, offers a cool place to rest, relax, and recreate without the extreme energy expenditure.

To get there, take exit 80 (Roslyn/Salmon la Sac) off Interstate 90 and

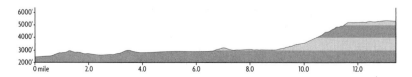

Scully cools off after a long trek through the valley. (Paul Gioia)

head north on the Salmon la Sac Road (State Route 903), passing through
Roslyn and past Cle Elum Lake about 15 miles to Salmon la Sac Campground and ranger station. Cross the river bridge and, before entering
the campground, turn right into the trailhead parking area.

Starting alongside the Cooper River, the trail deceives you into thinking it will be an easy stroll up the gentle valley. But as soon as that thought
occurs, the trail forks. Turn right and climb steeply away from Cooper River
as you switch back and forth up and over the ridge separating Cooper River
valley from Waptus River valley. Okay, so the climb over the ridge earned
you a net gain of 500 feet in just over 2.5 miles, at which point you reach
the Waptus River valley near the mouth of Hour Creek. A fine camp exists
here for those looking for a short backpacking trip. At the least, stop and
rest here while letting the dog splash and play in the water.

The trail angles up the south shore of Waptus River and sticks close to
the river for the next 4.5 miles as it climbs the gentle valley to Waptus
Lake. Along the way, as you weave in and out of the forest and riverside
meadows, enjoy periodic views of aptly named Cone Mountain—the best
views are found 4 miles in from the trailhead.

As the trail enters the lower lake basin, around 7.5 miles, the trail splits.
Stay right and cross the river on a new stout bridge. The trail follows the
path along the north shore of the long, broad lake, starting about 0.5

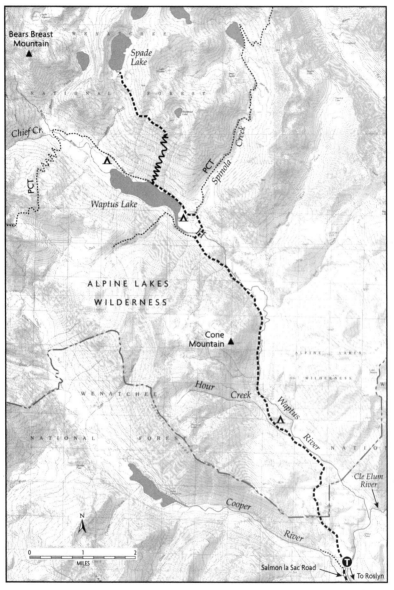

mile past the bridge. Campsites line the lake, but the best may be the first one encountered on the lake's lower end.

From this vantage point, enjoy long views uplake to Big Summit Chief Mountain and Bears Breast Mountain. The lake is positively perfect for humans and canines to swim away a day's worth of trail dust. Hikers looking for relaxation and alpine serenity should spend the night—or maybe several—here before returning to the trailhead. Adventure-seekers, though, should camp here then continue on to Spade Lake when well rested.

To get to Spade, hike west along the north shore of Waptus Lake to the second lake junction (the third trail junction) signed Spade Lake, about halfway up the lake (the side trail at the first junction leads up Spinola Creek). Turn right and climb the steep slope above Waptus Lake, as the trail weaves through tight switchbacks for more than 1.5 miles (gaining more than 1300 feet) before the slope moderates (slightly) as it continues to flip back and forth through long, looping switchbacks for another 2 miles. The steep, rough trail makes you wish you had four-leg drive like your canine companion, though she is probably panting and working just as hard as you are (make sure to water her frequently).

As you climb, you find great views of the Waptus valley and the tall peaks at its end. The trail traverses into Spade Creek valley, still climbing, still presenting fabulous views, then turns ruthlessly steep as it cuts straight up the last mile into Spade Lake Basin at 13.5 miles. Search out the best campsite, blessedly found near the outlet stream to minimize your need to scramble any farther up than need be.

44. Jolly Mountain

Round trip: 12 miles
Hiking time: 8 hours
High point: 6443 feet
Elevation gain: 4000 feet
Best hiking time: mid-July through early autumn
Map: Green Trails Kachess Lake No. 208
Contact: Wenatchee National Forest, Cle Elum Ranger District, (509) 674-4411

You'll feel jolly on top, but you'll jolly-well earn it. As you climb the trail, you'll be questioning the value of the views from the top, and whether they

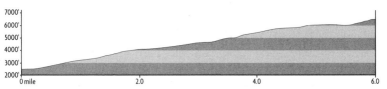

Sun-drenched ridge near the top of Jolly Mountain

are worth the thigh-burning, lung-popping workout of the ascent. But once you reach the top, the sweat and tears of the trail are forgotten as you soak in the mind-numbing panorama encircling you. Look in any direction and you'll find eye-pleasing scenery in unbelievable volumes. For the dog, the trail offers a chance to get a good workout and the top gives her a great chance to flop in the sun and smell the scents carried on the winds, which swirl over the peak.

To get there, take exit 80 (Roslyn/Salmon la Sac) off Interstate 90 and drive north on State Route 903 to Roslyn. Continue north on the highway, which becomes Forest Road 4330, to Salmon la Sac Campground and ranger station. Look for the trailhead on the right, between the Cayuse Horse Camp and the picnic area.

From the trailhead, find the trail behind the horse barn at the Forest Service workshop. The trail crosses Salmon la Sac Creek and starts upward immediately. The way zigs and zags for a steep 3.2 miles, through forest with occasional views into the Cle Elum valley, to reach a fork in the trail. Stay right and climb the southern face of the valley headwall to Sasse Ridge. In another mile, turn left at another trail junction, and climb even more steeply for another 0.5 mile to reach a third junction at 4.7 miles. Again, take the left fork and continue a long traverse around the north flank of Jolly Mountain.

The views now increase in frequency and magnificence. A half mile of traversing leads to the last trail junction at 6000 feet. You'll likely find lingering snowfields from this point on—the slippery snow may persist on the north face of the mountain into August. Be careful crossing these slick patches of winter remembrances.

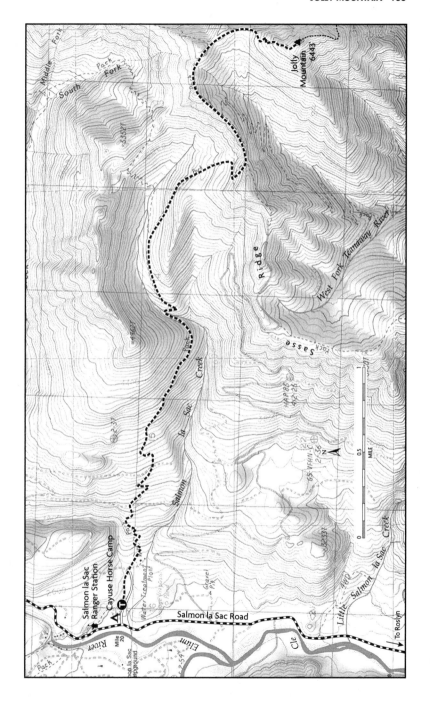

From the last trail junction at 6000 feet, turn right and climb a long, moderate mile to the summit of Jolly Mountain.

The 6 miles of this trail brought you and your dog up more than 4000 vertical feet. Congratulate yourself and your faithful canine companion (remember, you chose to do this trail—he didn't have any idea what you were getting him into) on a great achievement. Then, look out from your lofty perch. On a clear day, enjoy views of everything within 100 miles of your position. Soon, the fatigue of the trail falls away and the jolliness of the summit takes over.

45. Sasse Mountain

Round trip: 5 to 9 miles
Hiking time: 3 to 6 hours
High point: 5730 feet
Elevation gain: 1300 feet
Best hiking time: mid-July through early autumn
Map: Green Trails Kachess Lake No. 208
Contact: Wenatchee National Forest, Cle Elum Ranger District,
    (509) 674-4411

Sasse Ridge offers views nearly as good as those found from Jolly Mountain (Hike 44) without the muscle-ripping climb. You'll work hard for just more than a mile, but then you have several miles of ridgetop hiking, meandering through meadows and over view-rich peaks. Few hikers visit this trail, so you and your dog can romp and play to your hearts' content among the wildflowers on the wind-swept ridge.

To get there, take exit 80 (Roslyn/Salmon la Sac) off Interstate 90 and head north on State Route 903 about 16.3 miles, passing through Roslyn and past Cle Elum Lake. Turn right onto Forest Road 128 and drive up the steep, winding road about 5 miles to its end and the trailhead, near 4400 feet.

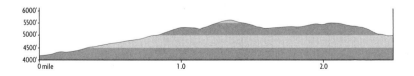

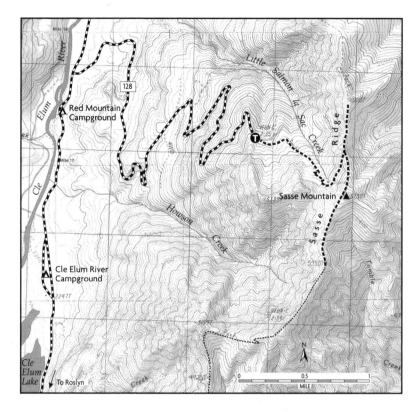

The trail begins by climbing steeply away from the road, cutting through an old clearcut and heading up the Little Salmon la Sac Creek drainage. For the next mile, the route angles upward without benefit of switchbacks or respite, gaining more than 1100 feet to attain the crest of Sasse Ridge at 5500 feet.

When you hit the ridgeline, you'll find a trail junction. Turn right and stroll south along the ridge crest, hopping over rocks and tripping through flowers, which sometimes grow right in the middle of the seldom-used trail. In the next mile, you'll climb to the 5730-foot summit of Sasse Mountain. Stop and enjoy the vast vistas found here. Jolly Mountain, Elbow Peak, and Hex Mountain fill the horizon to the north, east, and south. To the west, the blue chasm of Cle Elum Lake separates you from the tall summits of Domerie and West Peaks.

Walk as far south as you please along the ridge before turning and heading back to the trailhead. You can also hike north along the ridge from

the junction. Note that this is a dry route—there is no water but lots of sun and exposure. Pack plenty of fluids for both you and your canine to prevent dangerous dehydration. Also, be aware that some small species of cactus grow here, so you should have a pair of tweezers in your pack to pull spines from your dog's pads should he step on a spiny

This region's rocky ridge tops provide great views of surrounding countryside.

plant. (Better yet, teach Fido to walk in booties.)

46. Cathedral Rock / Peggy's Pond

Round trip: 11 miles
Hiking time: 7 hours (day hike or backpacking trip)
High point: 5600 feet
Elevation gain: 2200 feet
Best hiking time: mid-July through early October
Map: Green Trails Stevens Pass No. 176
Contact: Wenatchee National Forest, Cle Elum Ranger District,
(509) 674-4411

Doggy paradise, this trail is. Meadows, rivers, and lakes. Smooth trails, gentle climbs, and lots of grassy pastures in which to roll and romp. Oh, you humans will like it, too. The route offers a taste of some of the finest meadows, prettiest lakes, and craggiest mountains in the Alpine Lakes Wilderness, all in an easy hike along a picturesque ridge.

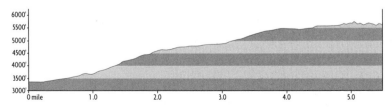

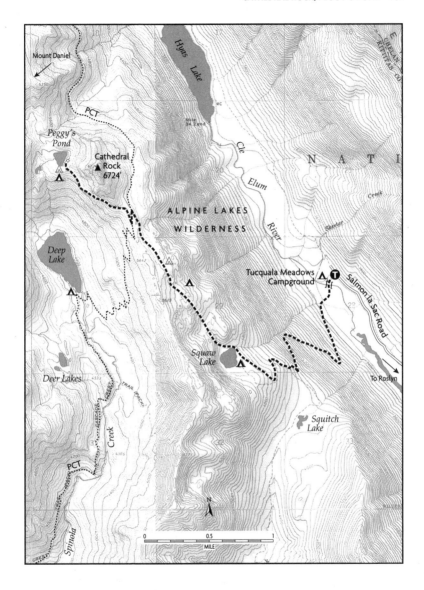

To get there, take exit 80 (Roslyn/Salmon la Sac) off Interstate 90 and head north on the Salmon la Sac Road (State Route 903) about 15 miles, passing through Roslyn and past Cle Elum Lake. At Salmon la Sac Campground, the paved road ends; stay right on the main road (rather than entering the campground) and continue up the Cle Elum River valley another 12 scenic miles through beautiful meadows to the end of the road.

On the trail in front of Cathedral Rock

Just before entering the Tucquala Meadows Campground, turn left into a wide trailhead parking lot.

From the parking area, hike down a short dirt road to the Cle Elum River, and find the trailhead at a bridge over the river. Head up the trail on the far side of the river and climb modestly for the first 2 miles (gaining just 1000 feet in the process) to a junction with Trail 1332 on the right. Stay left as the trail turns north along a long ridge crest. The forest on the ridge is broken and offers frequent views out across the Cle Elum River valley to the Wenatchee Mountains on the opposite valley wall.

At 2.5 miles, the trail passes Squaw Lake. This is a popular camping destination for families with small children, or for folks who just want to get far enough off the road to escape the noise and crowds but not so far they have to work excessively hard to get to their camp. The hiking distance isn't too great, and the shallow lake is perfect for wading or swimming. Stop for a break at the lake and let your dog paddle through the shallows or swim through the depths before continuing north along the trail.

Moving past Squaw, the trail follows the ridge north, alternating through grassy meadows and thin forest, with a few small tarns dotting the meadows along the way. Many of these cool blue pools sport gorgeous campsites nearby—you can pitch a tent on the edge of a ridge, with a small lake at your back and stunning views into the Cle Elum valley out your front door.

If you aren't looking for a campsite, though, keep hiking. At 4.5 miles, the trail ends at a junction with the Pacific Crest Trail (PCT). At this point, you're directly under the towering spire of Cathedral Rock. Look closely and you might see some Spiderman-wannabes scaling the rocky walls of the peak—Cathedral is quite popular with rock climbers.

Day hikers can stop here and find a place for a leisurely lunch along the meadows in the shadow of the Cathedral Rock monolith. Folks seeking a remote campsite, though, can turn south on the PCT and, in just 0.25 mile—about where the trail crosses a ridge and starts to descend—look for a small side trail on the right (north) side of the trail. This path contours north around the flank of Cathedral Rock, hugging the 5600-foot level, to reach the small pool of Peggy's Pond in about 0.75 mile. The trail is rough and rocky, with a few sections of exposure where the slope falls steeply away. Don't attempt this path if you or your dog have trouble with footing or stability. Peggy's Pond is a pretty alpine lake nestled in a rocky cirque with views down to the broad waters of Deep Lake and across to the ice-lined slopes of Mount Daniel.

For a less adventuresome journey, keep hiking south on the PCT to descend 3.5 miles to Deep Lake. This is a wonderful backpacking destination. The broad meadow is awash in purples and reds in midsummer with thousands of blooming lupine and paintbrush. On the north end of the lake, the glaciers and snowfields of Mount Daniel feed a score of thundering waterfalls that grace the steep wall above the lake. The best camps are on the west side of the lake. Return north to Cathedral Rock to complete the loop.

47. Scatter Creek

Round trip: 9 miles
Hiking time: 6 hours
High point: 6200 feet
Elevation gain: 2900 feet
Best hiking time: mid-July through early October
Map: Green Trails Stevens Pass No. 176
Contact: Wenatchee National Forest, Cle Elum Ranger District, (509) 674-4411

This route lets you explore a seldom-visited creek valley on the flanks of the Wenatchee Mountains. The trail ascends through steeply sloped

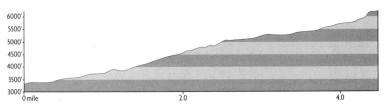

Luna loves the snow—as long as she has her jacket. Dogs are susceptible to the weather, too, so plan accordingly for them. (Carl Gronquist)

meadows into a broad wildflower basin at the head of the valley, and eventually to a high pass on the ridge, affording awesome views of both the Cle Elum River valley and east into the Icicle Creek drainage.

To get there, take exit 80 (Roslyn/Salmon la Sac) off Interstate 90 and head north on the Salmon la Sac Road about 15 miles, passing through Roslyn and past Cle Elum Lake. At Salmon la Sac Campground, the paved road ends. Stay right on the main road (rather than entering the campground) and continue up the Cle Elum River valley another 9.5 scenic miles through beautiful meadows to the trailhead on the right, just before the Scatter Creek ford (a concrete-lined vehicle ford).

The trail leaves the road and climbs gradually through thin forest to start up the slope on the south side of Scatter Creek. For the next 3 miles, the trail climbs 1500 feet through gentle switchbacks. The pine and fir forests are filled with green, flower-rich glades—the bulbous bear grass blooms, sitting atop their tall stalks, are particularly noteworthy early in

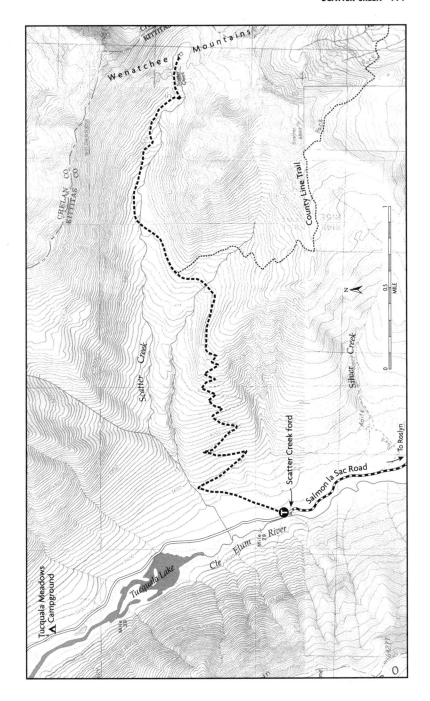

summer. Let your dog lead you through the brushy stretches of trail—the pup will keep you on track and will knock any morning dew off the dangling grasses before you get to it.

At 3.4 miles, find a trail intersection. To the right is the County Line Trail. You should stay left, continuing up the Scatter Creek valley and in 0.5 mile, cross the creek. Once across the creek, the meadows start to grow, slowly spreading out until you are hiking in a rolling field of native grasses and wildflowers. The lightly used trail can be overgrown and brushy in places, but generally it is easy to follow because it sticks close to Scatter Creek as it hooks southeast into the basin at the head of the creek valley. You can find plenty of places to camp along the creek in these upper meadows.

You could stop anywhere along here for a picturesque picnic site, with views out into the Cle Elum valley—Goat Mountain can be seen on the far side of the valley—and flowers stretching out under your feet. If you want more exercise, continue up the trail as it climbs the steep wall at the head of the valley, reaching the crest of the Wenatchee Ridge at Fish Pass, about 4.5 miles from the trailhead.

48. Esmeralda Basin/ Fortune Pass

Round trip: 7 miles
Hiking time: 5 hours
High point: 5900 feet
Elevation gain: 1700 feet
Best hiking time: June through early October
Map: Green Trails Mount Stuart No. 209
Contact: Wenatchee National Forest, Cle Elum Ranger District, (509) 674-4411

Vast meadows of wildflowers—one small clearing boasts several acres of purple shooting stars—line this trail, but that's just the icing on the cake.

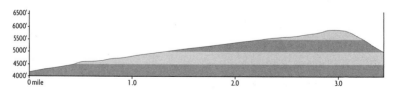

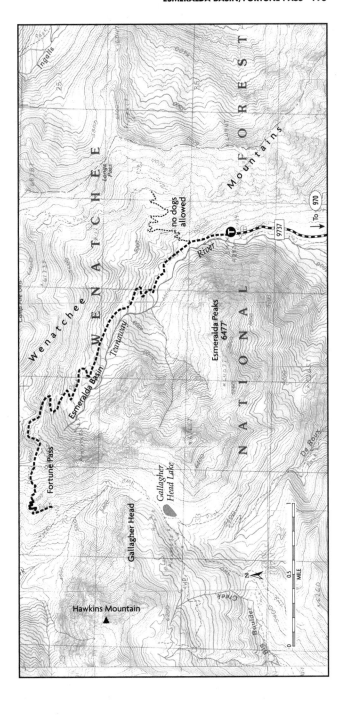

Field of shooting stars below Hawkins Mountain

The meadows provide local color, but the towering peaks surrounding the basin provide majestic highlights to your hike. The modest pitch of the trail makes this route ideal for hikers—two- and four-legged varieties—of all abilities, and the wonderful scenery will captivate everyone who visits.

To get there, from Cle Elum drive east on State Route 970, cross the Teanaway River Bridge, and in another mile, turn left onto Teanaway River Road, which becomes Forest Road 9737 at 29 Pines Campground. Continue to the road's end, about 13 miles from SR 970.

The trail starts up the path of an old miners road, though it has degraded to the point where only mossy-backed old timers remember this as anything more than a broad single-track trail. The path follows the Teanaway River upstream, staying just out of reach of the water for much of the way (though savvy dogs can and do find plentiful opportunities to drop the few yards down to the creek for a bit of wading and drinking). Less than 0.5 mile into the hike, you'll find a trail junction. The path to the right climbs steeply to Lake Ingalls, but dogs are banned on that path.

Stay left and continue up the North Teanaway valley, which in autumn is awash in color. Small meadows, separated by thin stands of forest, line the valley floor. Excellent campsites and plentiful photo opportunities (the meadows are so pretty, you'll swear every picture could be a future award-winner) are found in the first 2 miles of the trail.

At 2 miles, the path turns away from the river and climbs a gentle series of switchbacks into a slope scarred by a violent avalanche. Note the height of the stumps—this is the depth at which the less-stable surface snow slid to shear off the treetops a few years ago.

As the trail ascends the avalanche slope, keep a firm grip on Bowser's leash. The scattered tree trunks and rotting stumps are home to an army of small rodents and other burrowing mammals. These are the types of critters that attract the attention of even the most well-behaved dogs, so leashes are essential to keep the dog away from the log-dwellers.

Finally, at 3.5 miles, the trail makes one last switchback through the meadow and rolls up to the crest of the ridge between Ingalls Peak and Hawkins Mountain, ending at a trail junction at Fortune Pass. Turn around here, but before heading down, stop and rest, water the dog, and enjoy the views of the craggy summits of Hawkins and Ingalls, as well as the dual spires of Esmeralda Peaks.

49. Bean Creek Basin

Round trip: 5 miles
Hiking time: 4 hours
High point: 5600 feet
Elevation gain: 2000 feet
Best hiking time: June through early October
Map: Green Trails Mount Stuart No. 209
Contact: Wenatchee National Forest, Cle Elum Ranger District, (509) 674-4411
Warning: This trail crosses rattlesnake country. Dogs must be kept on-leash at all times when rattlesnakes are active (warm summer and early fall months) to reduce the risk of snakebite. This trail is best visited in spring and autumn when the vipers are less active. But at all times, be aware that rattlesnakes may be encountered and know the proper actions to take in the event of snakebite.

Mount Stuart dominates the eastern half of the Alpine Lakes Wilderness, towering so high above its surrounding peaks that it can be seen from trails

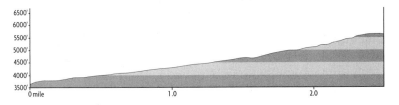

throughout the region. Bean Creek is one of those trails affording views of the spectacular rock slabs of Stuart. But there's more to this trail than mountain views. Indeed, there are splendid views of Mount Stuart, Ingalls Peak, and other summits in the Stuart Range. But it's the little things that make Bean Creek special. A plethora of blooming plants—wildflowers of all varieties—grace the valley pierced by this trail. An army of wild critters calls the basin home, from mule deer to deer mice, from gray jays to pileated woodpeckers.

To get there, from Cle Elum drive east on State Route 970, cross the Teanaway River Bridge, and in another mile, turn left onto the Teanaway River Road, which becomes Forest Road 9737 at 29 Pines Campground. Continue 3.8 miles past the end of the paved section of road to turn right (north) onto Beverly Creek Road (FR 9737-112). Drive about 1 mile to the road's end and trailhead.

Cross Beverly Creek on the stout bridge near the trailhead and climb 0.5 mile alongside Beverly Creek on an old, overgrown roadbed. At 0.5 mile, turn right at the first trail junction, away from Beverly Creek, and

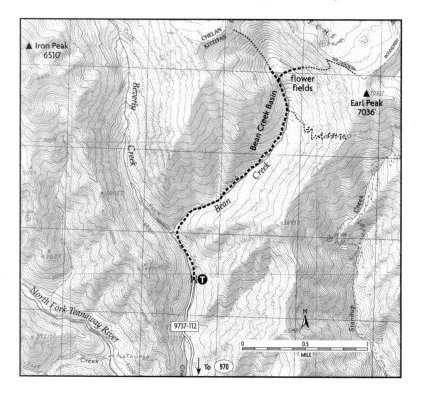

On a ridge near Bean Creek (Ken Konigsmark)

start up Bean Creek valley. This trail drives upward through a tight valley, lined lightly with trees and carpeted with bear grass, buckwheat, and other blooming plants under the waving branches of pines and firs.

Many of the trees that used to grace this valley can be seen rotting in piles at the bottom of the steep valley—dropped by a violent avalanche some years before. The trail continues a steep climb for nearly a mile, crossing the creek (the water can be fast and tough to wade early in the year when melting snows swell the creek) to access more, cool forest and small forest meadows higher up the valley.

At 2 miles, as the trail leaves a stand of forest, it erupts onto a broad swath of green, speckled with reds, blues, purples, yellows, and whites— that is, a vast grassy meadow filled with the odoriferous heads of blooming wildflowers. At this point, the trail forks. Stay left to climb into the flower fields of Bean Creek Basin. The trail leads to a wonderful camp along the creek, then angles up into a garden of color, dotted with alpine firs and stunted pines. As you ascend the 0.5-mile access trail from the last trail junction, you'll find the meadows growing larger and the stands of trees growing smaller, until finally, the meadows win out and take over all the basin before you. Here, at 2.5 miles and around 5600 feet, you'll be standing amidst flowers that stretch across scores of acres.

Above the meadows tower the jagged tops of Earl Peak, Mount Stuart, and Iron Peak. Let the dog roll in the fragrant grasses as you break out lunch; then enjoy a nap in the sun, with the pooch curled against you, before heading for home.

50. Navaho Pass

Round trip: 11 miles
Hiking time: 6 hours
High point: 6000 feet
Elevation gain: 3000 feet
Best hiking time: June through early October
Map: Green Trails Mount Stuart No. 209
Contact: Wenatchee National Forest, Cle Elum Ranger District, (509) 674-4411
Warning: This trail crosses rattlesnake country. Dogs must be kept on leash at all times when rattlesnakes are active (warm summer and early fall months) to reduce the risk of snakebite. This trail is best visited in spring and autumn when the vipers are less active. But at all times, be aware that rattlesnakes may be encountered and know the proper actions to take in the event of snakebite.

This route offers the best of the glorious Teanaway Country for hikers. Fantastic views, spectacular wildflowers, sparkling creeks, plentiful birds and wildlife, and a moderate trail await hikers here. What's more, this hike is perfect for dogs: plenty of water from the creek, lots of places to romp and play, and not too many hazards for our four-legged friends. In short, an ideal trail to explore and enjoy.

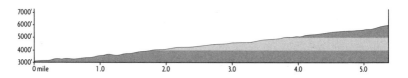

Spike and Koko near Navaho Pass (Ken Konigsmark)

To get there, from Cle Elum, drive east on State Route 970, cross the Teanaway River Bridge, and in another mile, turn left onto Teanaway River Road, which becomes Forest Road 9737 at 29 Pines Campground. Continue 1.3 miles past the end of the paved section of road and turn right (north) onto Stafford Creek Road (FR 9703). Drive 2.5 miles to the trailhead, found just after crossing Stafford Creek.

The orange-barked hulks of massive ponderosa pines line the lower section of this trail as it leads hikers into classic eastern Cascade ecology. The trail rolls upward slowly, if steadily, though the pine forest. Like all true old-growth ponderosa stands, this one is marked by a broken canopy that lets tons of sun streak down to light the forest floor, nourishing plenty of flowers around the trunks of the trees.

For 4 miles, the trail climbs alongside Stafford Creek, passing from ponderosa forest into Douglas fir stands, then into lodgepole and white pines and true fir, and then finally into spruce and hemlock forest. Through each forest type, the trail finds plenty of open clearings and sun-dappled glades. And of course, the creek is always near to keep the dog watered and refreshed.

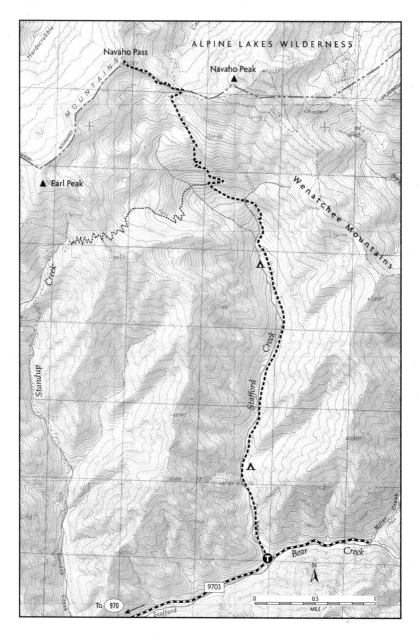

At 4 miles, the trail splits. To the left, a side trail drops into Standup Creek basin. Stay right, passing a modest campsite near the creek, and climb a few looping switchbacks as the trail moves up the valley's headwall to reach Navaho Pass on the ridgeline above the creek. Great views north to the long, rocky face of the Stuart Range captivate most hikers, but the views south, looking down into the green valleys of the Teanaway drainage, draw my eye. The varied hues of green mark the different types of forest and meadow, and there are still a few high, craggy peaks to punctuate the setting.

Enjoy the views on both sides of the pass, then head back down through the Stafford basin to the trailhead.

51. Tronsen Ridge

Round trip: 4 to 16.5 miles
Hiking time: 4 hours
High point: 5800 feet
Elevation loss: 1000 feet
Best hiking time: June through October
Map: Green Trails Liberty No. 210
Contact: Wenatchee National Forest, Cle Elum Ranger District, (509) 674-4411
Warning: This trail crosses rattlesnake country. Dogs must be kept on leash at all times when rattlesnakes are active (warm summer and early fall months) to reduce the risk of snakebite. This trail is best visited in spring and autumn when the vipers are less active. But at all times, be aware that rattlesnakes may be encountered and know the proper actions to take in the event of snakebite.

Start high, stay high, and enjoy the endless bounty of the wild country between the Cascade Crest and the dry, open deserts of eastern Washington. Tronsen Ridge provides a little of both worlds. Long, dry ridges topped with open meadows and wildflower fields resemble the desert gardens of the Yakima Plateau, but dense stands of fir and ponderosa pine offer up the

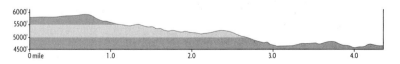

NOTE: *This profile shows just the first 4 miles (one way) of the route—additional hiking miles are possible.*

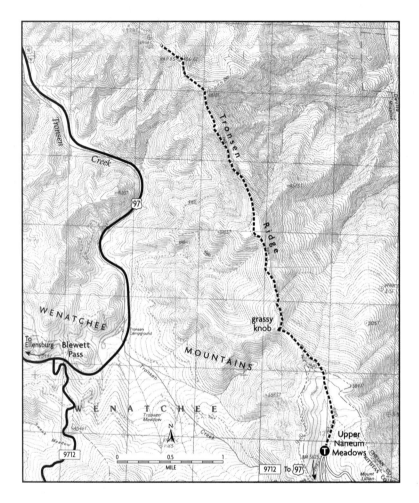

flavor of the mountains, with pine-scented valleys and cool woodland slopes. The glorious meadows and forests atop the long ridge are wonderful playgrounds for dogs and people, but the people will also enjoy the outstanding views from the high knobs of the route. At various points, Tronsen Ridge grants peeks out to Mount Adams, Mount Rainier, Mount Stuart, and countless other lesser peaks nestled in the eastern Cascades.

To get there, from Cle Elum drive 10 miles north on State Route 970, where the road merges into US 97. Continue another 14 miles to Blewett Pass and turn right (southeast) onto Forest Road 9716. In 3.7 miles, turn left onto FR 9712. Continue 5 miles to Haney Meadows and the Ken Wilcox Horse Camp. Drive another mile past the camp and, crossing Naneum

Creek, find the trail-head at 5600 feet in the Upper Naneum Meadows at a sharp, right-hand switchback curve in the road.

The trail heads north through the Naneum Meadows, climbing gradually (gaining a mere 100 feet) in the first 0.5 mile, before sloping downward for a slow, soft descent along the ridge for the next 4 miles. The high point of the ridge, an impressive grassy knob about 1 mile into the hike, provides un-

Hiking along the ridge

matched views of the eastern Wenatchee Mountains area and beyond. After leaving this knob, the trail heads into a roller coaster ride to the north, climbing short peaks and ridge knolls, then dropping into low saddles. The net elevation change over the hike past the knob is a loss of 1000 feet.

Many of the high points of the ridge are grassy bumps full of wild-flowers, while the low points are saddles timbered with thin stands of forest. Look for wildlife all along the ridge, but especially in the transition zones between forest and meadows.

For additional adventures, with map and compass in hand (and good skills in using those well in place) you can explore off-trail, letting the dog lead you out side ridges and onto rocky promontories with awesome views of Mount Stuart, Mount Rainier, and the Wenatchee peaks.

Note that this is a dry route, with no water sources and, in summer months, high daytime temperatures and lots of sun exposure. Provide lots of water for your dog, and check him often for dehydration. You might also apply some sunscreen to any areas of the dog's snout or ears where the fur is thin or skin is exposed.

SOUTH CASCADES

52. Snoquera Falls

Round trip: 4 miles (5 with side trip to river)
Hiking time: 3 hours
High point: 3400 feet
Elevation gain: 1100 feet
Best hiking time: March through November
Map: Green Trails Greenwater No. 238
Contact: Snoqualmie Ranger District, Enumclaw office, (360) 825-6585

The lush, moss-laden forest is reminiscent of the rainforests of the Olympic Peninsula, for good reason. The western foothills of the Cascades can get twice as much annual rainfall as the Puget Sound area, making the low forests of these regions wet, mossy, and rich in plant (and animal) life. In short, a rainforest. The loop trail here is short, but scenic, perfect for late season hikes when the days are short and hiking time is at a premium.

To get there, from Enumclaw drive east on State Route 410 (Chinook Pass Highway) through the town of Greenwater. From Greenwater continue about 9 miles, passing The Dalles Campground, and find a small parking area on the left (north) side of the highway, just a few yards south of the Sheppard Boy Scout Camp.

The trail angles into the forest on the northeast side of the highway, climbing gradually through the lush old cedar and hemlock forest.

Parka, Donna, and Bree near Snoquera Falls

Sweeping carpets of moss—spotted with splashes of yellow and white (skunk cabbage and trillium) in the spring, and garlands of red and umber (Oregon grape leaves and drying ferns) in the autumn. The trail steepens after the first 0.5 mile, as it slants up the lower slope of Little Ranger Peak. At the junction at 0.6 mile, turn right and continue climbing the valley wall.

Big leaf maples and a few scrub oaks now fill the spaces between the

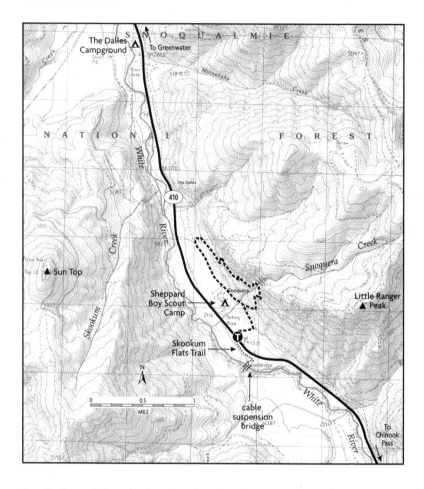

hemlocks and Douglas firs. In 1.2 miles, the trail drops into a little rocky basin, filled with maples, and crosses a small stream below the fantail waterfall on the Snoquera Creek. These pretty falls can roar in the spring as the winter's snowpack melts, but they can also turn off, leaving just a trickle, later in the fall. For the full experience, plan to visit the falls at least twice to see the difference in water levels and how it affects the whole basin.

From the waterfall basin, the trail continues north, rolling along the base of a steep, rocky slope for another 1.5 miles before descending a few short switchbacks to a junction with the lower valley trail. Turn left and follow this trail south 1.3 miles, passing the Boy Scout camp before returning to your starting point.

After your hike, if you have an extra hour, cross the highway from the trailhead to a trail leading into the woods. Hike south 0.5 mile on this trail to a long, steel-cabled suspension bridge over the White River. This bouncy bridge provides access to the Skookum Flats trail on the far side of the river. My dog won't cross it. Will yours? Enjoy the views of the river, then return to your car.

53. Noble Knob

Round trip: 7 miles
Hiking time: 5 hours
High point: 6011 feet
Elevation gain: 500 feet
Best hiking time: July through early October
Map: Green Trails Lester No. 239
Contact: Snoqualmie Ranger District, Enumclaw office, (360) 825-6585

Hike through meadows nestled more than a mile above sea level, but climb only 500 feet to get there. What could be better? Perhaps, having those meadows punctuated with stunning horizons capped by the snow-clad peak of Mount Rainier. Add in a large resident herd of elk; some pretty, doe-eyed mule deer; and a few hundred birds. Too much to ask? Perhaps, but what if we also toss in the fact that the trail is open to dogs?

It sounds unbelievable, but it's actually a noble destination: Noble Knob.

To get there, from Enumclaw drive east on State Route 410 (Chinook Pass Highway) about 31 miles and turn left (north) onto Corral Pass Road (Forest Road 7174). Drive 6 miles to the trailhead on the left, near where the road hooks south (elevation 5700 feet). If you reach the road end at Corral Pass, you've driven about 0.25 mile too far.

The trail angles north around the flank of Mutton Mountain, gaining only a few feet in the first mile. From the start, the trail slides through lush wildflower meadows with incredible views of the rocky top of Mutton Mountain and back south to Castle Mountain. About 1.5 miles from

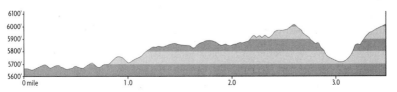

the car, the trail splits. Stay right and continue to contour through meadows below the jagged spine of Dalles Ridge. About 2.5 miles from the car, the trail crosses a low saddle (5900 feet) with phenomenal views over the surrounding meadows. Soak it in, before pushing on. With your dog in the lead, drop a couple feet in elevation over the next 0.5 mile to another trail junction. This time the left fork drops to Twentyeight Mile Lake. Stay right and in 0.25 mile, find a third junction, this one offering you three trails from which to choose. Look left (down toward Lake George), look right (down to Lost Lake), and go down the middle. Or

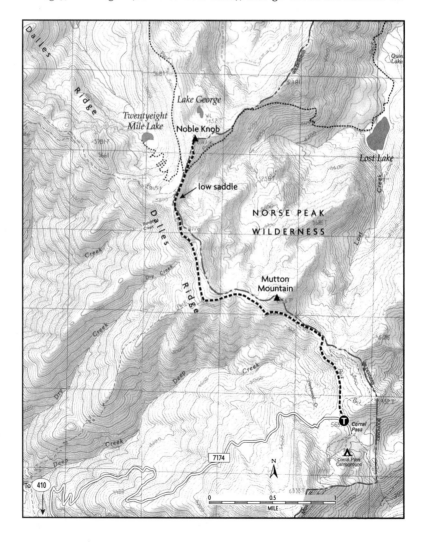

Bleached rootball on the slope of Noble Knob

rather, up the middle, as the center trail climbs a steep 0.25 mile, looping around the circular summit, to the 6011-foot crest of Noble Knob. Once upon a time, a fire lookout station was positioned here, from which the fire watch guard kept an eye on the forest in all directions, watching for lightning strikes and long fingers of smoke. Today, the lookout cabin is gone, but the views remain.

54. Greenwater Lakes and Echo Lake

Round trip: 14 miles
Hiking time: 8 hours (day hike or backpacking trip)
High point: 4100 feet
Elevation gain: 1600 feet
Best hiking time: June through early November
Map: Green Trails Lester No. 239
Contact: Snoqualmie Ranger District, Enumclaw office, (360) 825-6585

Lush old-growth forest; dark, mysterious forest lakes; and a wonderful chance to meet and see wildlife await hikers here. The trail sticks to a deeply forested river valley where it passes a wonderfully clear, cool lake with many fine campsites and good fishing opportunities. Dogs will love the cool forest and soft, duff-rich trail-tread. But for all that, few people (or dogs) visit, perhaps because the trail doesn't offer sweeping panoramas. The distant views may be missing, but the routes are remarkably scenic and solitude is a high probability.

To get there, from Enumclaw drive east on State Route 410 to the small town of Greenwater. About 1 mile east of the Greenwater Fire Station (at the eastern end of the community), turn left (north) onto the Greenwater River Road (Forest Road 70). Drive about 9 miles, crossing the Greenwater River, and turn right just past the bridge onto FR 7033. Drive up this narrow road (south) about 0.5 mile to the large trailhead parking lot.

Leave the trailhead and hike into the moss-laden forest, following the Greenwater River upstream. The trail is quiet and damp, even in summer it seems, providing soft footing for those who go without boots. As your dog pads up the trail beside you, watch him for any alerts to wildlife—he'll sense the critters before you do. Deer and elk browse through this valley, and where there are deer and elk, there may be cougar, coyotes, and bobcats.

The trail crosses the Greenwater River three or four times before reaching the long, shallow Greenwater Lakes about 2 miles up from the

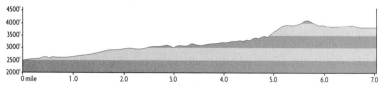

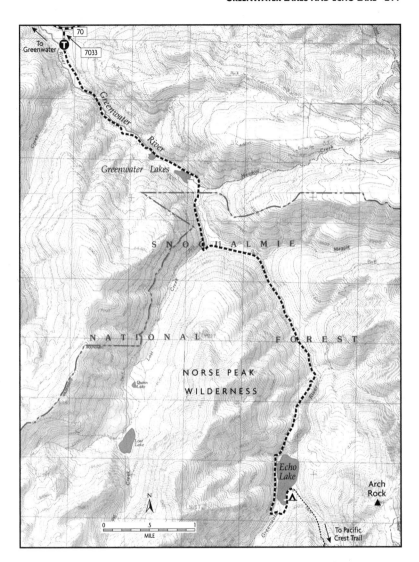

trailhead. There are some fine campsites along these forested ponds, but don't bother pitching the tent yet. Keep climbing up the valley. For the next 3 miles the route maintains a slow, easy ascent of the valley; but at 5 miles from the trailhead, the climb steepens substantially. For 1.5 miles, the path switchbacks up the valley wall before tapering off into a smooth, level glide into the Echo Lake basin at 7 miles.

This pretty forest lake offers excellent camping along its southern and

Hikers returning from Greenwater Lakes

eastern shores—the west shore is closed to camping—with many sites offering great views of the spires of Castle and Mutton Mountains to the southwest.

55. Arch Rock (Government Meadows)

Round trip: 12 miles
Hiking time: 7 hours
High point: 5200 feet
Elevation gain: 700 feet
Best hiking time: June through early November
Map: Green Trails Lester No. 239
Contact: Snoqualmie Ranger District, Enumclaw office, (360) 825-6585

Following the Pacific Crest Trail (PCT) south from the broad fields of Government Meadows, this route offers a chance to explore one of the most solitary sections of the PCT in the south Cascades. It provides hikers the chance to experience deep forests and rocky bluffs and gives dogs the

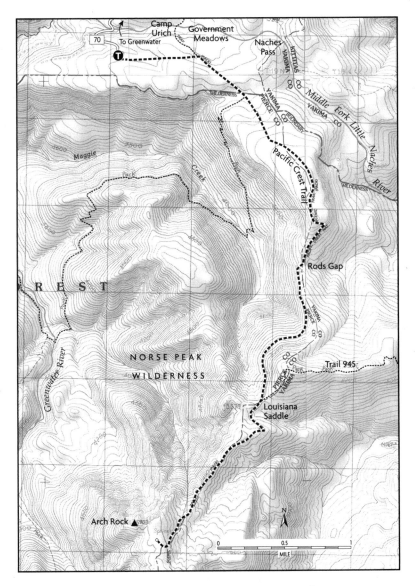

chance to walk with their humans without worrying about encountering too many other hikers along the way.

But all's not well with the PCT here. The trail starts in clearcuts just south of Government Meadows, the old wagon road through Naches Pass (now used extensively by four-wheel-drive fanatics). The PCT south of Naches Pass quickly enters the protective folds of the Norse Peak Wilderness, but

Signboard near Pacific Crest Trail

just north of Government Meadows, it literally disappears under roads and clearcuts. That's why we recommend heading south from the meadows.

Note that there's little-to-no water along the trail, so bring lots for your four-legged friend.

To get there, from Enumclaw drive east on State Route 410 to the small town of Greenwater. About 1 mile east of the Greenwater Fire Station (at the eastern end of the community), turn left (north) onto the Greenwater River Road (Forest Road 70). Drive about 15 miles to the trailhead at the road's end in an old clearcut. The last mile of road is dusty, rough, and at times deeply rutted. Use care when traveling it, especially in passenger cars and other low-clearance vehicles.

The trail leaves the clearcut at the trailhead on an old logging road that leads into the trees. In 0.5 mile the broad connector trail ends at a junction with the Pacific Crest Trail. Turning left leads you to Government Meadows in another 0.5 mile—these broad, marshy meadows are a haven for deer and elk and are worth a visit if you have the time and inclination to go look for critters. Once you've explored the meadows, head south once more, passing the access trail that brought you to the PCT and continuing south.

The trail is fairly flat for the next few miles as it weaves through the thick, old forests. About 1 mile from the trailhead, a secondary trail leads off to the right. Stay left on the PCT and in about 3 miles you'll find your first chance at a view. Just before the trail starts to descend into a few switchbacks down to Rods Gap you'll find a small clearing on the left side of the trail. Looking south and east, you'll enjoy the views of rolling hills and gray-green forests spread out before you but beware the dangers of looking northeast where you'll see huge scars on the land beyond the wilderness boundary.

Rods Gap is a small, forested saddle on the ridge separating the Greenwater valley from the Naches River valley. From the gap, the trail turns upward and climbs for the next 5 miles. Just 1 mile past Rods Gap, you'll cross Louisiana Saddle near a junction with a trail (Trail 945) on the left.

Continue upward on the PCT and you'll encounter a few clearings along the ridge where views of the nearby peaks present themselves. To the southeast you'll see the rocky top of Raven Roost while directly ahead lies the prominent peak of Arch Rock.

The trail reaches the open slope below Arch Rock about 6 miles from the trailhead. Stop here and enjoy the views to the east—Raven Roost cuts the sky just across the South Naches basin. Give the dog some water, enjoy some lunch, then return the way you came.

56. Norse Peak

Round trip: 12 miles
Hiking time: 7 hours
High point: 6856 feet
Elevation gain: 2850 feet
Best hiking time: mid-July through early October
Map: Green Trails Bumping Lake No. 271
Contact: Snoqualmie Ranger District, Enumclaw office, (360) 825-6585

Hike here in summer and you'll want to pack several quarts of water, then toss in two more once you've got all you think you'll need. This trail climbs steeply on sun-parched slopes, and you and your dog are going to need lots of water to stay hydrated and healthy. And you'll want to be healthy and feeling good, because the scenery you encounter on this short trail will be something you want to see and remember for a long time. The acres of wildflowers on all sides will capture your attention, and when you tire of the rainbow of colors on the ground, you'll find new, breathtaking vistas around every corner. Herds of elk frequent the meadows on the slopes to Norse Peak, and mountain goats dance and prance around the rocks at the ridge top. Hawks and golden eagles soar overhead, and small snakes and alligator lizards live on the sun-heated slopes underfoot. Keep your dog under control so she doesn't get excited and chase any of these critters.

To get there, drive east from Enumclaw about 34 miles on State Route

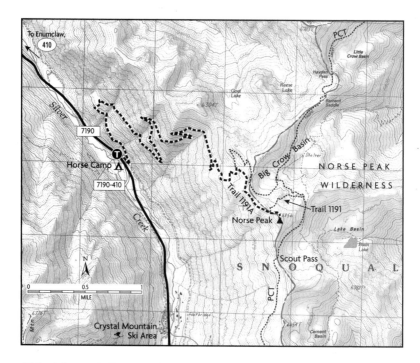

410 and turn left (east) onto the Crystal Mountain Road (Forest Road 7190) leading to the Crystal Mountain Ski Area. Drive about 3 miles to a large horse camp on the right (at a junction with FR 7190-410). Park in the lot at the upper end of the horse camp and find the trailhead on the left (east) side of the parking area.

The trail parallels the FR 7190-410 for about 0.3 mile before turning uphill for a steep, hot climb through open, rocky meadows. In the first mile, the views are few, but as you pause periodically for a rest, glance south to see Mount Rainier rising over the ridge of Crystal Mountain. Each switchback in the trail brings more of the mighty mountain into view. By the time you reach the first trail junction (6300 feet elevation), 4 miles from the trailhead, the entire peak towers over the ski area and its namesake mountain.

Go right at this junction onto Trail 1191A to continue your sweaty climb toward the summit of Norse Peak. In just 1.3 miles, you'll be standing atop the 6856-foot peak with 360-degree views. Because the former lookout site towers over the surrounding ridges and peaks, your views extend east past the Norse Peak Wilderness to Fifes Peak and Gold Hill. To the west, you'll see the sprawling patchwork forests of the central

Snow-covered ridge below Norse Peak

Cascades. This is checkerboard country—one square mile is Forest Service land, the next is private timber company land. The squares, unfortunately, are easily discernible because most of the private holdings have been scraped bare by clearcutting. Fortunately, that is just one small part of the view. Going down, you'll find Mount Rainier slowly disappearing behind Crystal Mountain, like a setting sun slipping below the horizon.

57. Bullion Basin

Round trip: 7 miles
Hiking time: 5 hours
High point: 6400 feet
Elevation gain: 1600 feet
Best hiking time: mid-July through October
Map: Green Trails Bumping Lake No. 271
Contact: Snoqualmie Ranger District, Enumclaw office, (360) 825-6585

Sure, it's a ski area, but powder hounds we aren't. We aren't dogging for soft, fluffy snow. We're leading out dogs on a gentle alpine ramble. This hike just happens to loop around the head basin of a major ski area. But

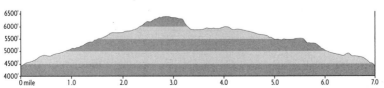

At Bullion Basin (Ken Konigsmark)

it also loops around the edge of a pretty, alpine wilderness area—the Norse Peak Wilderness.

The trail leads through steep, flower-filled alpine meadows, over narrow ridge spines, and under shady forest canopies. Views sweep over the dry, pine valleys of the eastern Cascades, the glacier-covered summit massive of Mount Rainier, and the craggy peaks of the central William O. Douglas Wilderness to the south. Best of all, despite the modest level of difficulty (not too long, nor too steep), the trail isn't heavily used so it's possible to find a quiet place for a peaceful lunch high on the ridge.

To get there, drive east from Enumclaw about 34 miles on State Route 410 and turn left (east) onto the Crystal Mountain Road (Forest Road 7190) leading to the Crystal Mountain Ski Area. Drive about 5 miles to the end of the road at the ski resort. Park on the left (east) side of the upper lot and find a faint trail behind the ski school building.

The trail (Trail 1156) climbs northeast away from the main ski lodge toward some cabins on the valley's east wall. In just a few hundred yards, you'll encounter a dirt, access road. Continue up this to the trailhead on left.

In the first 0.5 mile, the trail climbs gradually through open forests and meadows as it slants northeast before switching back to head up the Bullion Creek valley into the heart of Bullion Basin. The basin, a flower-filled meadow in a shallow cirque, is reached in just less than 2 miles. After crossing the creek, the path enters a deep thicket of woods then jumps back into the sunshine as it climbs steeply for 0.5 mile to reach the junction with the Pacific Crest Trail (PCT) at 6300 feet.

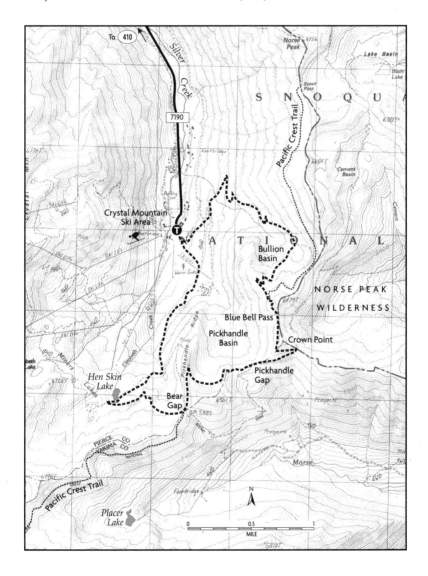

Turning south on the PCT, you'll follow the ridge down to Blue Bell Pass, along the side of Crown Point (see Hike 60), and through Pickhandle Gap to reach Bear Gap (elevation, 5882 feet) at 4.5 miles. The last 2 miles are all well above tree line and offer constant views of the wildflower pastures at your feet and the panoramic vistas beyond. Though there are many sights to see every step of the way through this section, each pass and peak has its own special view. From Blue Bell, look east to Fifes Peak. From Crown Point, look southwest to Mount Rainier. From Pickhandle, look southeast to American Ridge. From Bear Gap, look north to Norse Peak, south to Rainier, east to Fifes, and west to Crystal Mountain.

Leave the PCT at Bear Gap by taking the right fork at the four-way trail junction and heading toward Hen Skin Lake on Trail 1163. A gentle descent of 200 feet in 0.75 mile leads to the shallow, muddy-bottomed pond. There are a few small trout swimming in the lake but also a whole lot of mosquito larva early in the summer—keep moving quickly past the lake and most of the little biters will miss you. Turn right at the lake onto Trail 1192 and make a long, slow descent into the ski area. In 2 miles, you'll cross a creek near a couple of rustic cabins and burst out onto an open ski slope. Angle down the open slope to reach the parking lot and your starting point.

58. Sourdough Gap (Sheep Lake)

Round trip: 7 miles
Hiking time: 4 hours (day hike or backpacking trip)
High point: 6400 feet
Elevation gain: 1000 feet
Best hiking time: mid-July through October
Maps: Green Trails Mount Rainier East No. 270, Bumping Lake No. 271
Contact: Wenatchee National Forest, Naches Ranger District, (509) 653-2205

This section of the Pacific Crest Trail (PCT) seems tailor-made for kids and dogs. The trail is gentle, scenic, and easily accessible. It provides a

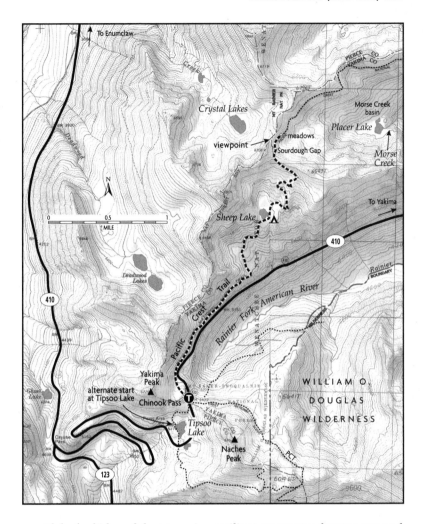

great lake for kids and dogs to swim, resilient grassy meadows to run and romp, and easy off-trail scrambles to burn some energy.

All this and more (huckleberries, wildflowers, wildlife, and great views) await hikers willing to share the trail with lots of fellow nature lovers and the occasional bear—where there are huckleberries, there are sure to be bears, and there are some wonderful huckleberry brambles above this trail. Of course, with lots of meadows for grazing, rocks for hiding in, and trees to perch in, Sourdough Gap is also popular with a host of bird and animal species. Deer, mountain goats, hawks, falcons, marmots, martens, chipmunks, and the ever-faithful friend of hikers, gray jays, are

Camp near the shores of Sheep Lake

just a few of the feathered and furred critters that thrive here.

With a modest elevation gain of just 400 feet in the first 2.5 miles, this trail can be enjoyed by hikers of all abilities. Kids will love it, and the idyllic little lake basin, with its lakeside meadows and shady groves of trees, makes a great destination for the little tykes' backpacking adventure.

Because the trail is popular, all dogs should be leashed at all times—except when they are swimming, when leashes are impractical and unsafe.

To get there, drive east from Enumclaw on State Route 410 to the summit of Chinook Pass. Just east of the pass and Tipsoo Lake, turn left (north) into a small, trailhead parking lot on the north side of the highway. The trailhead is found on the backside of the lot, behind the rest rooms. (**Note:** If the parking lot is full, return to the Tipsoo Lake parking lot at the summit of the pass and hike the 0.25-mile trail around the lake to the lower lot and the PCT trailhead.)

The trail traverses the steep hillside meadows east of the pass, staying above SR 410 for the first mile. Traffic noise can be heard, and sometimes seen, through the brush and trees below the trail, but the views beyond make up for that. The deep valley of the Rainier Fork of the American River, with Naches Peak rising on the far wall, is beautiful. Hikers with sharp eyes, or a good pair of binoculars, can often pick out hikers rounding the flank of Naches Peak on the PCT, some 3 trail miles to the south.

After the first mile, the trail veers north, climbing gently up to a bench below Sourdough Gap. Just past the 2.5-mile mark, you'll drop into the Sheep Lake basin. There are nice campsites around the lake, but the best are on the small tree-lined knoll to the south of the lake. The trail to the Gap rounds the east side of the lake and begins a moderately steep climb up the valley wall to the rocky saddle of Sourdough Gap at 3.5 miles. Along the way, the trail loops through a few switchbacks and offers wonderful views down to the lake and occasionally all the way back down to the trailhead.

Sourdough Gap is a small saddle in a jagged-edge ridge. You find a few spotty views of Mount Rainier during the approach to the gap, but for the really outstanding views, you'll need to scramble up the steep talus slope on the northwest side of the gap. A faint boot-beaten path leads to the ridge crest—be careful, though, because the far side of the ridge falls away as a 500-foot cliff. From this ridge, you'll look southwest onto the Emmons Glacier of Mount Rainier. Directly below your vantage point is the Crystal Lakes Basin—be sure to wave to the hikers clustered on the shores of those pretty lakes.

Those who'd rather stick to the established trail will have to forgo views of Rainier, but by continuing on the PCT about 0.25 mile north of Sourdough Gap, you'll find wonderful views east into the meadows of upper Morse Creek, with the blue pool of Placer Lake sitting dead-center in the valley. Far beyond, is the long spine of American Ridge in the William O. Douglas Wilderness Area.

59. American Lake

Round trip: 13 miles
Hiking time: 6 hours (day hike or backpacking trip)
High point: 5800 feet
Elevation loss: 500 feet
Best hiking time: July through October
Maps: Green Trails Mount Rainier East No. 270, Bumping Lake No. 271
Contact: Wenatchee National Forest, Naches Ranger District, (509) 653-2205

Dogs love lakes. People love lakes. Dogs love meadows and fields of grass. People love meadows and fields of huckleberries! This trail fills all those

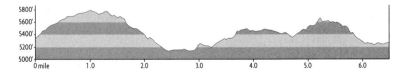

needs. The route follows the Pacific Crest Trail (PCT) south from Chinook Pass, weaving around alpine lakes of all sizes, cutting through dry-side old-growth forests, and pushing through wildflower meadows and tight brambles of fruit-rich huckleberry bushes. Oh, there are nice views, too, with Mount Rainier visible from the early sections of the trail and the peaks of the William O. Douglas Wilderness seen from the latter sections of trail.

To get there, drive east from Enumclaw on State Route 410 to the summit of Chinook Pass. Just east of the pass and Tipsoo Lake, turn left (north) into a small, trailhead parking lot on the north side of the highway. The trailhead is across the highway, where there is also a small parking area,

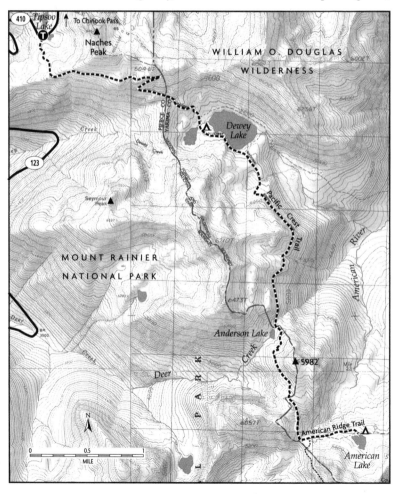

American Lake and rocky peak

but facilities are provided at the north-side parking lot.

After crossing the highway, join the PCT as it swings south along the east flank of Naches Peak. The trail traverses the slope through open hillside meadows. The first 0.5 mile pushes east, providing hikers with stunning views down the deep valley of headwaters of the American River. As the trail bends south, you'll find increasingly grand views of the long, tall spine of American Ridge before you. At 1.5 miles, you'll hit a trail junction. Stay left—the right-hand trail is off-limits for dogs—and begin a moderately steep descent, dropping about 600 feet in 1.3 miles.

The trail drops through a series of gentle switchbacks, passing through old, sun-dappled pine and fir forest, to reach a small forest clearing on the northwest shore of Dewey Lake. This broad, trout-filled lake is a great backpacking destination for families because the 3-mile hike (one way) is gentle and the lake is a great place to swim, fish, or just relax and enjoy the scenery.

Beyond Dewey, the PCT rolls nearly due south and brings you into the country that was loved so dearly by the late William O. Douglas—the Yakima native who grew up to become a U.S. Supreme Court Justice (who served from 1939 to 1975). Douglas was a sickly child—he nearly died of infantile paralysis—but he overcame his illness by trudging up and down the dry mountains west of Yakima. As his body grew stronger, so did his love of this pristine area and a lifelong bond was formed. The wilderness that bears his name sprawls over the eastern slopes of the Cascades all the way up to the PCT.

From the southeast end of Dewey Lake, the trail rolls gently south, cutting through huge expanses of huckleberry meadows—excellent places to savor the essence of pine forest, just be aware that berry hungry bears also like to gobble the juicy fruit. (See Part 1 for information on safe hiking with dogs in bear country.)

Douglas himself made this trek, enjoying the succulent berries along the way. His written account of it—in his autobiography *Of Men and Mountains*—describes hiking this stretch of the crest trail as a young boy. Just north of American Ridge, near Anderson Lake at the head of Deer Creek, Douglas and his brother hiked into a wide meadow on an open hillside on the eastern slope of the crest (where the PCT now lies).

"The hillside was filled with patches of low-bush huckleberries that were heavy with ripe fruit. We dropped our packs and sat on the ground and once more ate our fill. Some of the berries were twice as big as peas. We tossed them down by the handful, hungry for the sugar that sunlight had stored in them." (*Of Men and Mountains,* San Francisco: Chronicle Books, 1990, page 72.)

This enormous patch of huckleberries is just as rich in fruit today, and hikers can eat their fill before hiking on to Anderson Lake at 4.4 miles. The trail climbs gently for the next mile, rolling along the western flank of a small, unnamed peak (5982 feet) before reaching the junction with the American Ridge Trail at 5.8 miles. For a good campsite, hike east 0.75 mile on the American Ridge Trail to American Lake, where you'll enjoy more huckleberry fields and scenery that includes a rocky pinnacle to the south and the deep valley of the American River to the north.

60. Union Creek

Round trip: 14 miles
Hiking time: 7 hours (day hike or backpacking trip)
High point: 5900 feet
Elevation gain: 2500 feet
Best hiking time: July through October
Map: Green Trails Bumping Lake No. 271
Contact: Wenatchee National Forest, Naches Ranger District,
   (509) 653-2205

Pine and fir forests fill the valley of Union Creek, providing a cool retreat from the heat of summer for you and your furry friend. The trail follows the splashing creek upstream, sometimes climbing high above the water, sometimes swinging low along the creekside. There are open meadows to explore and shadow-laden forests in which to revel. Deer and elk browse through the valley, and birds swarm around the clusters of berry bushes and bug-rich creek bed. Look for gray jays, nuthatches, juncos, bushtits, sparrows, flickers, woodpeckers, and dippers. These last birds (also known as water ouzels) dance and dart along the rocks of the creek, diving and dipping into the plunging water to snatch up aquatic insects. Above the creek, hammer-headed woodpeckers and flickers drill into standing dead trees until the valley echoes with their drumming. The twittering nuthatches and trilling juncos provide a melody to the pounding bass line of the woodpeckers, creating wonderful woodland music. Not everyone will hear these feathered musicians—they have to take a break between sets—but everyone can enjoy the fragrant pine forest and, from the end of the trail, the spectacular views over the valley and beyond.

To get there, from Chinook Pass drive east on State Route 410 for 9 miles, then turn left into the Union Creek Trailhead parking area at the base of Union Creek.

Start up the trail on the soft path leading north out of the parking lot

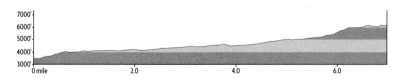

and in just 0.5 mile, enjoy the spectacle of pounding water at Union Creek Falls. Snap a picture or two to capture the pretty scene, then keep hiking. The trail crosses the creek and angles steeply up the nose of the ridge on the east flank of Union Creek valley. The trail zigs and zags up tight switchbacks before rolling into a long, climbing traverse of the valley wall, well above the creek. At just over a mile from the trailhead, the hiking path crosses the North Fork

Upper Union Creek

Union Creek above another waterfall, then descends to the main trunk of Union Creek to hug the water's edge before climbing onto the wall above the creek once more.

At 4 miles out, the trail returns to the creek for a long visit, passing

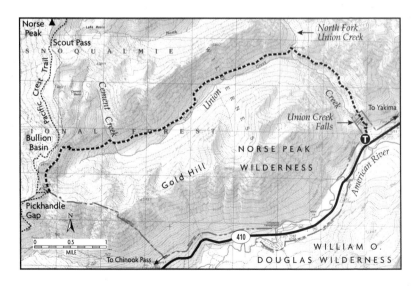

some wonderful campsites around 4200 feet elevation. Let the dog rest and splash in the icy cold waters here—she'll appreciate the opportunity to cool off and catch her breath, and so will you. Here the trail turns steep once more as it leaves the creek at 4.5 miles for a torturous 2.5-mile climb to the Pacific Crest Trail below Crown Point and Blue Bell Pass.

From this hard-earned vantage point, enjoy great views of the Norse Peak Wilderness and its rocky summits: Gold Hill, Norse Peak, Pickhandle Peak, and the Crystal Mountain Peaks. You can wander north and south along the PCT (see Hike 57) to explore the ridgetop meadows and alpine summits, or just return the way you came.

61. Mesatchee Creek

Round trip: 11 miles
Hiking time: 7 hours
High point: 5800 feet
Elevation gain: 2200 feet
Best hiking time: July through October
Map: Green Trails Bumping Lake No. 271
Contact: Wenatchee National Forest, Naches Ranger District,
     (509) 653-2205

Your dog may not appreciate the waterfalls, but she'll surely love the water pools found along the creek, and you'll both love the cool forest and plentiful wildlife (available for you to see and the dog to smell) found in this valley. The route climbs, steeply at times, along the Mesatchee Creek valley to the crest of the long, rambling American Ridge. You'll find great views from the wonderful alpine meadows lining the ridge top.

To get there, from Chinook Pass drive east on State Route 410 for 6.5 miles, then turn right onto a small road (Forest Road 460) leading south about 0.5 mile nearly to the mouth of Mesatchee Creek valley. Park at the road's end.

The trail starts up alongside the clear waters of the American River,

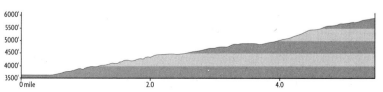

following an old roadbed for the first mile. A footlog over the river at 1.2 miles marks the start of the workout, as the trail, once over the river, turns away from the American and angles up into the Mesatchee Creek valley. At a trail junction in 0.25 mile, stay left—the right fork leads up the American River to Dewey Lake (another fine dog-hiking route for future exploration; see also Hike 59). The left-hand path stays in the Mesatchee valley but leaves the creek behind as it gets nasty-steep on a mile-long

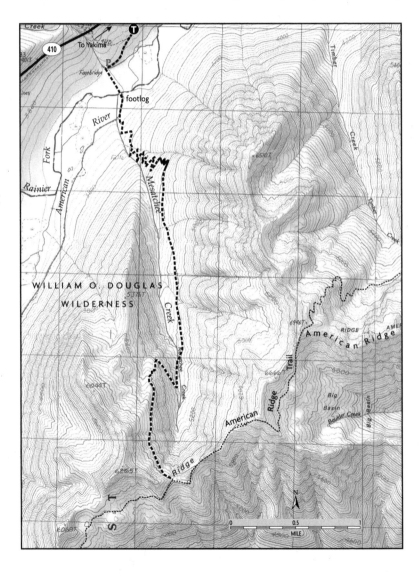

On American Ridge near Mesatchee Creek Trail (Ken Konigsmark)

series of switchbacks heading up the valley wall. Before the creek passes from sight, though, you loop close to it on one turn and come into view of a pretty horsetail waterfall cascading over a steep rocky rim.

Once well above creek level, the trail moderates a bit and enters a long, slope traverse, angling upstream before crossing the creek just short of the 4-mile mark. You'll find adequate campsites near the creek, but if you are merely day hiking, don't bother with a long rest here—take a break, and get yourself and your dog well-watered, then push on because there are prettier places to see and enjoy.

The trail moves farther up the creek valley, and slowly circles through the upper slopes of the meadow-filled basin at the head of the creek. At 5.5 miles, the trail ends at a junction with American Ridge Trail amidst a tangle of huckleberries and alpine firs. Enjoy the fruits of the bushes and the fruits of your labor as you bask in the sunshine and enjoy the views along the ridge and over the deep valley you just climbed. You can explore east or west along the ridge, or just stop here to rest in one of the local meadows before descending Mesatchee back to your starting point.

62. Fifes Ridge

Round trip: 8 miles
Hiking time: 7 hours
High point: 6500 feet
Elevation gain: 3100 feet
Best hiking time: July through October
Map: Green Trails Bumping Lake No. 271
Contact: Wenatchee National Forest, Naches Ranger District,
(509) 653-2205

The tightly clumped spires of Fifes Ridge present a formidable sight from any vantage point, but as you hike closer to them, the rocky ridge appears ever-more menacing and imposing. Perhaps that's partly because the trail you have to hike to get close to the precipitous ridge can be menacing and imposing in its own right. You'll climb steeply and steadily, earning the views with every step forward. Fortunately, the views are worth it, and not just the views at the end of the route. As you climb, you'll enjoy great local scenery as the trail climbs a rugged little alpine creek valley and occasionally darts out to great viewpoints midway up the mountain. The long, broad basin of the American River and the long, sweeping line of American Ridge stretch out before you every time you gain a vantage point, while Fifes Peak and its ragged, jagged ridgeline tower above you.

To get there, from Chinook Pass drive east on State Route 410 for 13.5 miles, passing Pleasant Valley Campground, and turn left onto a poorly marked dirt road just past milepost 82. Drive a short distance up to the lower parking area.

Start hiking up the dirt road, reaching an upper parking area (accessible only to high-clearance vehicles) in 0.25 mile. The trail starts here, crossing into the Norse Peak Wilderness Area just past the end of the road. The route follows Wash Creek upstream, meandering through a forest filled with

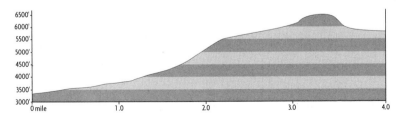

The top of Fifes Ridge provides good views of the American River Valley, William O. Douglas Wilderness, and Norse Peak Wilderness.

vanilla leaf and Indian pipe. Wash Creek has lived up to its name, having washed out a section of the old trail a few years ago, pushing the path up onto the low bench above the creekbed.

About a mile into the walk, the trail turns steep as it follows the now-steeply pitched creekbed up-valley. The heavily forested valley provides a cool environment in which to hike, even during the heat of summer, but the steepness of the trail will still have you sweating buckets. Fortunately, the trail crosses the creek frequently, providing ample opportunity for your dog to drink and dip to cool off.

Nearly 3 miles from the trailhead, the path climbs onto a low section of Fifes Ridge and turns east to ascend the ragged rocks of the upper section of the ridgeline. Just past the 3-mile mark, you'll cross a rocky summit, affording wonderful views west to the true summit of Fifes Peak— vertical walls of rock shoot skyward to form the craggy mountaintop. You can also look east along the ridge to view the rampartlike spires and towers of Fifes Ridge. Scan the treetops on the slopes below you and you might spot the nests of local raptors. During one early summer outing,

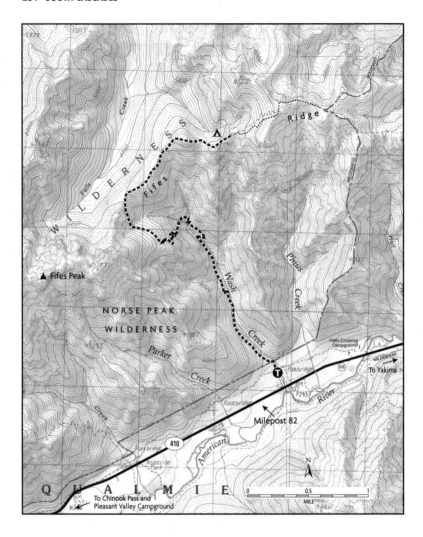

Parka and I watched a large hawk guard its nestlings just below us.

You can stop at this viewpoint and enjoy the panorama over a leisurely lunch, or push on another mile along the ridgetop trail, finding small meadows higher on the ridge with worthwhile campsites nestled among them (unless there is lingering snow to melt, the campsites are dry). At this point, around 4 miles, the trail begins to fade and disappear, and because there are few views and no campsites beyond this point, hikers should turn back here.

63. Cougar Lakes

Round trip: 12 miles
Hiking time: 7 hours
High point: 5400 feet
Elevation gain: 1800 feet
Best hiking time: July through October
Map: Green Trails Bumping Lake No. 271
Contact: Wenatchee National Forest, Naches Ranger District,
(509) 653-2205

The lakes may be named for big cats, but they were made for big dogs. Cougar Lakes are rimmed by gently sloped, sandy banks perfect for romping, swimming, and sunning after a long dusty hike. Too cold for you? Well, just toss a stick for the dog while you enjoy the sun-drenched beach and the stunning views of the House Rock monolith towering over the lake basin. Once you have tired of the stick-toss, and Bowser has tired of swimming and romping, pop up into the grassy meadows to the west of the lake. The dog can dry off by rubbing and rolling in the grass, and you can scan the talus slopes below House Rock, looking for the ever-present white specks of wildlife. Look closer and you'll see the blobs moving slowly across the steep (sometimes vertical) rock slopes. Look closer still and you'll see these are mountain goats doing what mountain goats do best—balancing on precarious perches high above green meadows.

Don't see goats? Then pull your gaze off the cliffs and scan the meadows below the talus. See any brown blobs moving through the greenery? These are likely big mule deer, or possibly even some of the resident elk, browsing through the rich forage of the upper lake basin. You can find these big beasts around the lake, or anywhere along the trail because a large stable herd of elk has made the greater Bumping River basin its home. But even if the deer, elk, and mountain goats stay in hiding, you'll find a host of airborne wildlife along the route: from fearless camp robbers

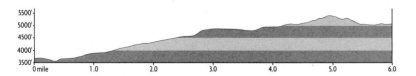

swooping in to help themselves to your sandwich, to brilliant blue scrub jays and Steller's jays screeching and whistling above camp (I think the screeching is out of frustration, because these timid birds must wish they were bold as their gray-hued cousins).

Note that encounters with horses and riders are likely on the Cougar Lakes Trail. It is important to restrain dogs by leash or strict voice command at all times to prevent your pooch from spooking one of the big beasts.

To get there, drive east from Chinook Pass for 19 miles and turn right (south) onto Bumping River Road. Drive 12 miles to the end of the paved road, at the entrance of the Bumping Lake Campground on the right. Continue south along the road, which becomes Forest Road 1800 near the end of the pavement. At 13.5 miles, the road forks. Stay right (still on FR 1800) and continue to the road's end and trailhead—about 4 miles farther on along the rough, dirt track.

The trail angles west of the large trailhead parking area (large, because it often accommodates numerous horse trailers), leading a level 0.5 mile through the open pine forest to the banks of Bumping River. Here, you'll have to get wet as the trail cuts through the river over a broad ford. Early in the year, when the snowpack is at full melt stage, the river can be deep and difficult to wade, but by midsummer on most years the water drops to no more than knee deep and the broad ford keeps the water flowing gently.

Once across the river, the trail starts a gentle climb—the route climbs nearly all the way to the trail's end, but never steeply—through the open forest. About 0.5 mile past the ford, the trail hits a four-way intersection. Our trail goes straight ahead, crossing the Bumping River Trail (Hike 64), which leads away to the left and right.

From this junction, the trail slants up the long, low ridge toward Swamp Lake. The trail here is badly routed and eroded from heavy use by hikers and horses for scores of years, and you and your dog might stumble and bumble over the exposed roots and hidden holes in the rough trail. Be careful. (The Forest Service has plans to reroute and rebuild the trail. Let's hope those plans come to fruition.)

At 3.2 miles, you'll pass the shallow (but still pretty) Swamp Lake. Good campsites can be found along the south shore of the lake, just off the trail. Continue past the lake and at mile 3.6, you'll break out of the forest into a broad meadow, only to dip back into the trees for a short,

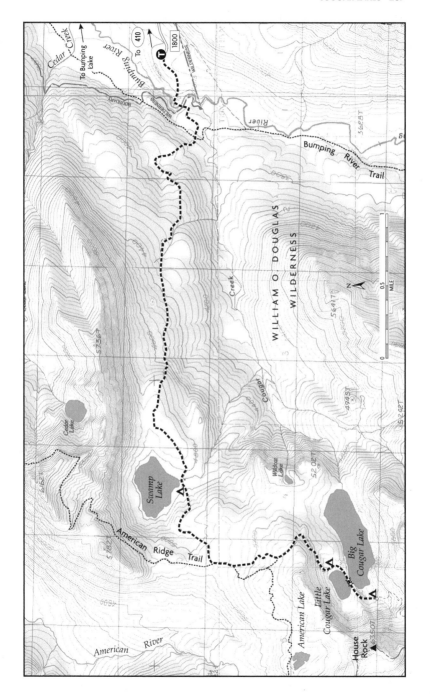

Small "bay" on Little Cougar Lake

forested section, then erupt back into meadow at a junction with the American Ridge Trail. Turn left on this long path and follow it a mere 0.25 mile before leaving it at another trail junction at 4.3 miles, this time turning left to climb the Cougar Lake Trail as it leads up a low ridge before dropping steeply into Cougar Lakes basin.

You'll find great campsites near the lower end of Little Cougar Lake (the first lake you encounter) and better camps on the west end of Big

Cougar at 5-plus miles. Note that the farther along the shores of the long, broad lake you go to find a camp, the longer your hike will be, with the farther camps sitting as much as 0.4 mile from the first camps. To get to these camps, skirt around the east end of Little Cougar and cross the small bridge between the two lakes. The meadows near the inlet stream of Big Cougar hold three good campsites, each with views of the lake and the towering hulk of House Rock to the west.

64. Bumping River to Fish Lake

Round trip: 14 miles
Hiking time: 7 hours
High point: 4200 feet
Elevation gain: 400 feet
Best hiking time: July through October
Map: Green Trails Bumping Lake No. 271
Contact: Wenatchee National Forest, Naches Ranger District, (509) 653-2205

Head up this trail anytime in September, pitch camp, and along about twilight, listen closely. If the weather has started to turn cold, with autumn obviously in the air, you might hear the most haunting sound of the American wilderness: bugling elk. A large herd of Rocky Mountain elk—known as wapiti to the Plains Indians—has established itself in the Bumping River valley. During its annual mating season, known as the rut, the males issue long, bugling calls, challenging each other for the rights to reproduce.

Autumn isn't the only time to visit, of course. This wilderness route can be enjoyed all summer, and though you may not hear the elk, you might very well see them as they browse through the rich forage of the forest and meadows along the river. The trail makes a great destination for hikers looking for an outing less intense than that on some of the higher alpine trails. The route from Bumping River to Fish Lake offers

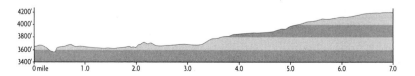

Elk herd along Bumping River near Fish Lake

modest ascents as it follows an easy grade along the river drainage, gradually gaining elevation to attain its upper reaches south of Crag Mountain. Good campsites are found at several sites along the way.

To get there, drive east from Chinook Pass for 19 miles and turn right (south) onto Bumping River Road. Drive 12 miles to the end of the paved road (at the entrance of the Bumping Lake Campground on the right). Continue south along the road, which becomes Forest Service Road 1800 near the end of the pavement. At 13.5 miles, the road forks. Stay right (still on FR 1800) and continue to the road's end and trailhead—about 4 miles farther on along the rough, dirt track.

Start out with a 0.5-mile hike along a level track to the edge of Bumping River, then—after stripping off your boots and socks—ford the river. Early in the year, when the snowpack is at full melt stage, the river can be deep and difficult to wade, but by midsummer (most years) the water drops to no more than knee deep and the broad ford keeps the water flowing gently.

From the river ford, the trail climbs gently for 0.5 mile to a four-way trail junction with the Cougar Lakes Trail (Hike 63). Turn left here and follow the Bumping River Trail up valley to its headwaters in Fish Lake.

The trail parallels the river for the next 8 miles, passing through the occasional forest glade and open meadow but generally sticking to open, airy pine forests, usually well above the river level. About 3 miles from the trailhead, you'll cross Red Rock Creek. There are decent forest camps here, on the banks of the creek. This is a good place for a rest stop if nothing more. Let the dog drink up and cool off in the creek before starting back up the trail. The trail ends at a junction with the Pacific Crest Trail (PCT), about 6.25 miles from the trailhead. Continue straight

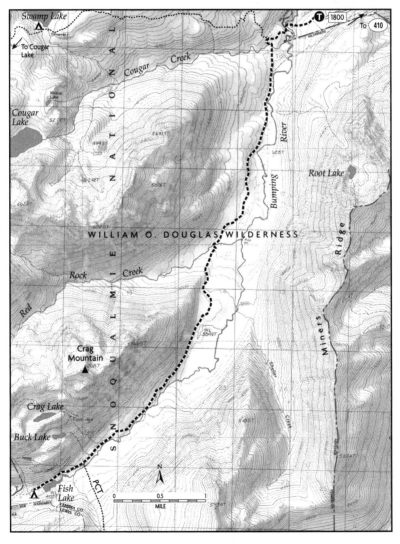

ahead on the right-hand fork of the PCT, staying along the river to reach Fish Lake in a little more than 0.5 mile. Fish Lake is a broad, swampy body of water at the end of the Bumping River valley. If you haven't seen elk yet, this is a likely place to spot them. The big ungulates love the rich grasses that grow around the lake basin.

65. Blankenship Meadows Ramble

Round trip: 9 miles
Hiking time: 7 hours (day hike or backpacking trip)
High point: 5400 feet
Elevation gain: 600 feet
Best hiking time: July through November
Maps: Green Trails Bumping Lake No. 271, White Pass No. 303
Contact: Wenatchee National Forest, Naches Ranger District,
(509) 653-2205

The William O. Douglas Wilderness is a haven for dog hiking, but it is best visited late in the summer and fall. The endless ponds, puddles, and lakes offer the reason why: bugs. This route crosses through Mosquito Valley, after all—you don't want to visit the area too early in the year when the bugs are at full strength. Wait until a few cold nights have knocked down the population before you bring the dog into this wilderness.

Once the biters are thinned out, though, the sprawling meadows and potholes offer unmatched opportunities for wilderness rambles, letting you explore on and off trail in an infinite array of loops. This route offers a good introduction to the varied wonders of the William O. Douglas Wilderness. It rolls around the octopus-shaped basin of the dual pools of Twin Sisters Lakes. It leads under the shadow of the cratered volcanic summit of Tumac Mountain. It ambles through the sprawling fields of Blankenship Meadows, around the Blankenship Lakes, and across the heart of broad Mosquito Valley. It leads through the home ranges of elk herds, mule deer populations, and black bears. You'll find yourself crossed

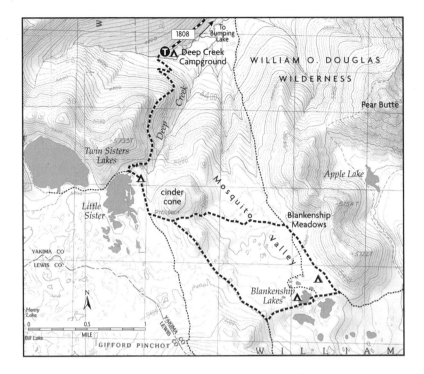

by the shadows of raptors aloft, and you'll be entertained by the antics of fearless camp-robber jays and flying squirrels. The dog, meanwhile, can romp through the long grassy meadows, paddle through the many deep lakes, and generally frolic with you under the wild blue sky.

To get there, drive east from Chinook Pass for 19 miles and turn right (south) onto Bumping River Road. Drive 12 miles to the end of the paved road (at the entrance of the Bumping Lake Campground on the right). Continue south along the road, which becomes Forest Road 1800 near the end of the pavement. At 13.5 miles, the road forks. Veer left onto FR 1808 and drive to the road's end, some 7 miles farther up the valley. The trailhead is found at the lower end of the Deep Creek Campground loop.

The trail climbs modestly from the trailhead, following around the end of a low ridge to reach the broad basin of Twin Sisters Lakes in about 1.5 miles. The forest along this early section of trail holds a good population of flying squirrels—you might catch a glimpse of them leaping and gliding from tree to tree. Also listen for the head-banging hammering of woodpeckers as they search for insects in the many dead snags standing in this old forest.

The trail past Twin Sisters is deeply eroded.

Twin Sisters Lakes provide many great campsites, and the sisters, though easily reached, are incredibly beautiful alpine lakes. But the easy hike in often means the lakes are crowded with noisy campers. Move on after a rest along the picturesque shores—enjoy a view over the Little Twin Sister to Tumac Mountain. Follow the trail as it leads south toward Tumac. About 0.5 mile after reaching the shores of the lake, the trail splits. To the right is a track that leads to the summit of Tumac Mountain. Stay left and skirt southeast around the flank of the cinder cone. In another 0.25 mile, reach another junction. This is the start of a loop. Stay right to complete the loop in a counterclockwise direction.

Hike nearly a mile south along this trail as it rolls gradually upward through thin forest and scattered clearings before reaching long broad meadows. About 3.5 miles from the trailhead, you'll find yet another trail junction (trails crisscross the William O. Douglas Wilderness like strands of a spider web—the loop-hiking alternatives are seemingly endless). At this most recent junction, turn left and amble east through the cluster of Blankenship Lakes. Find a campsite near these lakes, or continue on into the Blankenship Meadows. To find the meadows, continue on the trail, past the lakes, and turn left at 4.5 miles at yet another junction. This trail leads along the eastern fringe of a vast meadow area that stretches thousands of acres west and north, broken only by occasional narrow bands of forest. For assured solitude, head off into the meadows and find a campsite along the forest fringe deep in the meadow. Countless small ponds dot the area, providing drinking water for you and your dog.

To close the loop, continue along the Blankenship Meadows leg of the loop and at 6 miles, reach another junction. Turn left once more to hike a mile west, closing the loop at the junction just south of Twin Sisters Lakes. Hike north to those lakes and on out to the trailhead.

66. Yakima Rim

Round trip: 8-plus miles
Hiking time: 4 to 6 hours
High point: 3000 feet
Elevation gain: 1600 feet
Best hiking time: year-round
Maps: USGS 7.5-minute series Wymer, Ellensburg, Yakima East, Badger Pocket
Contact: Washington Department of Fish and Wildlife, (509) 575-2740
Warning: This trail crosses rattlesnake country. Dogs must be kept on leash at all times when rattlesnakes are active (warm summer and early fall months) to reduce the risk of snakebite. This trail is best visited in spring and autumn when the vipers are less active. But at all times, be aware that rattlesnakes may be encountered and know the proper actions to take in the event of snakebite.

Each spring, the desert hills near Ellensburg, Yakima, and the Tri-Cities burst with colorful blooms. During one short hike last spring, I counted

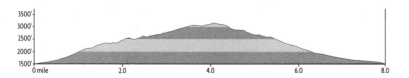

View of the cliffs above the Yakima River

more than two dozen species of wildflowers, all in full, glorious bloom. I also saw mule deer, bighorn sheep, ospreys, bald eagles, red-tailed hawks, an array of songbirds, and the signs of several small mammals, including an active badger burrow.

The eastern edge of the L.T. Murray Wildlife Refuge offers some of the best desert hiking in the state, with an amazing array of wildflowers filling the spring days with fragrant perfume and washing the dry brown hills with vibrant colors. Of course, come summer, the area is also home to rattlesnakes, scorpions, and black widow spiders, so watch where you and your dog tread. Note that this is a dry route with only one water source along the way. Provide lots of water for your dog, and check her often for dehydration.

To reach the Yakima Rim Trail, drive east on Interstate 90 to Ellensburg. Take exit 109 and drive south along State Route 821 (Canyon Road) through the Yakima River Canyon to a three-way junction with

SR 823 and Interstate 82. Turn right onto SR 823 toward Selah. In just under 2 miles, you'll encounter a T-intersection. Turn right (north) onto the North Wenas Road. Continue 2.6 miles to a small cinderblock fire station at a fork in the road. Veer right onto Gibson Road and proceed about 0.25 mile. Turn right onto Buffalo Road and follow this about a mile. You'll see a broad parking area on your left bounded by a high drift fence. You can park here, or drive through the gate (making sure to close it behind you) and proceed up a dirt track another mile to the

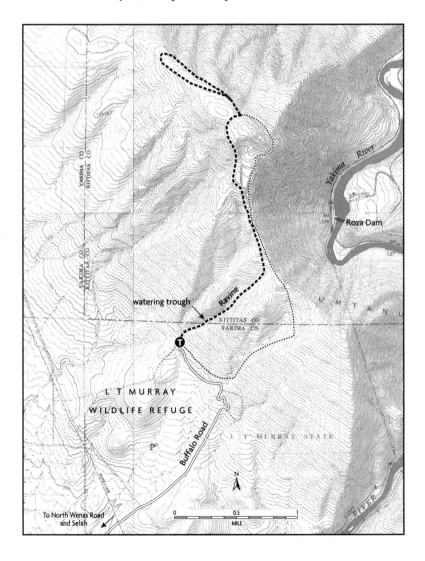

official trailhead. Start walking toward the rim from anywhere between these two parking areas.

The Yakima Rim Trail begins inside the elk drift fence—a tall stout fence used to prevent elk from drifting out of the refuge and into the adjacent rich farmlands. It climbs to the north through a broad ravine, passing a small A-frame shack—this is a feeding station of upland game birds. The ravine narrows in the first 0.25 mile, and the trail stays near the bottom of the narrow canyon, passing an old, spring-fed watering trough (the only water source along the route) about 0.5 mile from the trailhead. Keep your dog close at heel through the ravine section of the trail because there are porcupines and other critters lurking in the thick brambles of thorny bushes around the trail. There are also ticks aplenty, so be sure to check yourself and your dog for unwanted passengers.

In just more than a mile from the start, the ravine tapers away to nothing, and the trail reaches the rim of the Yakima River Canyon. Looking down the northeast side of the hill ridge, you see the blue-brown ribbon of the Yakima as it weaves through the tight rock-lined gorge. Roza Dam nestles astride the river far below your feet.

Turn left (north) and follow the trail as it hugs the rim of the river, keeping the river always in sight. Journey out as far as you like before returning.

For a little variety on the return, leave the trail as it turns back down the ravine section and continue south along the ridge edge. In less than a mile, you'll find a broad, gentle valley leading back down toward the trailhead. Hike cross-country down this side valley to experience the unspoiled desert country. Mingled with the ever-present sagebrush are an array of wildflowers: lupine, balsamroot, bitterroot, yarrow, sunflowers, and daisies.

As the flowers color the landscape, they also perfume the air. Sage provides a constant, steady background on the wind, but as the warm sun heats the new plant growth, an intoxicating blend of scents await you. The air itself becomes a veritable stew of odors as the ever-present sage is joined by the pungent odors wafting from the leaves of wild parsleys and onions. Through it all swirls the sweet aroma of new grasses and blooming flowers.

When you return home, remember to check for ticks, and also carefully check your dog's ears and eyes for foxtails—these spiny little grass seeds stick to hairs and can work their way into sensitive tissues if left in place.

67. Umtanum Canyon

Round trip: 8-plus miles
Hiking time: 4 to 6 hours
High point: 1900 feet
Elevation gain: 500 feet
Best hiking time: year-round
Maps: USGS 7.5-minute series Wymer, Ellensburg
Contact: Washington Department of Fish and Wildlife, (509) 575-2740
Warning: This trail crosses rattlesnake country. Dogs must be kept on
    leash at all times when rattlesnakes are active (warm summer and
    early fall months) to reduce the risk of snakebite. This trail is best
    visited in spring and autumn when the vipers are less active. But
    at all times, be aware that rattlesnakes may be encountered and
    know the proper actions to take in the event of snakebite.

This isn't your typical desert canyon. Though the hills around it are dry
and covered with sage and cactus, a pretty creek pierces the heart of the
canyon, providing a unique riparian ecosystem in the midst of the desert
ecology zone. In addition to all the critters you'd expect to see in the high
desert—deer, coyotes, rabbits, rattlesnakes, and raptors—you'll find other,
unexpected species, too. Beavers have claimed large sections of the creek,
creating vast pools behind tall dams. Aspen stands quiver and rustle along
the beaver pools. Badgers burrow in the banks of the creek. And a sizeable
herd of bighorn sheep roams the canyon bottom and the steep valley walls.

To get there, from Ellensburg, drive south on the Canyon Road (State
Route 821) along the Yakima River and turn west into a large parking area
near milepost 17.

The trail begins on a suspension bridge over the Yakima. Some dogs
may be hesitant to cross this wide, yet bouncy, bridge. Try a short leash
and a fistful of tasty treats to encourage the pooch to cross.

Once over the river, cross the railroad tracks (the tracks are active so check
both ways before crossing) and find the official start of the Umtanum Creek

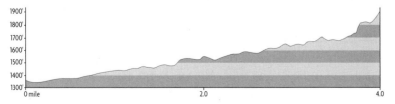

On desert hikes, dogs will need lots of water. (Kelly McCaffrey)

Trail. Head up the trail for 4 miles or so, then come back, for a nice day hike. The path rolls westward up the gentle canyon, passing an old homestead a mile up the trail. You can still spot the old foundation work and pluck sweet apples from the trees in the brushy old farm orchard.

The trail moves back and forth across the valley floor, sometimes nearly dropping into the creek, other times pushing against the valley wall. You can also ramble off trail to explore the many beaver dams and grassy meadows. Here and there, stands of aspen alternate with the more common locust and alders.

The route follows the creek upstream, crossing it once. Spring and fall

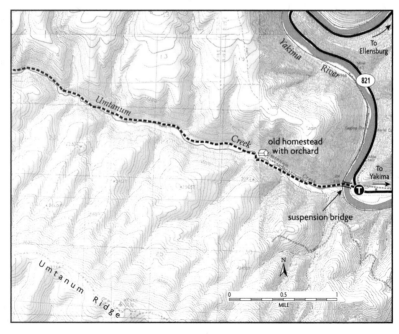

are the ideal times to visit this creek-side trail. Not only are the chances of encountering spectacular wildflower displays great in the spring but these are also the seasons when the wildlife is most active—with the notable exception of snakes. Come high summer, rattlesnakes are out in force in this region, so to avoid the vipers, visit in the cool months when they aren't active.

68. Tatoosh Lakes View

Round trip: 7 miles
Hiking time: 6 hours
High point: 5400 feet
Elevation gain: 2500 feet
Best hiking time: July through September
Map: Green Trails Packwood No. 302
Contact: Gifford Pinchot National Forest, Cowlitz Valley Ranger District, Packwood Information Center, (360) 494-0600

Thick old-growth forests of Douglas fir and western hemlock line the lower trail, while ridgetop meadows and clear alpine vistas await you on the upper trail. The path climbs steeply and steadily, giving you and your dog a good workout. But the payoff for that work includes glorious views of Mount Rainer and the Goat Rocks Peaks, as well as the many rocky summits of the Tatoosh Range. You can look down on the shimmering waters of Tatoosh Lakes, or if you are up for the extra effort, you can drop down a steep side trail to the lakeshore, finding great camps and fabulous views from around the lakes basin.

To get there, drive U.S. Highway 12 to the town of Packwood. Near the east end of town, turn north onto Skate Creek Road (the Packwood Ranger Station sits on the south side of the highway, opposite Skate Creek Road). Drive 4 miles on Skate Creek Road and turn north (right) onto Forest Road 5270. Continue 7 miles up this road along Butter Creek to the trailhead on the right. The trail is poorly marked, and the parking

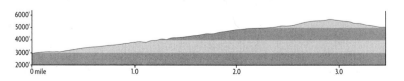

Josh and Moby on the Tatoosh Lakes Trail (Kelly McCaffrey)

area consists of a wide spot in the road. The trail is located about 1.5 miles past a junction with FR 5270-990 on the left.

From the road, you will climb steeply, starting with a scramble up the road bank and a dive into the forest. The path slants upward through the thick Douglas-fir forest, gaining elevation steadily as the trail settles into a long series of switchbacks. The old forest sports a broken canopy, which lets lots of sunshine filter through to the forest floor to support

the sprouting of many forest wildflowers around the path. Look for vanilla leaf, Indian pipe, avalanche lilies, trilliums, Canadian dogwood, and
more amidst the trees. As the trail climbs, the forest opens onto broad,
sidehill meadows filled with even more varied wildflowers.

At 2.5 miles, the trail crests the ridge and in a few hundred yards, reaches
a trail junction. To the left, a faint trail drops to the north, entering Mount
Rainier National Park. Skip this trail (remember, dogs are prohibited in the
park's backcountry) and turn right instead. This path leads south to another trail junction. To the left, a trail drops steeply into the Tatoosh Lakes
basin. Unless you're camping, you should stick to the ridge top because
you'll find better views for less work up here. Keep right once more to stay
on the main trail as it leads out the ridgeline. In a little more than 0.5 mile,
reach a rocky knob at the edge of the ridge. From here, you have unsur-
passed views of Mount Rainier, the Goat Rocks Peaks, Mount Adams, and
on clear days, Mount St. Helen's abbreviated top.

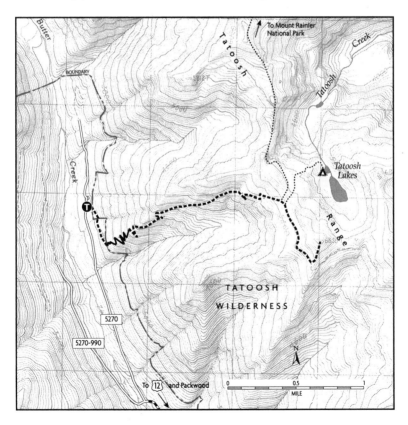

69. Packwood Lake

Round trip: 9 miles
Hiking time: 6 hours (day hike or backpacking trip)
High point: 3200 feet
Elevation gain: about 500 feet
Best hiking time: May through November
Map: Green Trails Packwood No. 302
Contact: Gifford Pinchot National Forest, Cowlitz Valley Ranger
District, Packwood Information Center, (360) 494-0600

Sometimes, all a dog wants is a gentle walk, followed by a leisurely swim and a relaxing evening in camp. Indeed, this is a recipe for relaxation that many human hikers appreciate, too. Packwood Lake is the perfect place to practice this laid-back trail lifestyle, especially late in the spring and early in the autumn when the hordes of summer hikers have gone home.

This route provides an experience in deep river valley forests and along a broad, low-elevation lake. The trail leads to sprawling Packwood Lake with its popular campgrounds and excellent fishing opportunities (make sure that after fishing, you account for all your lures and broken strands of line—you don't want any hooks or monofilament to entangle a dog during a paddle around the lake).

To get there, from Packwood, follow U.S. Highway 12 to the east end of town and turn southeast onto Forest Service Road 1262 (found right next to the USFS Packwood Ranger Station). Continue southeast on Road 1262 for 6 miles to the trailhead parking lot.

The Packwood Lake Trail (No. 78) weaves through older second-growth forests for 4 miles, with views limited to the trees around you. As the trail nears the lake, you'll find peak-a-boo views up the valley to the jagged crest of Goat Rocks. At 4 miles, the trail reaches an old ranger station at the end of the lake (2900 feet). A wide wooden footbridge crosses the outlet stream. Pass the campground just after crossing the bridge. The

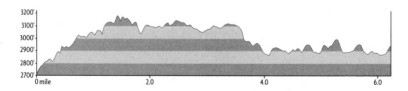

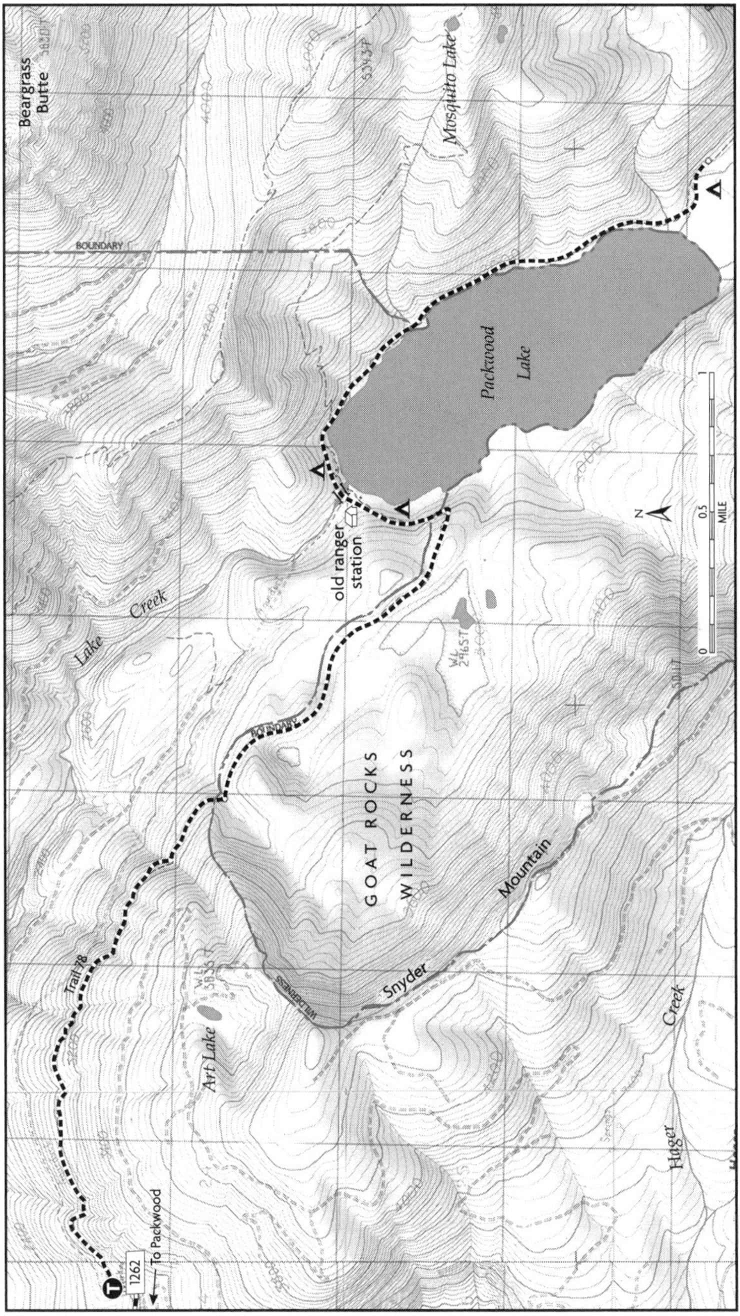
Beargrass Butte
BOUNDARY
Lake
Creek
old ranger station
Packwood Lake
Mosquito Lake
N
0
0.5
1
MILE
BOUNDARY
GOAT ROCKS
WILDERNESS
Mountain
Snyder
WILDERNESS
Trail 78
Art Lake
Creek
Hager
1262
To Packwood

Here's a good reason why fires aren't recommended in wilderness areas—they mess up your dog. Parka after a swim and a roll.

trail continues around the end of the lake and leads east along the north side of the mile-long lake. Many campsites can be found along the lake, with great views south and east up into the Goat Rocks Peaks and wilderness area.

70. Sand Lake

Round trip: 6.5 miles
Hiking time: 4 hours
High point: 5300 feet
Elevation gain: 900 feet
Best hiking time: June through late October
Map: Green Trails White Pass No. 303
Contact: Wenatchee National Forest, Naches Ranger District,
   (509) 653-2205

This is a trip for the whole family. Load up the kids, the dog, and even the grandparents for this easy walk in the pristine Northwest forest. The elevation gain is minimal, the scenery is pretty, and the lake at the end of the hike offers a perfect swimming experience. While many wilderness lakes stay ice cold throughout the summer, Sand Lake is just shallow enough for the sun to warm it to a comfortable temperature for cooling off during a hot summer hike. The smooth, sandy bottom is a comfort to boot-tired feet, too.

Indeed, there are a slew of lakes in the southern half of the William O. Douglas Wilderness worth visiting, and Sand is the second you'll pass on this trip. Deer Lake is the first you'll encounter, and between them you'll find acres of wildflower meadows and cool stands of pine forests.

To get there, drive U.S. Highway 12 to White Pass. The Pacific Crest Trail-North Trailhead is found just east of the ski area and the White Pass Campground. Turn onto a poorly marked road on the east end of Leech Lake and drive a few hundred yards to the trailhead, found between the horse camp and car campground.

Your pooch will be eager to lead you up this trail—be sure that the leash is secure—because there are multitudes of scents awaiting an eager nose. Deer, elk, and mountain goats roam the forests and hills. There are bobcats, cougars, coyotes, and black bears. Badgers, mountain beavers, snowshoe hares, weasels, martens, and foxes dodge and scurry through

the brush. Ptarmigan, grouse, and quail flutter through the air and roost in the trees. And birds of prey, from golden eagles to small kestrels, soar the thermal winds overhead.

Starting north on the Pacific Crest Trail, you'll enter the forest at the trailhead and stay under cover of trees nearly all the way to Sand Lake. The trail gains more than 900 feet in elevation over the first mile, but then it levels for the rest of the trek to the lake. After that first mile, the forest opens onto a scattering of clearings and small meadows, allowing sun to filter down to the blooming flowers and ripening berries that line the trail.

At 1.3 miles, a small side trail on the right leads downhill to Dog Lake (see also Hike 71). On your return trip, you can take this 1-mile trail if you want a little variety; though from Dog Lake, you'll have to return the way you came or hike a mile along the shoulder of US 12 to get back to your vehicle.

To continue on to Sand Lake, stay on the main track and in another mile, reach a second spur trail, this time on the left. Take a few minutes to hike the 100 yards down this trail to Deer Lake, a forest-lined lake. Dogs and kids alike will enjoy a dip in this cool mountain lake before continuing on with the hike.

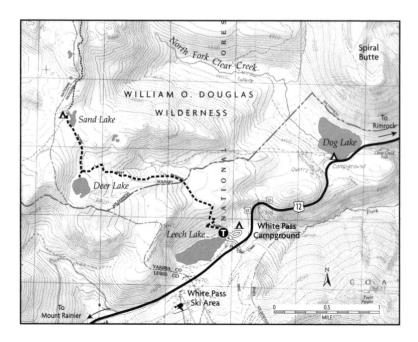

Snow-swollen lake invades the trail

The last mile to Sand Lake crosses several broad meadows (in early summer, the meadows are more like marshes) and offers the best chance of seeing big critters like deer and elk. Meadows push right up against Sand Lake, though so do stands of timber. The lake is actually a catch basin for runoff from melting snow. There is no permanent stream running into the lake, nor out of it. As snow melts, the water rolls into the lake basin, where it gathers, swelling the lake in early summer. After the majority of the snow has melted off, the lake waters slowly recede as some evaporates and some perks down through the porous volcanic soil.

Ideally, you'll visit here in late July to early August, when the waters are low enough to be off the lakeside trail but still high enough to be clear and cool. Folks who want to spend the night (it's a great destination for the kids' first backpacking trip) will find plenty of high, grassy campsites around the lake basin—just be sure to stay well back from the water so as not to intrude on the scenery and to protect the clean waters of the lake itself.

71. Dumbbell Lake Loop

Round trip: 11 miles
Hiking time: 7 hours (day hike or backpacking trip)
High point: 5200 feet
Elevation loss: 1000 feet
Best hiking time: June through late October
Map: Green Trails White Pass No. 303
Contact: Wenatchee National Forest, Naches Ranger District,
    (509) 653-2205

From Dog Lake(!), canine hikers and their human companions are swept north around Cramer Mountain and back under the shadow of conical Spiral Butte. This loop explores the forests, meadows, lakes, and mountains of the southwestern section of the William O. Douglas Wilderness. All hikers—two- and four-legged varieties—will appreciate the gently rolling nature of the route. No big ascents, no big descents, as the trail weaves among the lakes and meadows.

The loop is a good length for a day hike, and because the route is relatively flat and the trail generally well maintained, hikers can maintain a good pace; you should have no trouble exploring the basic loop in a single

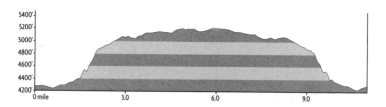

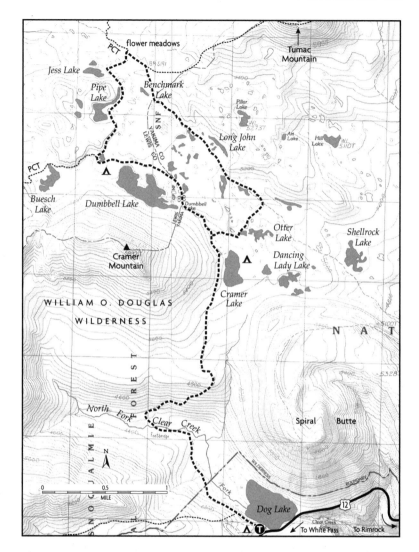

day. The recommended way to enjoy this trip, though, is as an overnight backpacking trip, especially if you are an angler. Dumbbell Lake supports a strong population of cutthroat and eastern brook trout. Nonanglers will also enjoy camping at Dumbbell—the lake tends to warm nicely by mid-summer (at least, the glacierlike chill is removed by the ever-present sunshine) making it a fine option for swimmers who lack a thick coat of fur to block out the cold.

You can add extra miles by using the many different connector trails

Parka wading in twilight

that lead further north into the wilderness, past additional lakes and meadows.

To get there, drive U.S. Highway 12 to White Pass and continue east about 1.5 miles to Dog Lake Campground on the left (north) side of the highway. Park here.

Head up the trail as it climbs around the west side of Dog Lake and skirts north around the tall cone of Spiral Butte. The path rolls north through forest and swampy meadows, climbing modestly from the lake. The route gains just 800 feet in the 4 miles needed to reach Cramer Lake on the eastern flank of Cramer Mountain.

A quarter mile north of Cramer Lake, you'll reach a trail junction. Stay left and head north through fields of flowers and small stands of trees to reach Dumbbell Lake at 4.5 miles (named for the shape of the lake, not the intelligence of those who camp here). Fine campsites are found all around the long, narrow lake. Scramblers can find a route to the top of Cramer Mountain (5992 feet) from either lake—just push through the brush on the lower flank of the mountain and you'll have an easy climb on the treeless upper slopes. From the top of the Cramer, you'll find fabulous views of the entire William O. Douglas Wilderness.

To continue with the hike, follow the trail around the north side of the lake to reach a trail junction that heads left toward Buesch Lake about

5.3 miles from the trailhead. Turn right here and follow a short, 0.75-mile trail east and then north through pond-dotted meadows to another trail junction (Pacific Crest Trail) just past Jess Lake in a long, broad meadow.

Turn right at this junction and head south, still in meadows and thin stands of trees, to another junction at 6.3 miles with a trail that heads left (southeast) past Shellrock Lake. Turn right to complete the circle. Pass pretty Otter Lake in 0.25 mile, then reach the main trail just north of Cramer Lake in another 0.5 mile. Turn south on the trail and retrace your steps to the trailhead.

Throughout this hike, the trail passes a slew of tiny unnamed ponds and potholes—some are big enough to be clear and refreshingly cool, others are tiny and good for little besides breeding mosquitoes (early summer hikers take note: bring plenty of good bug repellent!). The meadows and forest clearings offer frequent views of Mount Adams and the Goat Rock Peaks to the south, Mount Rainier to the northwest, and Spiral Butte to the east.

72. Shoe Lake

Round trip: 14 miles
Hiking time: 8 hours (day hike—no camping allowed at lake)
High point: 6600 feet
Elevation gain: 2200 feet
Best hiking time: July through October
Map: Green Trails White Pass No. 303
Contact: Wenatchee National Forest, Naches Ranger District, (509) 653-2205

This is what the Pacific Crest Trail (PCT) is all about—dancing along a steep, knife-edged ridge at the top of the mountain range. The trail from White Pass climbs through thin forests and crosses stunning alpine meadows,

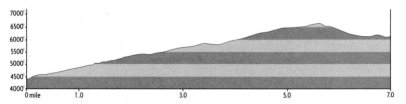

reaching a gorgeous little alpine lake, but it's the section in the middle—the long traverse under Hogback Mountain—that sets this off as an excellent example of the PCT.

Still, as beautiful as that section may be, it's unfair to suggest it is the only highlight of the route. The Shoe Lake Basin is simply stunning in its beauty, despite having been nearly loved to death. Indeed, the area is recovering nicely from years of extensive use (some argue, overuse). The heavy use and abuse of the meadows around the lake forced the land managers

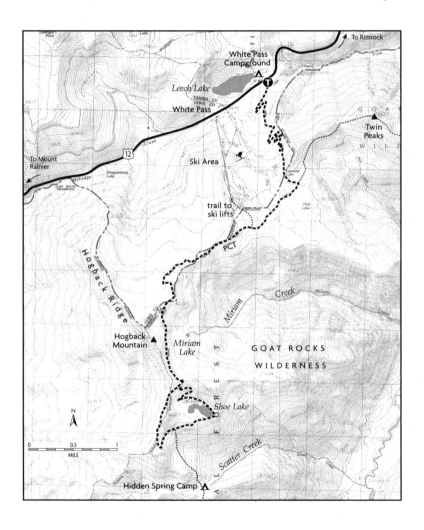

Shoe Lake is named for its horseshoe shape.

(U.S. Forest Service) to close the area to camping. Despite the camping closures, though, the lake—and the hike to it—is stunning enough that a long day hike to the area is well worth the effort. Note that backpackers can find fine campsites just a mile south of the lake basin near Hidden Springs.

Campers overran Shoe Lake in the 1980s, and the fragile meadows around the pond were crisscrossed with social trails and dotted with bare-earth tent sites. In the years since camping has been prohibited, the vegetation has slowly recovered, though faint trails still show through the wildflowers.

To get there, drive U.S. Highway 12 to White Pass. The PCT-South Trailhead is located just east of the ski area on the south side of the highway just across US 12 from the White Pass Campground.

The trail angles southeast for the first 2.5 miles, skirting the edge of the White Pass Ski Area. This initial section climbs modestly through open pine forests, gaining 1000 feet in those 2.5 miles, to a junction with the Twin Peaks Trail. There, our route bears west (right) and the forests opens even more, as the trail weaves between sun-dappled woods and sun-filled meadows. At 3.5 miles, a short spur trail leads north to the top of the ski lifts. The PCT, though, continues southwest along the east flank of Hogback Mountain.

This remnant of the once-great Goat Rocks volcano is a jagged peak with long, knife-sharp ridges leading north and south from the summit. The trail hugs the southern ridge, contouring along the 6400-foot level. A few wildflowers struggle for survival on this steep slope, but mostly the trail slides across scree slopes and pika-playgrounds on the curving ridge wall. At just more than 6 miles from the trail, the PCT crosses a narrow shoulder of the mountain at 6600 feet. Pause here to soak up the incredible views before you—the horseshoe-shaped Shoe Lake lies 400 feet below, while far beyond the lake to the southeast is the cliff-lined Pinegrass Ridge.

From the ridge top, it is another 0.5 mile down to the lakeshore and then there's 0.5-mile trail around the lake to explore. Wildflower meadows surround the lake, with a small grove of shade-providing evergreens on the peninsula in the center of the lake's horseshoe. Those who insist on camping nearby should return to the PCT and continue south about a mile to Hidden Spring Camp.

73. Juniper Ridge

Round trip: 7 miles
Hiking time: 5 hours
High point: 5600 feet
Elevation gain: 2000 feet
Best hiking time: July through October
Map: Green Trails McCoy Peak No. 333
Contact: Gifford Pinchot National Forest, Cowlitz Valley Ranger District, Randle office, (360) 497-1100

Ridgetop meadows stretching for miles await you here, though you'll work hard to reap those rewards. The trail climbs steeply from the low valley bottom to the high ridgeline, but once aloft on those airy plains, you'll stroll through endless fields of flowers, basking in the glorious views

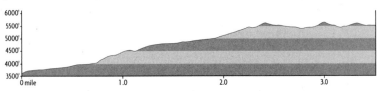

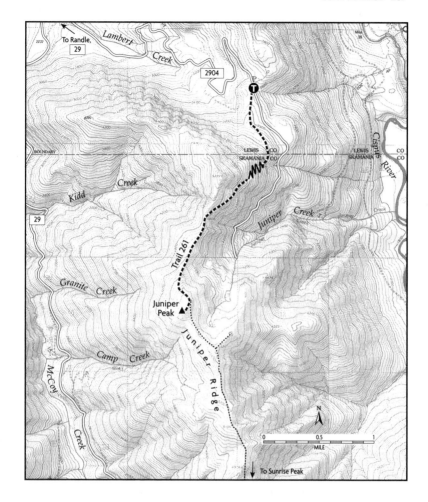

of the south Cascades peaks, from the mammoth volcanoes—Mount Rainier, Mount Adams, Mount St. Helens, and even Oregon's Mount Hood—to the modest little knobs and knolls that make up the heart of the range—Juniper Peak, Jumbo Peak, Sunrise, and Dark Mountain, among others.

To get there, from Randle on U.S. Highway 12 drive 1 mile south on Forest Road 25. At the first main road junction, turn left (east) onto FR 23. Continue south 9 miles and turn right onto FR 28. Continue 1 mile and turn left onto FR 29. Four miles down FR 29, turn left onto FR 2904 and in another 4 miles, look for the trailhead on the right (south) side of the road at about 3600 feet elevation.

Thin forest near base of Juniper Peak

The Juniper Ridge Trail (No. 261) climbs south from the trailhead, passing through an old clearcut before ascending through long, looping switchbacks up the snout of the ridge. For more than 2 miles the trail climbs, fortunately offering frequent photogenic views out over the forest and mountains to the north. The path rolls in a long, straight ascent from here, following the ridgeline up and over knobs and knolls, through long, unbroken fields of flowers, to reach the rocky top of Juniper Peak at about 3.5 miles. Stop and rest here. Take lots of pictures, provide lots of water for your dog, and pass some time dozing in the sun or just gazing out over the grand panoramas laid out before you. Mount Rainier dominates the northern skyline. The ragged line of the Goat Rocks Peaks, punctuated at their southern end by the tall cone of Mount Adams, captures the eastern horizon. Nearby, Sunrise Peak and Shark Rock can be seen across the long, green valleys of the Dark Divide. Your dog can romp and play, fetching sticks and scenting the wind, while you rest. If you want to extend your hike, continue south along Juniper Ridge—all the way to Sunrise Peak (7 miles from the trailhead) if you have the time and energy—before returning to the trailhead.

74. Dark Meadow

Round trip: 5.6–plus miles
Hiking time: 5 hours
High point: 4450 feet
Elevation gain: 600 feet
Best hiking time: July through October
Map: Green Trails McCoy Peak No. 333
Contact: Gifford Pinchot National Forest, Cowlitz Valley Ranger District, Randle office, (360) 497-1100

Dogs dig Dark Meadow. The trail passes through deep old forest, ascending modestly to high meadow-rimmed ridgelines. As the trail ascends, the views begin to develop, and the thick fir forest thins and fades away entirely when the trail enters Dark Meadow near the ridge top. The stunning meadow is filled with wildflowers, panoramic vistas, and a wide variety of wildlife. The views encompass Mount Adams, Mount St. Helens, and Jumbo Peak just to the north. There's no stable water source so hikers must carry plenty of fluids for themselves and their canine companions.

To get there, from Randle drive 1 mile south on Forest Road 25. At the first main road junction, turn left (east) onto FR 23. Continue south on FR 23 for nearly 25 miles, turning right (south) onto FR 2325. Drive 5.3 miles on this road and locate a small, unmarked trail on the right (west) side of the road, elevation 3900 feet.

From the road, head up the faint trail as it enters the forest, climbing gradually through the trees. If you have a savvy trail dog, trust her nose and eyes to pick out the sometimes-overgrown path, or just keep climbing, knowing that you'll eventually reach the Dark Meadow Trail no matter where you crest the ridge.

The path leads upward, slanting southeast. The trees give way to forest glades, laced with fruit-rich huckleberry brambles, and then broader fields of berries. Soon, even the huckleberry bushes fall back and the trail enters

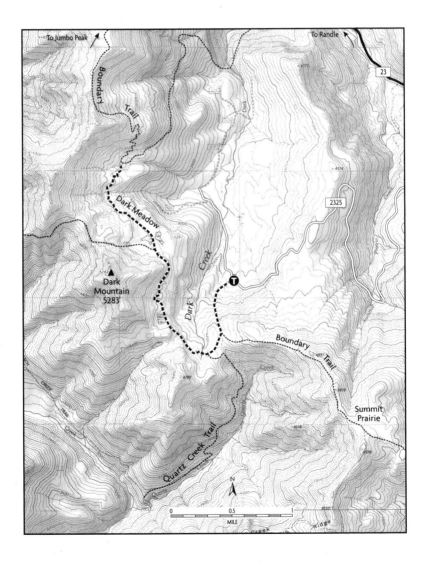

The sandy meadows below Dark Mountain

long, sweeping meadows atop the ridge. At the junction with the Boundary Trail at about 1 mile, turn right and hike north along the long ridgeline on the flank of Dark Mountain. The trail drops off the ridge and enters the broad, shallow cirque of Dark Meadow about 2.8 miles from the car, and for the next mile the trail crosses these fragrant flower fields. A good turn-around point is the Boundary Trail junction at about 4 miles.

To continue your trek and make a longer day of it, continue north (turn left at the junction) on the Boundary Trail, reaching Jumbo Peak about 2.5 miles past the meadows.

75. Snowgrass Flats/Goat Lake Loop

Round trip: 11.25 miles
Hiking time: 8 hours (day hike or backpacking trip)
High point: 6550 feet
Elevation gain: 1920 feet
Best hiking time: late July through October
Maps: Green Trails White Pass No. 303, Blue Lake No. 334, Walupt Lake No. 335
Contact: Gifford Pinchot National Forest, Cowlitz Valley Ranger District, Packwood Information Center, (360) 494-0600

The loop up through Jordan Basin, Goat Lake valley, and Snowgrass Flats makes a wonderful outing for all hikers, but the open meadows and modest climbs are perfect for trail dogs. The path lets you wander alongside

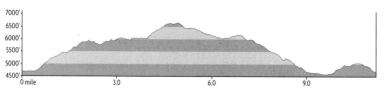

Resting at a frozen Goat Lake (Ken Konigsmark)

your pooch, with enough water along the route to keep her fully hydrated and cool even in the heat of summer. The trail makes a long day, or a comfortable overnight, but the elevation change is modest and not too taxing.

But what does the trail really offer, you ask. Simple: It offers nearly everything you could want on an alpine ramble. Vast wildflower fields, stunning panoramas that include towering glaciated peaks, high alpine meadows, cold alpine lakes, tons of birds and wildlife, and a good chance at solitude despite the incredible beauty of the route.

To get there, from Packwood drive west on U.S. Highway 12 for 2 miles and turn left (south) onto Forest Road 21 (Johnson Creek Road). Continue about 15.5 miles on the sometimes-rough gravel road before turning left (east) onto FR 2150, signed Chambers Lake Campground. In 3.5 miles, turn right onto a short dirt road that leads into the trailhead parking area, just above the Chambers Lake Campground.

Hiking the loop clockwise, start up the Goat Ridge Trail (No. 95) as it climbs the snout of Goat Ridge. The first part of the route ascends through old pine and fir forests. The airy woodlands present an open canopy with

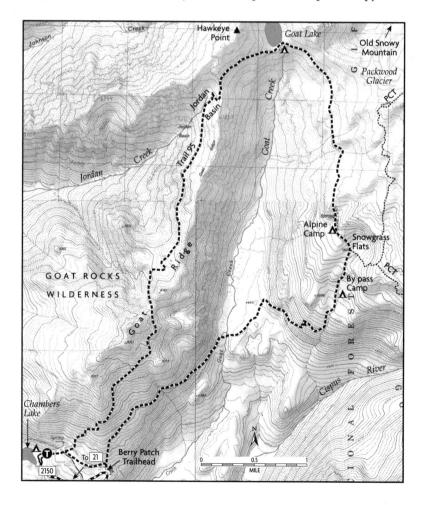

lots of sunshine reaching the forest floor. Taking advantage of that plentiful light is a sprawling mass of huckleberry bushes. The berries aren't as big and juicy as some found in more open meadows, but the fruit offers a tasty treat to hikers plodding up the steep trail. The berries are so tasty and so plentiful that you shouldn't be surprised if your dog starts plunking them off the bushes herself. Even dogs can't resist this succulent fruit.

A small side trail branches off to the left at 1.5 miles—this is merely a scenic alternative that loops out around the steep west slope of Goat Ridge while the main trail hugs the meadow-dotted east side of the ridge. Just over 0.5 mile down the main trail, the secondary trail rejoins it (taking this alternative trail adds a mile to the main route).

Just after the first trail junction, the forest begins to open up: small forest glades scattered along the ridge finally give way to broad, rolling meadows as the trail crosses under a large talus slope at 2.5 miles. Marmots thrive in this rocky slope, and so do predators—it was here that I encountered the largest coyote I've ever seen, hunting the whistling marmots. That's good cause to keep Fido on a firm leash—you don't want your dog caught in a dustup with a coyote.

Above this point, the trail climbs steeply into the flower-filled meadows. The views gradually improve as you ascend until, at 3.8 miles, the trail crosses over Goat Ridge in a deep saddle under Hawkeye Point. This ridge provides outstanding views west into the wildflower wonderland of Jordan Creek basin to the west and Goat Creek basin to the east. Far beyond, look out over the gray-green forests of the Cispus River valley to the west.

From the ridge crossing, the trail traverses around the upper basin of Goat Creek to reach Goat Lake at 5.3 miles. There are a few campsites along the shores of the intensely cold lake. The lake is nestled in a north-face, rocky cirque and frequently has an ice shelf covering a portion of the water year-round.

Continue southeast as the trail completes the traverse around the head of Goat Creek basin and at 7 miles, reach Alpine Camp in the meadows above Snowgrass Flats. Camping is prohibited in the flats, but excellent tent sites can be found in Alpine Camp. To close the loop, from Alpine Camp descend through Snowgrass Flats and drop down to the Berry Patch Trailhead in 4 miles, then take the 0.5-mile connection trail to the Goat Ridge Trailhead where you started.

76. Nannie Ridge/Sheep Lake

Round trip: 9 miles
Hiking time: 9 hours (day hike or backpacking trip)
High point: 5800 feet
Elevation gain: 1800 feet
Best hiking time: early July through early October
Map: Green Trails Walupt Lake No. 335
Contact: Gifford Pinchot National Forest, Cowlitz Valley Ranger
   District, Packwood Information Center, (360) 494-0600

While hiking trails like this, Parka learned to pick berries. The endless
tangle of huckleberry bushes offers such a bounty of sweet fruit that humans and dogs alike find themselves unable to resist the temptation.
Parka picked up the berry-picking pastime from me. During every rest
stop (which tend to come far more frequently during berry season than
during other times of the year), I would pick as many ripe berries as I
could find in easy reach, and about every third berry was flipped to Parka.
Soon, she learned to follow my hand, leaning in and nipping the berries
off the bush before I could get them.

In addition to plump berries, the trail to Nannie Ridge provides stunning views of the peaks of the south Cascades—including the near-perfect
cone of Mount Adams—and ample opportunity to witness wildlife.

To get there, from Packwood drive west on U.S. Highway 12 for 2 miles
and turn left (south) onto Forest Road 21 (Johnson Creek Road). Continue about 19 miles on the sometimes-rough gravel road before turning left (east) onto FR 2160, signed Walupt Lake Campground. The
trailhead is about 5 miles farther on at the end of this road near the pretty
campground on the shores of Walupt Lake.

The trail begins near the eastern end of the campground. The Nannie
Ridge Trail (No. 98) climbs north through dense pine forests for more
than a mile, crossing a couple shallow creeks (often dry late in the year)

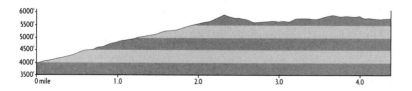

and gradually gaining elevation. As you hike, note that the soil here poses extra concerns for your dog. The many volcanoes in the area have dumped a lot of light ash into the soil, making it gritty and powdery. In fact, by midsummer, the dirt trail is churned into several inches of billowy dust. Your dog, panting happily up the trail, needs plenty of water breaks to clear that dust from his throat.

As the trail nears the 1.5-mile point, the forest begins to open with spacious clearings scattered throughout. Here's where the fun begins. Hit the trail in late August and you'll find these clearings a deep shade of purple, provided you get there before the other hikers—and the bears. Because bears frequent the berry fields, it is vital that you keep your dog—even if it is superbly trained to voice command—on leash.

At 3 miles the trail tops the ridge crest just below the summit of Nannie Peak. A short, 0.5-mile way trail leads to the summit of the peak, and it is well worth the effort to scramble up this boot-beaten path to enjoy

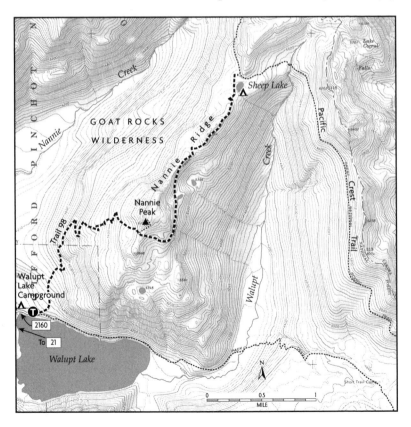

Camp set up on Nanny Ridge meadows

the outstanding views and wonderful mountaintop meadows. The views are dominated by the big three southern volcanoes—Mount Rainier to the north, Mount Adams to the south, and Mount St. Helens to the southwest—but the jagged crests of the Goat Rocks peaks to the northeast are also not to be missed.

The trail continues east from Nannie Peak, following just below the crest of Nannie Ridge—the trail drops several hundred feet below the ridge for a while in order to avoid some towering cliffs. At 4.4 miles, you'll find Sheep Lake at the junction with the Pacific Crest Trail. The best campsite is on the knoll to the south of the lake where you'll enjoy evening views of alpenglow on Mount Adams.

The lake is large enough to be clear and cool but shallow enough that the summer sun takes the bone-chilling cold out of the snowmelt water. That makes it a fine place for you and your dog to enjoy a refreshing swim.

77. Killen Meadows

Round trip: 9 miles
Hiking time: 6 hours (day hike or backpacking trip)
High point: 6900 feet
Elevation gain: 2300 feet
Best hiking time: late summer
Map: Green Trails Mount Adams No. 367s
Contact: Gifford Pinchot National Forest, Mt. Adams Ranger
District, (509) 395-3400

Meadows. Lush, green meadows filled with fragrant wildflowers and juicy berries. High, alpine meadows with low, hardy heathers and grasses. Rocky subalpine meadows littered with rocks and patches of slow-melting snow. This route explores a rich cornucopia of meadow types. Because many of the meadow types are fragile, neither you nor your dog should venture out onto them. On the higher elevation meadows, make sure to stay on the trails; it is only the hearty grass meadows of the lower mountain that can withstand much paw or footfall.

This simple climb along a ridgeline to the high snowline of Mount Adams offers more than mere meadows, though. Hikers will find stunning views of Mount Adams all along the trail. Along the way, you'll study the mountain's rocky cliff faces, heavy ice glaciers, rippled ridges, and rockfalls.

To get there, from Randle on U.S. Highway 12 drive 1 mile south on Forest Road 25. At the first main road junction, bear left (east) onto FR 23 and drive 32 miles to a junction with FR 2329 (signed Takhlakh Lake Campground); turn left. Continue 6 miles on FR 2329 to the Killen Creek Trailhead on the right, elevation 4580 feet.

First, a word of warning. The pumice and basalt rocks that comprise most of Mount Adam's slopes are highly abrasive. If your dog is willing to walk while wearing booties, this is the place to use them. If booties

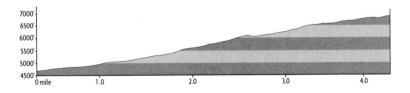

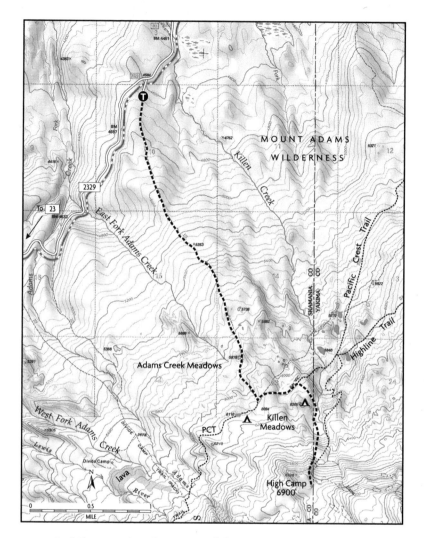

are out of the question, keep a careful eye on your dog and make sure she doesn't show any signs of limping or worrying about her paws during rest stops. If there are indications of foot pain, stop and check her pads. Cuts and abrasions should be dealt with immediately—and even if the dog doesn't like booties, have them along because they are a great way to keep sterile bandages in place on a torn paw pad.

Now, as you start up the trail, you'll find yourself entering a world of wildflowers—the colorful blooms fill the meadows as well as the open forest along the trail for most of its length and throughout much of the

Donna and Parka among huckleberries

hiking season. Early on, the bulbous white blooms of bear grass wave you on, while later in the summer, the trail is lit with brilliant displays of gaudy colors, thanks to the prolific wildflowers, including paintbrush, marsh marigolds, shooting stars, columbine, and lupine, to name just a few. The trail climbs gradually through forest clearings and open, sun-dappled stands of old growth for the initial 2 miles before running into a denser and cooler forest of old growth. This ancient cathedral continues for less than a mile more before the way opens once again onto bright sunlit meadows with glorious views of Mount Adams ahead.

At just over 2.5 miles, the trail crosses a stream in the meadow—East Fork Adams Creek—and reaches the first of the countless possibilities for camping. This is the start of the sprawling meadow country, and the broad fields around East Fork Adams Creek are quite properly known as the Adams Creek Meadows. You can scramble off away from the trail to find a suitable, solitary campsite here and then spend days exploring the rest of the area from your base camp, or you can press on.

At just over 3.5 miles, the Killen Creek Trail dead-ends at the Pacific Crest Trail (PCT), at 6100 feet elevation amidst heather meadows with wide-open views of Mount Adams. A faint, way trail leads seemingly straight toward the summit from this junction. This is the route to High Camp, a rocky plateau at the edge of the life zone—the line where vegetation gives way to a world of rock and ice. High Camp, at 6900 feet, is often crowded on hot August weekends, so it's usually best to camp lower, in Killen Meadows, and visit High Camp merely as a side trip.

The trail to High Camp covers the 800-foot gain in just 1 mile, and a second trail, about 1.3 miles long, descends to the northeast along the headwaters of Killen Creek, to join the PCT near its junction with the Highline Trail at 5900 feet.

At this junction, Killen Creek tumbles north through green meadows. A slew of ponds and small pools dot the meadows, and good campsites can be found on the higher knolls of Killen Meadows. To return to the trailhead, hike west along the PCT about 1.3 miles back to the Killen Creek Trail junction.

78. Blue Lake

Round trip: 13 miles
Hiking time: 8 hours (day hike or backpacking trip)
High point: 5000 feet
Elevation gain: 900 feet
Best hiking time: July through early October
Maps: Green Trails Wind River No. 397 and Lone Butte No. 365
Contact: Gifford Pinchot National Forest, Mt. Adams Ranger District, (509) 395-3400

It could just as well be called "Labrador Retriever Heaven" because waterdogs love Indian Heaven Wilderness Area. Parka, a typical Labrador retriever, bursts with excitement when hiking here, because there

seems to be a small lake or pond for her to swim in every few miles. This hike is a rare gem with its multitude of sparkling lakes, acres of flower-filled meadows, fields of rich berries, and herds of deer and elk.

To get there, from Trout Lake head west on State Route 141 for about 8 miles to Peterson Prairie Campground and a junction with Forest Road 24. Turn right onto FR 24 and drive 5.5 miles to the Cultus Creek Campground on the left. The starting trailhead is found near the back of the campground loop and heads southwest.

The 1.5 miles gain nearly 1200 feet in elevation as the trail ruthlessly ascends the Cultus Creek alley along the south flank of Bird Mountain. About a mile into the hike, the trail breaks out on a small ridge. Stop here to wet your dog's tongue and to catch your breath. Look east from this rocky point and Mount Adams dominates the horizon. Below the viewpoint, the slope drops steeply away to a broad expanse of blue-green forest sprawling between you and Mount Adams. Face north on clear days and Mount Rainier can be seen. Between the two great volcanoes stretch the craggy summits of the Goat Rocks Wilderness.

From here the trail turns sharply south as it draws near the cliff faces of Bird Mountain. Pine forests enclose the trail, with occasional meadow breaks and views of the towering cliffs, until the trail passes the first of the dog's swimming holes—Cultus Lake—at 2.5 miles. This is a fine lake in which to swim or just to sit beside and enjoy during a leisurely lunch. Beyond the lake, Lemei Rock scrapes the sky. This 5925-foot rock is the remnant plug from the core of a long-gone volcano.

Just a few hundred feet past the lake, a side trail leads off to the left. This path leads to Lemei Rock and beyond. Stay right on the main trail and, in another 0.25 mile, reach a second trail junction. This is the Lemei Lake Trail, No. 179. Here, you'll take the left-hand trail and hike south past the second dog-dipping hole, Lemei Lake. More like a vast puddle, Lemei Lake is a shallow, somewhat dirty lake—dogs will love it!

Continuing south through the broken forest (stands of pine and fir intermingled with open meadows and clearings) you'll find Junction Lake at 5.1 miles from the trailhead. Junction Lake, so named because two side trails merge into the Pacific Crest Trail (PCT) at the lakeshore, is a muddy, frog-filled pond at the base of East Crater. This cinder-cone volcano is heavily wooded with spindly pines, and though no trail leads to the top, it is possible to bushwhack to its summit for a view of the crater for which the formation is named.

Junction Lake offers a few fine campsites, but these are best passed

Cultus Lake along trail to Blue Lake

up. The warm, shallow lake breeds a healthy population of mosquitoes, and the forest that rings the lake breaks any wind that might sweep the little biters away. In other words, camp here during the summer and you let yourself—and your dog—in for a bloodletting.

From Junction Lake, continue south on the PCT, following it around

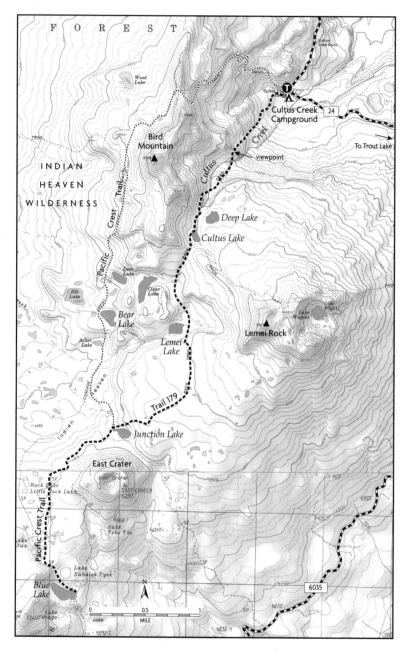

the west flank of the crater, before starting a long, gentle descent to Blue Lake near the base of Gifford Peak.

Blue Lake, 6.5 miles from the trailhead, abounds with campsites and a strong population of rainbow trout, with excellent views of the various small volcanic cones that dot this part of the south Cascades. The area is also rich with huckleberry brambles. The lush, purple fruit typical ripens in early August, and the berries tend to bring out a variety of pickers, including the natives—black bears!—so you and your dog take care while enjoying the sweet treats.

79. Siouxon Peak

Round trip: 15 miles
Hiking time: 8 hours (day hike or backpacking trip)
High point: 4106 feet
Elevation gain: 2400 feet
Best hiking time: July through October
Map: Green Trails Lookout Mountain No. 396
Contact: Gifford Pinchot National Forest, Wind River Information Center, (509) 427-3200

If you are backpacking to Siouxon Peak, bring lots of water or hit the trail early while there's still snow along the route to melt. If you're day hiking, you—and your dog—better be in good shape. This trail in the Gifford Pinchot National Forest challenges hikers with four legs nearly as much as it challenges two-legged hikers. The route climbs steadily and steeply for the first two-thirds of its length before moderating into a gentle roll along the ridge. But for all the sweat you pump out and all the calories you burn, you'll earn great rewards. Fabulous wildflower fields, stunning scenery, and glorious views await you, as you cross one old fire lookout site and climb to the summit of another tall mountain.

To get there, from Cougar south of Mount St. Helens, drive toward Amboy on State Route 503. Before Amboy and just north of Chelatchie, turn northeast onto Healy Road (found near a small country general store). This road soon becomes Forest Road 54. Drive 9 miles and turn

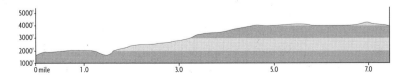

left onto FR 57, then in 1.25 miles, turn left onto FR 5701. In less than a mile, the road switches back sharply to the right. As you drive out of this corner, look for the trailhead on the left (north) side of the road.

Start up the trail as it descends gradually through old, dense successional forest to the banks of Siouxon Creek at about 1.5 miles, crossing the creek on a rustic old bridge and starting a long, steep climb onto Huffman Ridge. The trail is the one used years ago by the attendants of a fire lookout station atop Huffman Peak, and as such, it heads straight for the top (the thinking being then that the fire watchers needed to get to their posts as quickly and in as direct a manner as possible).

The trail climbs for nearly 5 miles from the creek, ascending through forest with only occasional views out over the south Cascades, before rolling up to the high, windswept summit of Huffman Peak, 4106 feet. Enjoy sweeping views in all directions here, and if you have pushed yourself too hard, consider making this your turnaround point. If you want more views, though, roll down the trail on the north side of Huffman and follow the ridgeline east for more than 2.5 miles to the top of Siouxon Peak. You'll find more views here. (Not necessarily any better than those on Huffman—just more.)

As you start back, you can change your route by descending the rough,

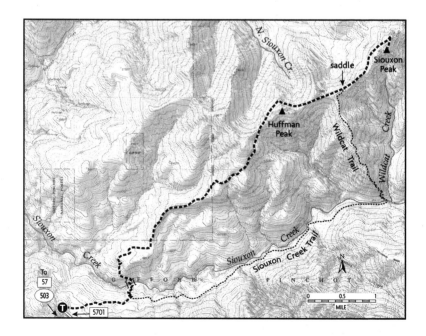

Rutted trail heading toward Huffman Peak

brushy Wildcat Trail from the saddle between Huffman and Siouxon Peaks. This side trail drops to the Siouxon Creek valley, where you can pick up the Siouxon Creek Trail and follow it back to the intersection of the Siouxon Peak Trail and continue 1 mile back to the trailhead.

80. Dog Mountain

Round trip: 8 miles
Hiking time: 6 hours
High point: 2948 feet
Elevation gain: 2800 feet
Best hiking time: February through December
Map: Green Trails Hood River No. 430
Contact: Columbia River Gorge National Scenic Area, (541) 386-2333
Note: Dogs must be leashed on this trail.

With a name like this, is it any wonder this trail made it into this book? Of course dogs should hike Dog Mountain but not just because of the name.

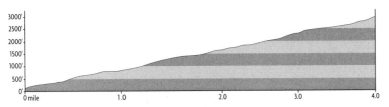

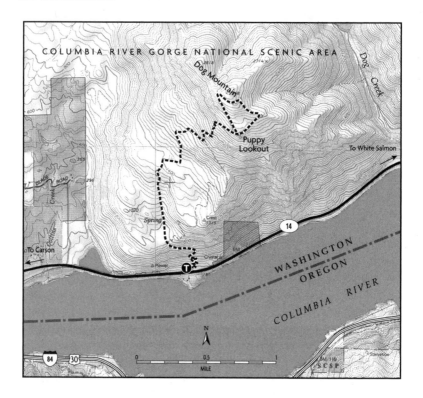

The long, steep climb on this low-elevation trail provides an excellent opportunity for canines and their two-legged friends to stay in hiking condition all year-round.

But it's more than a training hill. With a trailhead in the Columbia River Gorge, this mountain offers wonderful views of the deep cut of the Columbia as it slices through the Cascades. This is a popular trail that offers great views and a pleasant trail experience—wildflowers grace the forest meadows and clearings, and wildlife such as black-tailed deer, raccoons, skunks, coyotes, and bobcats roam the area. Water is scarce on this hike so make sure to bring plenty to keep both you and your trail dog hydrated. Also note that because of the popularity of this trail, leashes are required on Dog Mountain!

To get there, from Carson drive approximately 9 miles east on State Route 14 to the trailhead, just beyond milepost 53. The parking area and trailhead are on the left (north) side of the highway.

From the large parking area, the trail begins with a steep, 0.5-mile climb to a junction. At the junction, both trails before you lead to the top. My

Balsamroot on the flank of Dog Mountain

recommendation is to go right, because the left fork climbs more steeply up the northern flank of the mountain. Use the longer, more gradual route on the right as it loops around to the east and climbs through broken forest that offers periodic views across the gorge. You can descend by the steeper northern route.

The trails climb steeply, reconvening near the 3-mile mark, before the combined path crosses a little knoll known as the Puppy Lookout. From here, another choice awaits you. The trail splits again. Left or right: There's not much difference either way. Choose one direction for the ascent and one direction to come back down. You're only 500 vertical feet below the top of Dog Mountain at this point, so keep pushing and soon, at 4 miles from the trailhead, you'll be striding through the broad meadows of balsamroot blooms to look out into the fabulous views south and west into the Columbia River Gorge.

APPENDIX A

Hike Summary Table

Trail Name	Distance (miles, round trip)	Hiking Time	Difficulty	High Point (feet)
1 Colonel Bob	14	9 hours	more difficult	4510
2 Fletcher Canyon	3.5	3 hours	easy-moderate	1320
3 Leadbetter Point	4+	3+ hours	easy	49
4 Tubal Cain Mine Meadows/Buckhorn Lake	10	7 hours	moderate	5300
5 Silver Lakes	10	8 hours	moderate	5500
6 Camp Mystery/Marmot Pass	11	8 hours	more difficult	6100
7 Mount Ellinor	5	6 hours	strenuous	5900
8 Dry Creek	12	6+ hours	moderate	3600
9 Skyline Divide	6	4.5 hours	more difficult	6215
10 Damfino Lakes	2	4 hours	difficult	5700
11 Tomyhoi Lake	10	7 hours	moderate	5400
12 Welcome Pass	6	5 hours	more difficult	5200
13 East Bank Baker Lake	up to 28	4 hrs to 4 days	moderate	1000
14 Watson Lakes/Anderson Butte	5	5 hours	difficult	4900
15 East Creek to Mebee Pass	16	2 days	difficult	6500
16 Cutthroat Pass	10	6 hours	difficult	6800
17 Cutthroat Lake	4	3 hours	moderate	5000
18 Blue Lake	4+	4 hours	more difficult	6300
19 Remmel Lake	33	3 days	difficult	6870
20 Horseshoe Basin/Louden Lake	14	8 hours	difficult	7200
21 Scatter Lake	9	8 hours	difficult	7050
22 Boulder River	9	6 hours	easy-moderate	1600
23 Round Lake	11	8 hours	more difficult	5500
24 Poodle Dog Pass/Silver Lake	11	8 hours	moderate	4400
25 Phelps Creek/Spider Meadows	14	8 hours	difficult	5500
26 Chelan Lakeshore Trail	18	2 to 3 days	moderate	1700
27 Eagle Lakes	12	2 to 3 days	moderate	7200
28 Cooney Lake/Martin Lakes	17	2 to 3 days	moderate-difficult	7240
29 Sunrise Lake/Foggy Dew	13	8 hours	difficult	7240
30 Pear Lake	12	8 hours	moderate-difficult	5200
31 Surprise and Glacier Lakes	11	7 hours	difficult	5200
32 Chain Lakes	22	2 days	moderate-difficult	5790
33 Twin Falls	3	2 hours	easy-moderate	1000
34 Big Creek Falls (Taylor River)	10	5 hours	easy-moderate	1750
35 Dingford Creek to Hester Lake	11	7 hours	moderate-difficult	3900
36 Williams Lake	15	2 days	difficult	4600

Elevation Gain (feet)	Seasons Hikeable	Best Season	Prime Features
4280	spring, summer, fall	early summer	old-growth forest, views, wildlife
1029	spring, summer, fall	late spring	old-growth forest, wildlife
35	year-round	fall–spring	beach, wetland ecology, birds
2000	spring, summer, fall	summer	wildflowers, historic sites, birds
2600	summer, fall	late summer	lake, meadows, views
3700	summer, fall	early fall	mountain views, meadows, forests
2100	summer, fall	late summer	views, meadows, wildflowers
2800	spring, summer, fall	autumn	lake views, forest ecology
2000	summer, fall	late summer	mountain views, wildlife, wildflowers
1500	summer, fall	midsummer	lake, mountain views
1600	summer, fall	midsummer	lake, meadows, mountain views
3000	summer, fall	late summer	alpine meadows, views
300	spring, summer, fall	late spring	lakeside ecology, wildlife, fishing, old-growth forest
600	late spring, summer, fall	midsummer	lake, alpine views, forest ecology
4000	summer, fall	late summer	forest ecology, alpine views, wildflowers
2000	summer, fall	early autumn	alpine views, meadows, autumn colors
500	summer, fall	early autumn	lake ecology, wildflower meadows, wildlife
1100	summer, fall	early autumn	birds, lake ecology, alpine views
3400	summer, fall	late summer	lake ecology, forest ecology, wildlife
1200	summer, fall	late summer	wildflowers, wildflowers, wildflowers
3900	midsummer, fall	early autumn	lake, wildflowers, autumn colors
600	year-round	spring	waterfall, forest and riparian ecology
3600	summer, fall	midsummer	lake ecology, wildlife, bird watching
2000	summer, fall	late summer	meadows, lake, mountain views
2000	summer, fall	late summer	wildflower meadows, wildlife
800	spring, summer, fall	late spring	lakeside ecology, mountain views
2900	summer, fall	early autumn	alpine meadows, views, wildflowers, lake
2500	summer, fall	early autumn	alpine meadows, views, wildflowers, lake
2500	summer, fall	midsummer	alpine meadows, views, wildflowers, lake
1400	summer, fall	late summer	alpine meadows, views, wildflowers, lake
3000	summer, fall	late summer	forest ecology, lakes, wildlife, meadows
3700	summer, fall	late summer	forest ecology, riparian ecology, birds
500	year-round	spring	waterfalls, old-growth forest, riparian ecology
700	year-round	spring	waterfall, historic sites, forest ecology
2600	spring, summer, fall	early summer	forest ecology, riparian ecology, lakes
1600	summer, fall	early autumn	forest ecology, lakes, wildlife, meadows

Trail Name	Distance (miles, round trip)	Hiking Time	Difficulty	High Point (feet)
37 Kendall Kat (DOG) Walk	11	7 hours	difficult	5760
38 Tinkham Peak/Silver Peak Loop	8	6 hours	difficult	5605
39 Margaret Lake/Lake Lillian	6	4 hours	moderate-difficult	5200
40 French Cabin Creek	5.6	4 hours	difficult	4900
41 Thorp Mountain	7	4 hours	more difficult	5850
42 Pete Lake	9	6 hours	easy-moderate	2980
43 Waptus and Spade Lakes	16-27	2 to 4 days	difficult	3000
44 Jolly Mountain	12	8 hours	difficult	6443
45 Sasse Mountain	5+	3+ hours	moderate	5730
46 Cathedral Rock/Peggy's Pond	11	7 hours	moderate-difficult	5600
47 Scatter Creek	9	6 hours	difficult	6200
48 Esmeralda Basin/Fortune Pass	7	5 hours	moderate-difficult	5900
49 Bean Creek Basin	5	4 hours	difficult	5600
50 Navaho Pass	11	6 hours	more difficult	6000
51 Tronsen Ridge	5+	4 hours	moderate	5800
52 Snoquera Falls	3.25	3 hours	easy-moderate	3400
53 Noble Knob	7	5 hours	easy-moderate	6011
54 Greenwater Lakes and Echo Lake	14	8 hours	moderate	4100
55 Arch Rock (Government Meadows)	12	7 hours	easy-moderate	5200
56 Norse Peak	12	7 hours	difficult	6856
57 Bullion Basin	7	5 hours	moderate-difficult	6400
58 Sourdough Gap (Sheep Lake)	7	4 hours	moderate	6400
59 American Lake	13	6 hours	moderate-difficult	5800
60 Union Creek	14	7 hours	more difficult	5900
61 Mesatchee Creek	11	7 hours	difficult	5800
62 Fifes Ridge	8	7 hours	more difficult	6500
63 Cougar Lakes	12	7 hours	moderate-difficult	5400
64 Bumping River to Fish Lake	14	7 hours	moderate	4200
65 Blankenship Meadows Ramble	9	7 hours	moderate	5400
66 Yakima Rim	8+	4+ hours	moderate	3000
67 Umtanum Canyon	8+	4+ hours	easy	1900
68 Tatoosh Lakes View	7	6 hours	difficult	5400
69 Packwood Lake	9	6 hours	moderate	3200
70 Sand Lake	6	4 hours	moderate	5300
71 Dumbbell Lake Loop	11	7+ hours	moderate-difficult	5200
72 Shoe Lake	14	8 hours	moderate-difficult	6600
73 Juniper Ridge	7	5 hours	difficult	5600
74 Dark Meadow	5.6	5 hours	moderate-difficult	4450
75 Snowgrass Flats/Goat Lake Loop	11.25	8 hours	more difficult	6550
76 Nannie Ridge/Sheep Lake	9	9 hours	difficult	5800
77 Killen Meadows	8	6 hours	more difficult	6900
78 Blue Lake	13	8 hours	difficult	5000
79 Siouxon Peak	15	8 hours	strenuous	4106
80 Dog Mountain	8	6 hours	difficult	2948

Elevation Gain (feet)	Seasons Hikeable	Best Season	Prime Features
2700	summer, fall	midsummer	forest ecology, wildflower meadows, views, alpine lakes
2600	lsummer, fall	midsummer	forest ecology, wildflowers, views, alpine lakes
1300	summer, fall	late summer	huckleberries, forest ecology, alpine lakes, views
1100	late spring, summer, fall	midsummer	forest ecology, wildflowers, views, alpine lakes
1800	summer, fall	late summer	sprawling meadows, wildflowers, wildlife, views
200	spring, summer, fall	early summer	forest ecology, lake ecology, views, wildlife
600	summer, fall	late summer	forest ecology, lake ecology, views, wildlife
4000	summer, fall	late summer	meadows, forest, wildlife, views
1300	summer, fall	early summer	meadows, forest, wildlife, views
2200	summer, fall	midsummer	wildflower meadows, forest, wildlife, views
2900	summer, fall	late summer	forest ecology, wildflowers, birds
1700	summer, fall	late summer	wildflower meadows, mountain views, wildlife
2000	late spring, summer, fall	midsummer	wildflower meadows, forest, wildlife, views
3000	summer, fall	late summer	wildflower meadows, forest, wildlife, views
minus 1000	late spring, summer, fall	early summer	wildflower meadows, deer, elk
1100	year-round	mid-spring	waterfalls, deer, song birds
500	summer, fall	midsummer	wildflowers, mountain views
1600	late spring, summer, fall	early summer	lakes, wildlife (deer, elk), forest ecology
700	late spring, summer, fall	midsummer	meadows, forest, wildlife
2850	summer, fall	late summer	wildlife (mountain goats, elk), wildflowers, views
1600	summer, fall	late summer	wildflowers, mountain views, wildlife
1000	summer, fall	late summer	wildflowers, lake, views, huckleberries
minus 500	summer, fall	late summer	lake, views, wildflowers, huckleberries
2500	summer, fall	midsummer	forest ecology, wildlife
2200	summer, fall	midsummer	forest ecology, wildlife, birds
3100	summer, fall	midsummer	forest ecology, views, birds
1800	summer, fall	late summer	forest ecology, lakes, wildlife, meadows
400	summer, fall	late summer	forest ecology, riparian ecology, elk, birds
600	summer, fall	late summer	meadows, lakes, wildlife
1600	year-round	spring	elk, bighorn sheep, desert ecology, views
500	year-round	spring	beavers, bighorn sheep, creek ecology, desert ecology
2500	summer, fall	late summer	alpine views, wildflowers, forest ecology
500	spring, summer, fall	late spring	forest ecology, lakeside ecology, fishing, wildlife
900	late spring, summer, fall	early summer	lake, wildflower meadows, wildlife
minus 1000	late spring, summer, fall	late summer	lakes, wildflower meadows, wildlife, birds
2200	summer, fall	late summer	wildflowers, meadows, lake, views
2000	summer, fall	late summer	wildflower meadows, wildlife, views
600	summer, fall	late summer	wildflower meadows, wildlife, views
1920	summer, fall	early autumn	wildflower meadows, wildlife, views, lake
1800	summer, fall	late summer	wildflower meadows, wildlife, views, lake
2300	summer, fall	late summer	wildflower meadows, forest ecology, views
900	summer, fall	early autumn	meadows, lake, forest ecology, wildlife
2400	summer, fall	early autumn	views, meadows, mountain views
2800	early spring, summer, fall	late spring	wildflowers, forest ecology, views

APPENDIX B

Resources
Books

LaBelle, Charlene G. *Guide to Backpacking with Your Dog.* Loveland, Colo.: Alpine Publications, 1992.

Mullally, Linda. *Hiking with Dogs: Becoming a Wilderness-Wise Dog Owner.* Missoula, Mont.: Falcon Guides, 1999.

Smith, Cheryl S. *On the Trail with Your Canine Companion: Getting the Most out of Hiking and Camping with Your Dog.* New York, NY: Howell Book House/Macmillan, 1996.

First Aid

Acker, Randy, DVM. *Dog First Aid: A Field Guide to Emergency Care for the Outdoor Dog.* Gallatin Gateway, Mont.: Wilderness Adventure Press, 1999.

Acker, Randy, DVM. *Dog First Aid.* An instructional video tape designed to help teach how to perform basic canine field first aid, 1994.

Dr. Acker also offers a comprehensive Dog First-Aid Kit with most of the items discussed in the first-aid section of Part 1, all packed in a compact fanny pack–style case. For information, contact him at the Sun Valley Animal Center, 1-800-699-2663, or visit *www.svanimal.com.*

Ruffwear, Inc., offers pre-packaged dog first-aid kits containing the basic essentials. These are available at many outdoor retail shops or by visiting *www.ruffwear.com.*

Dog Gear

www.cascadedesigns.com

Cascade Designs, Inc., invented the self-inflating sleeping pad more than three decades ago for human hikers. now, they offer a line of fleece-covered Therm-a-Rest pads just for dogs.

www.granitegear.com

Granite Gear makes doggy backpacks.

www.planetdog.com

Planetdog makes gear for active dogs, including toys, bowls, beds, leashes, leads, and collars. The company also donates a portion of its proceeds to environmental charities.

www.ruffwear.com
This Bend, Oregon company specializes in products specifically for active outdoor dogs. Ruffwear offers dog backpacks, high-visibility safety vests, booties, toys, beds, canine first-aid kits, safety equipment, flotation vests, collapsible food and water bowls, and more.

INDEX

ABOUT THE AUTHOR

DAN A. NELSON is executive editor of *Signpost for Northwest Trails,* a monthly backcountry recreation magazine published by The Washington Trails Association (WTA). He wrote *Best of the Pacific Crest Trail: Washington, Predators at Risk in the Pacific Northwest,* and *Snowshoe Routes: Washington,* all published by The Mountaineers Books, and was the writer and editor for a 1995 release from The Mountaineers Books—the WTA-authored *Accessible Trails in Washington's Backcountry: A Guide to 85 Outings.* Nelson is also co-author of *Pacific Northwest Hiking: The Complete Guide* (Foghorn Press, 1995). He is a contributing writer for the *Seattle Times* and a frequent contributor to *Backpacker* magazine.

THE MOUNTAINEERS, founded in 1906, is a nonprofit outdoor activity and conservation club, whose mission is "to explore, study, preserve, and enjoy the natural beauty of the outdoors . . . ." Based in Seattle, Washington, the club is now the third-largest such organization in the United States, with 15,000 members and five branches throughout Washington State.

The Mountaineers sponsors both classes and year-round outdoor activities in the Pacific Northwest, which include hiking, mountain climbing, ski-touring, snowshoeing, bicycling, camping, kayaking and canoeing, nature study, sailing, and adventure travel. The club's conservation division supports environmental causes through educational activities, sponsoring legislation, and presenting informational programs. All club activities are led by skilled, experienced volunteers, who are dedicated to promoting safe and responsible enjoyment and preservation of the outdoors.

If you would like to participate in these organized outdoor activities or the club's programs, consider a membership in The Mountaineers. For information and an application, write or call The Mountaineers, Club Headquarters, 300 Third Avenue West, Seattle, WA 98119; 206-284-6310.

The Mountaineers Books, an active, nonprofit publishing program of the club, produces guidebooks, instructional texts, historical works, natural history guides, and works on environmental conservation. All books produced by The Mountaineers Books fulfill the club's mission.

Send or call for our catalog of more than 500 outdoor titles:

 The Mountaineers Books
1001 SW Klickitat Way, Suite 201
Seattle, WA 98134
800-553-4453

mbooks@mountaineersbooks.org
www.mountaineersbooks.org

 The Mountaineers Books is proud to be a corporate sponsor of Leave No Trace, whose mission is to promote and inspire responsible outdoor recreation through education, research, and partnerships. The Leave No Trace program is focused specifically on human-powered (nonmotorized) recreation.

Leave No Trace strives to educate visitors about the nature of their recreational impacts, as well as offer techniques to prevent and minimize such impacts. Leave No Trace is best understood as an educational and ethical program, not as a set of rules and regulations.

For more information, visit *www.LNT.org*, or call 800-332-4100.

Other titles you might enjoy from The Mountaineers Books
Available at fine bookstores and outdoor stores, by phone at (800) 553-4453, or on the World Wide Web at *www.mountaineersbooks.org*

50 Trail Runs in Washington by Cheri Pompeo Gillis. $16.95 paperbound. 0-89886-715-0.

100 Classic Hikes in™ Washington by Ira Spring and Harvey Manning. $19.95 paperbound. 0-89886-586-7.

Hiking Washington's Geology by Scott Babcock and Bob Carson. $16.95 paperbound. 0-89886-548-4.

Hidden Hikes in Western Washington by Karen Sykes. $16.95 paperbound. 0-89886-859-9.

Best of the Pacific Crest Trail: Washington: 55 Hikes by Dan A. Nelson. $16.95 paperbound. 0-89886-703-7.

Washington State Parks: A Complete Recreation Guide, 2nd Edition by Marge and Ted Mueller. $16.95 paperbound. 0-89886-642-1.

75 Scrambles in Washington: Classic Routes to the Summits by Peggy Goldman. $18.95 paperbound. 0-89886-761-4.

Snowshoe Routes: Washington, 2nd Edition by Dan A. Nelson. $16.95 paperbound. 0-89886-884-X.

100 Classic Backcountry Ski and Snowboard Routes in Washington by Rainer Burgdorfer. $17.95 paperbound. 0-89886-661-8.

Best Hikes with Children in® Western Washington and the Cascades, Volume 1, 2nd Edition by Joan Burton. $14.95 paperbound. 0-89886-564-6.

Best Hikes with Children in® Western Washington and the Cascades, Volume 2, 2nd Edition by Joan Burton. $14.95 paperbound. 0-89886-626-X.

A Field Guide to the Cascades & Olympics, 2nd Edition by Stephen R. Whitney and Rob Sandelin. $19.95 paperbound. 0-89886-808-4.

Northwest Trees by Stephen F. Arno and Ramona P. Hammerly. $14.95 paperbound. 0-916890-50-3.